Butterfly

Orion Monroe

All rights reserved.

Copyright © 2025 by Orion Monroe

Cover Design by Caspian C. Waters

Edited by Travis Hunt

Library of Congress Control Number: 2025916583

ISBN: 979-8-9989953-7-8

No part of this book may be reproduced transmitted in any form or by any means, electronic or mechanical, including photocopying, recording, or by any information storage and retrieval system, without permission in writing from the publisher.

 For Information address:

Greylander Press, Dayton, Ohio

Published in the United States of America

FIRST PRINTING

20 19 18 17 16 15 14 13 12 11 10 9 8 7 6 5 4 3 2 1

Foreword

Innocence should never be a casualty of assumption and bias.

Butterfly is not just the story of one young man—it is the story of thousands. Across the United States and around the world, men and boys are being falsely accused of sexual assault, and the consequences are devastating. These are not isolated incidents. They are part of a growing crisis that demands attention, reform, and courage.

False accusations have led to arrests, expulsions, public shaming, vigilante actions, irreparable reputational damage, and prison sentences—even in the absence of evidence. And this speaks only to the accused. The ripple effects on their families and loved ones are profound and heartbreaking.

As a passionate advocate for the falsely accused, I've spoken directly with representatives from the Office on Violence Against Women, hoping to raise awareness and push for change. What I encountered instead was silence—dismissal of the issue's gravity and a refusal to acknowledge the harm inflicted on innocent individuals. When institutions designed to uphold justice ignore one side of the story, they fail us all.

This book does not seek to silence survivors. It seeks to amplify a truth too often ignored: justice must be impartial. Every accusation deserves a thorough, evidence-based investigation—not blind belief. When we abandon due process, we risk replacing justice with vengeance, and truth with narrative.

The young man at the heart of this story is not alone. He stands among countless others whose lives have been shattered by lies. Their pain is real. Their fear is real. And their voices deserve to be heard.

This book is a call to action—for fairness, for reform, and for a justice system that protects the innocent as fiercely as it pursues the guilty. Let it remind us that integrity is not a luxury—it is the foundation of any society that claims to value truth.

Read with conviction. Listen with empathy. And above all, question what you think you know.

-Lori DeBolt

> Co-Founder, Advocates for the Falsely Accused
>
> Mother of a son wrongfully convicted
>
> Friend to many across the world who have endured this injustice
>
> Nona to three loving grandsons who deserve a world where truth stands strong

Preface

This is neither an easy story for me to share nor an easy one for you to read. What unfolds within these pages is a visceral and candid exploration inspired by events that deeply affected me. I'm taking you into the uncomfortable corners of our shared human experience, where accusation, consequences, and the shattering impact of both truth and falsehood have played out in lives I know intimately.

Sexual assault is a horrific act, a violation that leaves indelible scars on survivors. There is no minimizing its deep and lasting damage. This narrative approaches it with the gravity and empathy demanded because I have witnessed the immense suffering it inflicts.

However, this novel also navigates more treacherous ground, one that emerged from the complexities of a real situation: the delicate and often fraught space where allegations are made, and a life is irrevocably altered, based on untruths. The intent is not to diminish the overwhelming prevalence of sexual assault, but to acknowledge a harrowing and often silenced aspect of human nature. The power of accusation can be wielded in ways that inflict their own severe harm. This is a reality that has unfolded around me and within the life experiences that shaped this book.

Butterfly does not seek to provide simple answers or comfortable resolutions. Instead, it aims to immerse you in the intense emotional world of an individual caught in a web of suspicion and judgment, a setting directly informed by meaningful experiences. It is a narrative that demands introspection, challenging our assumptions and forcing us to confront the subtleties often lost in the urgency of social discourse.

My hope is that by engaging with this complex account, drawn from the wellspring of real life, we can foster a more layered and empathetic dialogue about the complexities of accusation, the devastating consequences of both assault and false allegation, and the urgent need for a justice system that seeks truth with unwavering diligence. This story, though unsettling, is offered in the spirit of fostering understanding and prompting a vital conversation about the realities we often prefer to ignore. These realities have shaped the lives involved in the events you are about to read.

Prepare to be moved, challenged, and perhaps even angered.

This is Butterfly, a fictionalized story I feel compelled to share, born from the intricate tapestry of an actual American tragedy.

Acknowledgement

It is difficult to express the extent of my gratitude to Chris, Terry, Lori, and Caspian. Your steady support, your belief in me, and your willingness to remain by my side throughout this process have shaped this work. Without you, this book would not exist.

You stayed when the writing stopped, when the silence grew loud, and when I questioned whether this story should be told at all. Each of you brought a different kind of strength. Patience. Clarity. Loyalty. Honesty.

Lori, your determination runs through every page of this novel. You did more than encourage me. You offered connection. Through you, I found a wider community of people who have lived through experiences that echo my own. You introduced me to voices that are often ignored, individuals who have endured silence, isolation, and judgment.

Their courage reminded me that stories like this do not disappear when the legal battles end. The narratives continue on in the lives of the accused. You gave me access to a place where truth still matters, where people continue to fight for justice, even after the world has stopped paying attention.

To Advocates for the Falsely Accused (AFFA) and the National Coalition for Men (NCFM). Thank you for your relentless pursuit of justice. You confront institutions that have no interest in listening. You speak up when most turn away. You remain when others retreat. Your work has brought light into places that are often left in darkness. You give people the courage to keep moving. You provide guidance when the path forward is unclear. You offer the structure and clarity needed to reclaim lives torn apart by false allegations. I am proud to acknowledge your efforts here and to say that your mission is vital.

This book is for every person who has been accused and punished for a crime not committed. It is for those who sat behind cold walls while their names were ruined. It is for those who watched their lives unraveled with no chance to speak.

You have been doubted. You have been ignored. You have been labeled. But you are not forgotten. Your story is real. It deserves to be heard.

This book is not an argument for those who refuse to listen. It is a reminder that you are not invisible. That you are not erased. That you are still here, even if the world pretends you are not. You are not broken. You are not beyond repair. You still carry your truth, whether others see it or not. That truth still has power. And no one can take it from you.

Your story matters.

You matter.

3

Chapter 1: Davis

Davis lay like a king in his realm as the morning sun sliced through the slats of the plastic window blinds over his bed. Light streamed over his body, casting a morning glow over him and fading onto the crumpled soccer jerseys, half-read comic books, and discarded energy drink cans scattered haphazardly throughout his room. At thirteen, he carried himself with the restless command of something wild and untamed, even in sleep.

Splayed across the pillow was his dark brown hair, which he often styled with care, but in this moment, it was a militant halo. He was handsome; his sharp facial features and high cheekbones, dusted with a faint scattering of nearly invisible freckles, enhanced the smirk playing on his lips that bordered on contempt. His brooding eyes held a spark of raging fire. A chiseled body, developed from years of training, was evidence of his athleticism.

The silence in the room felt dense, rife with tension lingering beneath the surface. It wasn't peace but, instead, an eerie stillness that is commonly felt before a catastrophe. Being a soccer prodigy wasn't a gift. It was a burden. It was a shield raised against the pressure of expectation. This wasn't arrogance born of ignorance. It was a defense crafted by a boy who'd felt too much, seen too much, and learned too early that kindness was a weapon as potent as hate. The cruelty he sometimes inflicted was a desperate effort to contain the unrest which lived within him.

A shrill sound from the digital alarm clock broke the quiet. Its piercing cry demanded consciousness. Davis silenced it with a powerful swat and sat up slowly. The bed sheets clung to his skin like damp parchment. His shirt, plastered to his back as he stretched, gently tugged at his shoulders. He yawned and raised his arms far over his head to jump start his reluctant body. A faint scent of fabric softener clung to the clothes he wore. It was a strange comfort. It soothed him but tethered him to the world he couldn't seem to understand.

The day ahead loomed with uncertainty. It could be thrilling. It might be disastrous. He didn't care. His wide eyes already scanned for the fight in it. He was a contradiction, and he knew it. He wasn't proud of it. It was simply accepted as truth. Conflict lived inside him so fully that peace felt dangerous. Losing it meant losing himself.

Feeling the pressure of the day, he took a deep breath. Then, planting his arms on the mattress, he lifted himself and stood with the cold floor pressed beneath his bare feet. Every slight shift drew a creak from the wooden boards. Each sound carved the quiet.

He dropped to his knees with a thud and bent low until his cheek nearly touched the surface. Beneath his bed stretched a dim, narrow cave. It seemed undisturbed, with the flecks of dust clinging to the slats above. For a moment, he stared into the darkness, waiting for his vision to adjust. Holding his breath, he reached in. His arm slid forward. His elbow nudged the floor as his fingers swept across forgotten toys, a single sock, the curled edge of a faded drawing. Something rough touched his knuckles. Burlap.

With halted breath, he pressed forward. His shoulder met the bed frame as he closed his hand around the bag, which was barely within reach. It was coarse and scratchy, but it felt exactly right. He pulled it from the dark. It sagged in his grip, familiar in shape and weight. Rising, he held the bag against his chest. He stood straight and looked around. The room felt smaller. It felt charged. Retrieving it had changed something. He stepped back and loosened the drawstring. The fabric rasped beneath his fingers as he opened his cache.

One by one, he removed the contents and placed them at the foot of the bed. The hand mirror came first. It was small and oval, framed in smooth, forgettable plastic. He had stolen it from the bathroom months ago. It had hung behind the cabinet door, hidden behind toothpaste and cotton balls. It had remained unseen... until it wasn't. When his mom asked where it went, he lied. He said he dropped it. The truth was, he had waited until the house was empty and took it. He claimed it like it had always belonged to him.

The bottle of lotion was nondescript. Its label was peeling away at the corners. Not long ago, he had taken it from the hallway cabinet and replaced it with an empty one. No one noticed. He didn't like the scent, but it had become part of the process. It was familiar. It was fixed. A soft, synthetic sweetness clung to the edges of everything it touched. The bottle sat light in his hand. It was almost toy-like, yet its presence was serious. Its original purpose no longer mattered. It belonged to this place now.

He was proud of the razor. He didn't acquire it from someone else. He had bought it with his own money. Coins and crumpled bills from his soccer bag had been saved over weeks. He walked to the drugstore alone, heart pounding, trying to appear like he belonged there. It wasn't expensive. It felt like it should have been. The handle was polished steel. It was cool in his palm and sharper than it looked. It caught the morning light like a shard of silver.

It wasn't just any grooming tool. It was his. It was sacred. It was honed to the edge of danger. Its mirrored surface caught his eyes and returned them to him. They looked hollow. They looked like they were burning. He ran a fingertip along the blade.

Cold metal met warm skin. The clash stoked the heat in his chest. He respected it completely. One slip could ruin everything. Even the smallest cut, leaving a stain on his clothing, might expose him.

This was a ritual. It involved setting each piece the same way. He followed a specific order. This quiet rite was his personal alchemy, born from fear and imagination. For him, it was a final stand for his youth. These objects were talismans. They were instruments in a war against time. They were weapons against the approaching threat of age turning him into something unrecognizable.

He moved to the mirror standing in the corner. He had always been drawn by its quiet gravity. It was situated exactly where it always had been, an antique passed down from his grandmother, its wooden frame carved in swirling vine patterns. It had become part of the routine now, just as constant as the items he placed at the foot of the bed. The glass caught him mid-step, and for a second, he didn't move. The boy in the mirror stared back at him. The relic that contained him had always managed to reveal something that felt slightly removed from real life. Real life felt somewhat removed from him. The image presented wasn't entirely true, but it wasn't a lie either. It was a version he might keep if he fought hard enough.

Now, he stood before it, wearing only his sleeping shirt and blue plaid boxers. A shiver rose through his legs as his toes shifted beneath him. His body felt oddly disconnected from the rest of the room, as if the boy in the mirror weren't really him. Locking onto his reflection, he studied it closely, scanning for signs of the maturity he feared might be creeping in. His face was a collision of features: the angular jawline, the cheekbones that still held a trace of softness, and his dark, restless eyes burning a wisdom he hadn't quite grown into.

He leaned closer and exhaled. His breath fogged a portion of the glass and stopped. It was there; a faint shadow tracing the space above his lip. It was soft. Uncommitted. Barely there. But it was real. His stomach tightened.

It hadn't been there yesterday. Or maybe it had, and he hadn't allowed himself to see it. It looked like nothing. It looked like a smudge. But it was enough. It meant something. It was a signal. A line had been crossed.

He wanted to erase it. He wanted to rub it out with his thumb. He wanted to pretend it hadn't happened and would never return. He stood frozen, just staring. The boy in the glass didn't blink. The image didn't breathe. He wondered if it was waiting, too.

Without breaking eye contact, he reached back toward the bed and picked up the hand mirror. His fingers closed around the plastic edge with practiced care. He lifted it slowly, angling it so it reflected his jawline, then his cheek, then the spot above his lip. That blur of darkness was nearly invisible unless caught in the light just right. But it was definitely there. It was taunting him.

A faint smell of soap hit him. Nausea crept through his throat. Memories rushed in without consent. His thoughts instantly shifted, dragging him back to the previous week. The locker room, with its slippery tile floors, the loud clang of locker doors, and the stale, humid air, carrying sweat and confidence in equal parts. The setting had once felt comfortable. Now, it felt like it belonged to someone else.

He remembered the game victory, the shouting, and the laughter that still echoed off the walls. The boys moved through the space like they were part of it. Steam rose from their skin. Voices overlapped in teasing and celebration. No one covered up. They stood naked in clusters, leaning on lockers, crowding mirrors, and talking over one another. Their bodies told different stories. Some were still boyish. Others had surged ahead. Their every movement was a display of effortless pride.

Ollie was the focus of most of the teasing. His body had developed faster than the others, and not just in the usual ways. The boys had started calling him "The Beast" because of how much further along he was and how much larger he was, compared to everyone else. Ollie took it all in stride, grinning widely as he swayed his hips, making his body move in exaggerated motions, swinging his dick back and forth like a grandfather clock pendulum.

"Look at Ollie, man," Travis said, his voice high with mock awe. "That thing's like a weapon." The others roared. Ollie shrugged and stepped in closer to the mirror, his grin widening. He knew exactly what they were looking at. He wasn't ashamed. He flaunted it.

Their jokes weren't mean. They were spirited. Young men were bonding in an undefined ceremony. They were celebrating their growth like it was a game. Davis watched from the edge. He saw everything. Ollie's muscle tone. The confident stance. The knowing eyes. What shook him wasn't the physical difference. It was the way Ollie carried himself. No shame. No hesitation. He had accepted change. He embraced what Davis simply couldn't.

The others followed Ollie's lead. They pointed. They laughed. They tugged at the hair on their legs, compared trails down their stomachs, and puffed out their chests like actors in a comedy with no script. They teased. They joked. They stood tall, loud, and unbothered.

Jacob had stepped forward, too. He was usually quiet. Soft-spoken. But that day, he stood taller and more confidently. He had something to prove. A small patch of light-brown, downy hair under his navel darkened his torso. It wasn't much, but it was something. He didn't hide. He didn't cross his arms. They teased him, but gently. Encouragingly. He laughed along. There was joy in it. Not boastful swagger. Just proud to be seen as becoming one of them.

Travis always laughed the loudest and threw jabs with ease. He eagerly played the part. On this day it was different for Davis, and something in him cracked. It wasn't about modesty. It wasn't about nudity. It was the comfort they displayed. The seamless transition to belonging. The way they had moved forward was horrifying.

Davis hadn't moved forward. He hadn't moved at all. He defied it. He stood there with his arms folded and eyes drawn to his feet, locked in place while everyone else ran ahead. The teasing didn't bother him. It was the voice. Travis's voice. His tone no longer felt like it belonged to him. It belonged to them. It had shifted. It had changed, too. Davis felt the rift, quietly and sharply growing.

What hurt him the most wasn't the laughter. It was the distance. Travis, his best friend for as long as he could remember, no longer seemed to need him in the same way. The bond they'd shared seemed to be unraveling day by day. Davis didn't know how to stop it. He didn't even know if he could.

A school bus picking the kid up from across the street screeched to a halt, distracting him. He was back in his room with his mission and his solitary war. The vision of the lockers left him as abruptly as it arrived. Davis paused for a moment and took a confident breath before returning to his reflection.

Determined thumbs grasped the waistband of his boxers and slid them down past his hips, slowly. The thin fabric floated along his thighs and calves, settling in a pool around his ankles. The cool air on his skin was oddly grounding. He stepped out carefully and used the top of his foot to nudge the plaid fabric aside. It came to rest near his bed in a soft ripple.

He stood now, bare. His heartbeat hard as he faced the mirror, his eyes drawn downward, transfixed by the quiet betrayal unfolding in his groin. The specks of emerging quills, stubborn, wiry things, sprouted like tiny invaders, each one infiltrating the territory he thought was still his. They signaled a deadly assault on his childhood, a place he defended constantly. Every dark hair felt like a trespass, an incursion he hadn't agreed to. This discovery wasn't progress. It was a potential loss.

His reflection stared back like an enemy. Not monstrous, not even frightening, just wrong and menacing. It was a counterfeit version of the boy he knew himself to be, standing on the edge of something colder, duller. It was someone he didn't recognize, and someone he never would become.

He turned toward the bed, where the items lay at the foot, just as he'd arranged them. The mirror. The bottle. The razor. He reached first for the lotion. The cap clicked open with a soft pop, and the scent rose immediately, sweetly and artificially. He squeezed a small amount into his palm, then began to smooth it over his lower abdomen, methodical in his movements. The cool cream spread evenly, his fingers working in small circles. The sensation was familiar, but no less jarring. Like painting over something he wasn't ready to fully erase.

He wiped his hands carefully on a towel he'd brought over earlier. Then he reached for the razor. It rested there like something omnipotent, something that demanded more than just a motion. He picked it up slowly, wrapping his fingers around the cool handle. It felt heavier than it looked. Or maybe, what it represented carried far more weight than its form.

He returned to the mirror, the blade in his hand now. He moved gingerly, guiding the blade through the thin layer of lotion. His hands, steady from years of training and control on the soccer pitch, trembled here. Not from fear of cutting himself but from the fear that he wouldn't. That he'd do it perfectly. That he'd get used to it.

He worked in silence, the room still except for the occasional soft scrape of metal against his skin. He avoided looking up. He couldn't face the reflection just yet, not while he was in the middle of becoming something he didn't want to be. This wasn't like taping an ankle or tightening cleats before a match. It seemed somewhat more final than that. Each swipe of the razor felt like a lie, deepening the chasm between who he was and who he pretended to be.

When he finished, he wiped the blade with the towel and looked with satisfaction and relief at the smooth, untainted skin he left behind with relief. It was another day of triumph, not loud or celebratory, but something quieter, purer. A hard-won calmness filled his chest, the kind that came from fighting off something bigger than himself, even just for a little while. The tension didn't totally vanish, but it softened.

Then, he lifted his chin to face the mirror. He saw the reflection, honestly showing him what was there and, more notably, what was not. His eyes, twin pools of obsidian, burned with a fierce, unsettling intensity, watching his reflection as if it held the answers he so desperately sought. The war within him was relentless, a battle between defiance and fear, with vulnerability lurking like a predator just beneath the surface. His body, muscular and taut but still carrying the innocence of boyhood, felt like a cruel reminder of what he needed to escape. The boyish curve of his hip, the new lines of muscle that defined his frame, and the unmistakable evidence of growth seemed to mock him.

He stood there, transfixed by his reflection, surrounded by the unfamiliarity of it all. "I will never grow up," he whispered fiercely. The words were a mantra designed to hold back time. His labored breath fogged up the mirror again. It was then, as if to prove the truth of his own words, that his hand, trembling from a determined mix of fear and defiance, moved involuntarily. His fingers violently gripped himself with force and shook. The ever-increasing weight and pressure were undeniable as he squeezed until he could feel it in a desperate attempt to assert his intentions.

"I'm a boy with a big thing. That's all. I'm not a man." The words defined his control and reminded himself of the boy he still was.

The mirror offered no comfort, only a reflection stripped of reassurance, unyielding, impersonal, and unkind.

Everything about this moment felt exposed, but essential. This pursuit was a performance, yes, but one steeped in agonizing self-awareness, an effort to wrangle control from the current that threatened to drag him under. It was not vanity. It was survival. With every stroke of the blade, every careful application of balm, he carved out a space for himself, a small sanctuary of desperation against the expectations that pressed in from all sides. This was where he pushed back, not with words, but with motion, with precision, and with pain.

He noticed pinpoint spots of blood from tiny razor nicks stinging his tender skin, bright red confirmations of his resolve. He groaned as he pressed against the minor wounds, ending the threat of discovery… today. It was a victory in a war fought with the ferocity of a cornered animal. And yet, in that wooden-framed, mirrored cage, a boy stood insolently, a solitary figure in a battle he knew he would win. Because of this, he refused to surrender or be swept away by the unforgiving tide of what his parents called "science."

"Davis!"

His mother's call shattered his moment. The word crashed through the air like a thunderclap, ripping him from his thoughts and unleashing a torrent of fury. His muscles stiffened, and his stomach seared with intense anger.

He dropped to the floor without thinking, aimlessly grabbing for his clothes in a frantic scramble. It wasn't from shame. It was an urgent and immediate need to cover himself before the boundary between worlds could be crossed. If she opened the door, his plan would be revealed. In a burst of motion, he pulled up his discarded underwear. The elastic band caught on his privates before releasing them with a voluble snap, compounding his emotion with a smarting, dull ache.

His skin, still raw from the razor, stung with every abrupt movement. Rational thought evaporated, consumed entirely by primal rage. Across the room, the blue robe lay on the bed. With anger mounting, he rapidly advanced toward it with purpose. In one explosive motion, he snatched it up and threw it over his shoulders. The fabric snapped into place, nearly tearing under the sheer force of his motion.

His chest constricted with furious breaths as he turned and stormed toward the door. Heavy, stomping steps reverberated with an all-consuming feeling of hate, which dominated him.

"What?" he shouted, a sudden, explosive cry that shattered the quiet.

His hand immediately clamped on the doorknob like a vise. Every muscle in his arm tensed. His heart pounded loudly. In that instant, the bed littered with remnants of sleep, the casually discarded clothes, and the soccer trophies proudly displayed on shelves along the wall all melted away. None of it mattered. Only the overwhelming urge to break through the intrusion remained.

The wild surge of his annoyance condensed into a focused, unsettling calm. His eyes, once wide with frantic fury, narrowed with clear, determined focus. It wasn't rage anymore. It was intent.

Without hesitation, he turned toward the stereo. His fingers flew over the controls with urgency and force. In a single, decisive motion, he slammed the power button. The stereo roared to life. The red indicator light flashed brightly. The speakers shook under the weight of the bass, vibrating with the impact of his command.

He cranked the volume, pushing it to the edge of distortion until the stereo unleashed an assaultive rhythm. The floor trembled. The walls buzzed. The room closed around the sound. There was no space for thought. No room for interruption. The bass exploded outward, filling every corner and crevice of his world.

It was control.

And he stood in the center of it.

Unapologetically.

Chapter 2: Ellen

Ellen paced in the living room with a grace that opposed the simmering energy beneath. She did not want to rush to work again today. Sable brown hair rested on her shoulders, framing a face cycling through expressions from understanding, to frustration, to anger, and back again. Her sapphire-blue eyes revealed an incompetence that disputed the composure she presented to the world around her.

She looked at her watch. Her son's alarm sounded twenty minutes ago. "Ten more minutes", she whispered to herself before stopping to look in the mirror. The charcoal grey suit she wore complemented her complexion, which was flushing by the minute. Her skin often acted as a mood ring, changing color with her temperament.

Stepping from the mirror, she wished she could depend on the authority she commanded at work to also manage her life at home. The helplessness she felt, especially in the mornings, was a feeling she had become used to. Communicating with her son was much more challenging than managing a finance department at the office.

A blue spiral bound notebook left on the coffee table attracted her attention. She sat on the sofa and thumbed through the algebra homework she had completed the night before. She got past feeling guilty about doing his work for him months ago. The fact was that if somebody didn't do it, he would fail. He may not care about his academic progress, but she did. To Ellen, the options were clear. Checking her work seemed to be more productive than checking her watch.

Her focus was hard to maintain. She had to get out of the house but first needed to sit with her son to lay out his home-school expectations for the day. There was no time for this and also no willingness to address it… yet. Fighting her compulsion to stare at the clock, she returned to the time-passing busy work of math.

Verifying the first half of her algebra solutions were correctly solved, she stopped to listen for signs of movement from behind Davis's door. The occasional creak of floorboards was enough to, at least, let her know that he was up and moving, albeit slowly. She knew better than to open his door to speed him up. She didn't want a fight, and he would only become more difficult afterward. Experience was a ruthless teacher.

"Come on, Day," she nagged at herself.

Discomfort persisted when it came to him. A nervous shifting of her feet, while she impatiently waited, confirmed its presence. The binder gently found its way back to the table accompanied by hope that when she returned home in the afternoon, there would be no more to do tonight.

Her son's untouched school laptop sat folded on the table as its own confirmation of her weakness. She moved it every other day or so to hide the evidence it had not been touched for weeks. This activity was more for her than anyone else. It was somehow soothing in its irrationality.

Looking at his unused study area was a face punch, a wrenching reminder of her inability to encourage him. She had spent a great deal of time transforming part of the dining room into a school to make him feel comfortable, yet he couldn't care less. She was the one who used it. Someone had to. The chore of completing homework nightly ate at her but not doing it... seeing him held back would destroy her. The current educational arrangement was humiliating enough for all of them.

Homeschooling wasn't a fight she had chosen. It was a demand placed upon her by the board of the expensive private school which lured her in with promises of excellence. The academic superiority they sold her seemed to be only evident when it stood without challenges. Davis needed help. He was being bullied. Of course he became physical. Who wouldn't have? Instead of offering solutions, they abandoned him.

Their expulsion of her son, after only a few occurrences, seemed unfair. The determination was absent of empathy or understanding for his challenges. As a result, Ellen felt unable to trust the educational system as a whole. This one critical event added to the agonizing weight of her burden. She knew that public school would not be any better. How could it be? A chilling fear took hold: somehow losing all control.

"Davis?" she called, probably too softly to be heard. It had been fifteen minutes. Without hearing a response, she decided to wait a little longer before trying again. It took him longer than most kids to get moving in the morning. It was something to work on. Maybe she would speak with him later about setting his alarm to wake him a bit earlier.

Ellen's inability to confront Davis felt like the ultimate betrayal of her son. It eroded a deep chasm of guilt through her conscience. She had vowed to contribute to his success… and his pride. The triumphs in her professional life felt like a shirking of her responsibility as a parent. Managing his studies wasn't a simple matter of education. To her, it was an opportunity to be a good role model. It wasn't working out, but all other reasonable inlets had been exhausted.

Ellen stood stately, her eyes scanning her home until her attention fell upon the family photographs adorning the credenza. A thin layer of dust provided an opportunity to get her mind on something more positive for a moment. To pass the time, she began wiping down the framed snapshots of her, Max, and their beautiful son, Davis.

As she picked each one up and cleaned the surface beneath, she wondered if it all was a carefully crafted illusion. Were these snapshots of her life merely deceptions of static happiness and harmony, reminiscent of the TV families she had grown up watching and striving to emulate? No pictures showed the long nights, the breakdowns, the quiet decisions that led to the isolation she now lived in. She brushed the thought away. "Who would have pictures like that, "She asked herself.

Ellen's life, the life she had worked so hard to create, seemed to be under the constant threat of her scrutiny. She couldn't help but ask herself, "Why me?" The answer, when it came, was not comforting. "Why not me?" It was a blunt realization that her reassurances had been an illusion all along. The dream that had led her to this very moment laughed at her through snapshots.

The frozen memories before her felt like theatrical masks. Each radiant smile opened a fresh wound. As her hand brushed the wood beneath them, she noticed the frigid surface on her fingertips. Its coldness echoed the despair that gripped her. Captured mirth, eternally fixed in time, felt like stifling lies.

"Calm down, Ellie. You are running late and letting it get to you. Everything is fine. He is doing the best he can with what he has." Talking to herself sometimes helped, but not today.

The diagnosis of Davis's bipolar disorder was a poisoned dart. It was a source of contention that floated heavy, like steam, in her head. Even the word "disorder" sent a chill down her spine. The word, by definition, did not align with the image she longed for and worked for since her own childhood.

Max's dismissal of it was also a thorn. She witnessed its insidious impact ravaging her son, claiming more of him... more of her... with each passing day. His denial stabbed at her because it was the only explanation that relieved some accountability for the boy's problems from her. She understood her husband's position that it was a phase, but this insight did not discount the evidence presented daily.

Ellen wasn't living the idyllic life of motherhood she always dreamed of: the version peddled by television shows and glossy magazines. Hers was torn between the unwavering devotion to nurturing a child and the desperate pursuit of professional success. She needed to have purpose.

Motherhood, she knew, was paramount; her world revolved around Davis's well-being. Had she erred in not sacrificing her career to dedicate every moment to him? Was she even capable of excelling in either role while attempting both? Davis's future, delicate as a soap bubble, balanced on the thread of her decisions. Had she, in her efforts to protect him, inadvertently crippled him? Was Max right? Did she screw up by excusing his refusal to study? Should she not have completed his neglected homework to insulate him from disappointment and failure? A powerful self-doubt resided within her. This was not an uncommon feeling, but it felt stronger today.

The voices inside her hurled accusations of incompetency. She wanted to maintain peace but also needed to nurture her son. Experience had shown this combination to be impossible. She faced the pressure of trying to maintain balance, and the all-too-familiar sense of danger picking at her every day. Months... years... a lifetime of resentments grew. Despite this, she knew her son was hurting. Davis was also keenly aware of his problems. She hated he had to live with that knowledge.

A half hour passed. Like it or not, she needed Davis to come out. She could practically feel the signals of Davis's reaction vibrating through the floorboards, carbon copies of the ghouls she imagined were always watching and tearing at her own soul. Beyond that door was her brilliant, volatile son, wounded by her pursuit of an unattainable ideal. He was consumed by a rage as cold and sharp as shattered glass.

The rasp of her voice, a dry whisper like sandpaper on bone, was a reticent call through the stifling nothingness. She prepared herself for the aftermath history had proven was coming.

"Davis?"

The silence that followed was a wall of cold energy pressing against her chest. Each beat of her heart was a muffled drum against the building pressure. The clock in the hall became a metronome and measured the moments. Each second pronounced a hammer blow against her. She dropped into a chair at the dining room table surrounded by the makeshift schoolroom and waited with her head balanced on her hands.

The oak of the dining table, cold under her elbows, paralleled the chill spreading through her. Then, a sound. Not a voice, but a low, guttural moan, shot through the narrow hallway. A sound that spoke not just of teenage defiance but of simmering hatred, of a detachment that cut her to the core.

"What?!" The word spat out with venomous precision, a cobra strike. Cynicism dripped from it, thick and oily, coating the room and everything in it with its acrid stench. A misplaced nervous laugh revealed the solitude that had become her constant companion. She slammed her fist on the table hard enough to rattle the breakfast dishes.

The sharp sting of the oak against her fist was nothing compared to the dull ache of helplessness that grasped at her heart. Fatigue settled on her shoulders even though she had only been awake for three hours. It weighed her down and made her into a prisoner of her own lack of conviction.

She tried again, a plea lost in the chasm that yawned between them.

"Davis? Honey? Are you almost ready?" The silence, another rejection, thwarted her hope that a less authoritative tone might be better received. Her second attempt rapidly threw more coldness in her direction. Then, a volcanic eruption of fear moved through her. Her hope disintegrated, leaving only flailing loose ends, snapping chaotically like bullwhips. She rose from her chair. The legs screeched across the floor, sounding like a banshee's wail.

"DAVIS! I KNOW YOU'RE IN THERE! GET OUT HERE NOW, OR SOCCER IS CANCELLED! I SWEAR, I WILL RIP YOU OUT OF THAT ROOM MYSELF! GET…OUT…HERE… NOW!"

Her uncharacteristic demand was a roar that tore through the house. It shattered the silence and left behind the wreckage of her broken morning, the disappointing crush of defeat, and the cold, hard certainty that something had irrevocably changed in her. The house groaned beneath the *THUD, THUD, THUD,* of Davis's descending stomps.

She sat, remaining attuned to the pounding. She was accustomed to his slamming and stomping when he did not get his way. Each thud drilled against Ellen's already fractured patience, a brutal percussion that vibrated into her teeth. At the same time, it did not have the effect on her he wanted. She refused to let it. Ellen crossed her arms and waited.

Anticipation was a press crushing her ribs, stealing her breath, leaving her gasping. Pompeiian air carrying ashes from the past encased her, ensuring every inhalation was a wasted effort. She was suffocating in her own feelings of helplessness.

Then, the vocals: "Arghhhh!"

It was a guttural outcry racing from his room that lacerated the very soul of the house. It broke through the silence like a siren. It scraped against her sanity and exposed nerve endings which howled in agony. This was the opening salvo of a never-ending war she had been fighting, and losing, for years. She wasn't a mother facing a tantrum; she was a prisoner facing execution, a vessel splintering under the pressure of a bomb about to explode.

"What...now?" she whispered, her voice a threadbare sigh against the silence that followed. It was the silence, dead as a tomb, loaded with the weight of undeniable accusations, that concerned her. Quiet was definitely not usual, and it made her nervous. Davis's silence was never empty; it was a weapon, sharpened to lethal perfection by his years of honed experience. He knew how to frighten her. Something was going on.

The polished oak of the bedroom door throbbed with a malevolent pulse, a heartbeat echoing the frantic drum in her temples. The stillness pulsed with a single, terrifying question, a question that manifested into a physical presence: What is next?

Davis's temper was not a monster she'd created; it was a beast she had birthed, nurtured, and now inevitably faced. Her question was answered in spades as her ears were overwhelmed by electric guitars and bass notes hurling cannonballs at her. Davis's stereo, an offensive attack, had met its target. Each boom was a critical hit designed to compromise the fragile peace she attempted to build.

Ellen's counterattack came as a raw shriek. "Stop, Davis, stop!" But it was swallowed by the sound. Ellen was perishing in the war zone her home had become. The space around her felt gelatinous, choking her with fear and stale sweat, a plague sticking to the walls. She knew better than to confront him, so she bowed her head and sobbed.

Then, a sliver of hope emerged. The jarring slam of the front door was a miracle against the chaotic attack. The very sight of her husband provided respite from the torment she found herself in the center of. "Max!" The relief in Ellen's cry was desperate, a ripple that ran through her, propelling her towards him. She pleaded with her eyes because her voice was rendered useless.

She depended on Max for the steadfast strength only he possessed. He was the man who understood the labyrinthine shadows of her soul, the man who knew her better than she knew herself.

Her husband felt the tremor in her body, the ungraded panic radiating from her like heat. He crushed her against him.

The bass was a malevolent presence. It was a painful manifestation of Davis's inner demons. Eruptions of rage pulsed through the timbers of the house in time with the noise flooding the hallway.

Ellen stood, hanging onto Max in confused wonder. The house groaned, exhibiting a sadness that squatted like unwanted tenants in her head. Her fear was not about this moment. From where she stood , it represented the constant storm of failure raging within her fractured family.

Chapter 3: Max

Waves of heat rose from the top of Max's freshly washed sedan. Stepping into the sun, he pressed his key fob with a firm thumb. The click of the doors locking sounded sharp against the chirping of crickets in the overgrown verge behind him. His six-foot frame supported the physique of a man built for hard work. Olive skin glistened from a thin layer of perspiration clinging to his forehead. Dark, jet-black curls barely met the nape of his neck. A goofy, careless grin pulled the corners of his mouth toward his ears.

Worn jeans and a tight polo shirt hugged his body. His wife often teased him about wearing clothing too small for his build. The stretched fabric enhanced the muscle definition he worked hard to develop and maintain. What was wrong with showing it off a little, he wondered?

He stood still in the driveway for a moment, taking in the morning air. He appreciated having the luxury of spending some time with his family before heading to the construction site. He let out a satisfied breath. The muscles in his back reminded him of the hard work out he finished twenty minutes ago. The gym was his therapy. He glanced at himself in the tinted driver's side window. He had never been one to shy away from his image.

He was huge. Thick through the chest and shoulders. His skin was darkened from spending hours in the sun. He considered the deep tan to be a benefit of his employment. His face was sharp like his son's, with high cheekbones, a squared jaw, and steady brows that didn't move much. His eyes were dark, calm, and hard to read. He stood still and enjoyed the moment. He knew it was his.

Max slapped a hand onto the roof of his car, projecting boyish confidence. The impact disturbed the softer sounds in the upper-middle-class neighborhood around him. A lawnmower hummed in the distance. A dog barked at him from somewhere beyond his range of sight, piquing his curiosity. He scanned the street to look for the source, but the distraction didn't hold his interest for long.

A half-smile formed as he tossed the car keys high, catching them as they quickly descended. The jingle, as he closed his hand around them, served as a reminder that he was right where he wanted to be at this point in his life. As he approached his house, he chuckled at something he'd heard at the gym.

"Those guys," he muttered, the words carrying a hint of affectionate amusement. "Always trying to one-up each other. Good luck with this one here."

He removed his sunglasses and placed them in the pocket of his shirt. For a moment, he stood, squinting, while his eyes adjusted to the brightness of the morning. His contented stride was long and powerful but not hurried. He moved with the casual confidence of a man completely at home in his own skin.

A strike of bass notes and drums slammed against his chest before he reached the concrete stairs leading to his front porch. A moment passed before Max registered that it was coming from inside his house. A horrible percussion vibrated through the soles of his shoes and rattled the storm windows in their frames. The quiet suburban street was assaulted by a sonic earthquake. His smile, beaming only a moment before, vanished.

Ellen's thin voice sliced through the racket. It was a screeching plea over the earsplitting surges of sound: "Davis! Please, turn it down!"

A rolling thunder rose from Max's core and the jovial expression melted from his face. "Damn it, Day-Day," he mouthed, the words laced with a mixture of weary resignation, unfortunate familiarity, and smoldering rage.

"Fucking why? What now?" He bounded up the porch steps and ate up the ground between him and the house. The door burst inward, and his wife ran to him, slamming herself against his torso. Tears soaked his shirt as she pressed into him. He held her close; his arms, corded and strong, were armor.

"Here we go again," he sighed, with budding exhaustion. Ellen's nod was sharp and jerky. Her tears were a silent accusation waged against her son. She didn't speak but pointed in the direction of Davis's room with resignation. Max's regard, usually warm and gentle, hardened. Beyond Ellen, the chaotic living room swam into focus. The salt of her tears continued to moisten his skin as he held her.

For a moment, he remembered the glowing fire in her eyes when they'd first dreamt of a family, a life brimming with laughter. Reality served them something very different. Davis... his boy, his worshipped son, wasn't bad. No, the word was too blunt, too simplistic for the stinging truth. Davis was gunpowder primed for explosion and starved for connection.

The arrangement Ellen and he had come to was not working out. Davis needed the harsh grind of public school, the chaotic judgement of peers, to learn about compromise, to understand the weight of consequence. Home schooling was not the answer. "Social skills," Max thought.

The entitlement his son personified infuriated him. It was a poison, slowly consuming them all. Ellen, in her fierce, desperate love, had unwittingly fostered the problem. She meant to shield their son from failure, but instead, she'd dulled him to struggle and denied him the lessons usually acquired from life's challenges.

His wife's over-protectiveness and consistent rescue were both the sun that warmed Max's soul and the shadow that choked his spirit. He loved her for the way she never gave up on their boy. At the same time, he hated the way she never let him fall. He resented her compulsion to sacrifice the boy's growth to feed the fire of her own pride.

He crushed her closer. Her heartbeat was a drum against his ribs. He had to do something. Now. His whisper, bitter with a grief that nicked in his throat, was a sincere prayer, "I love you, Ellie. God, how I love you." Then, like a lightning strike, his voice tore through the house. It boomed, washing over Ellen. The loudness of his call resonated in her body and settled in the base of her skull. "Davis Day! Turn that down now, or I swear to God, I will beat your bare ass with a belt in the front yard in front of every single one of your friends!"

Max knew there was no way his challenge would go unheard. The intensity of his threat, coupled with its volume, was a pronounced warning shot. He may just do it. He feared he would enjoy putting him in his place.

The uncharacteristic savagery of Max's expression, the steely callousness in his eyes, and the way his knuckles clenched into massive fists frightened Ellen. She usually met Max's outbursts with calm acceptance, but this time she felt a cold dread gripping her soul. He had gone too far. She pulled from his embrace and glared at him. Max had never struck their son. She knew he wouldn't today, but the unfiltered fury, the certainty of his threat, still shocked her.

As if on cue, the music ceased. Silence rang through the halls. A deafening but welcomed emptiness stretched and strained with the sudden end of the audio assault. Ellen offered Max a look that was both imploring and reverent. He could read the anger and disapproval reflected in her eyes. With the crisis averted, the aggression in his posture swiftly departed.

He brushed the tears from his wife's cheek. His hand felt rough but surprisingly gentle, a comparison that only amplified the intensity of the preceding moments. Then, Max slowly approached the door at the end of the hallway. Floorboards groaned under his weight. Each step toward Davis's room landed like a countdown. The atmosphere became consumed with impending consequence.

He opened the door with force.

A draconian call greeted him. "ARRRGH!" Davis stood his ground defiantly. The tears streaming down his face opposed his confrontational stance. His eyes fixed onto Max's. This wasn't the rage of a child; it felt like something ancient, dark, like something chillingly adversarial to the man facing him. His father was always the disciplinarian. The history between them mattered. The shared burden of a legacy rife with failed understanding was a liability they both carried.

Angst, sweat, and fear filled the room as they stared at each other without speaking. The silence of the moment felt worse than the noise preceding it. Davis stood panting while Max towered over him, assessing his son with disappointment. He could only bring himself to shake his head dismissively.

He didn't want to escalate the boy's anger, not now. Seeing Davis in fear of him was painful, even when his son was at his worst. The truth was that Max's pride in the boy knew no bounds.

His mood lightened as he remembered Davis as a toddler, his chubby legs stumbling over a soccer ball in a world of determination and joy as he chased it across the grass. As he grew up, he stayed focused on the game. His passion for soccer never diminished. The kid was loyal.

Max remembered watching Davis on the field the night before; a gifted, competent teen with lightning-quick reflexes. Davis danced across the pitch, a graceful athlete, the ball glued to his feet as he weaved and feinted, leaving defenders in his wake. His son was a prodigy, an elite player with a bright future. Max's admiration followed Davis's every move, his heart pounded with excitement and pride.

The way Davis moved with the ball was a testament to his natural talent and hard work. He was a force of nature, an unstoppable juggernaut when he built up speed, leaving everyone else in his dust. Max recalled his eyes widening as his son executed, for the first time in actual play, a perfect Maradona turn, a move he had practiced for months in their backyard, preparing for that single opportunity.

The crowd roared with its approval, but Max remained silent, his throat tight with emotion. As Davis later lined up for a corner kick, Max remembered countless afternoons spent in the park, the two of them practicing set pieces until the sun dipped below the horizon. The memory of Davis as a young boy, lit up with determination, overlapped with the vision of him now, a confident young man on the cusp of potential greatness... if he could only hold it together. As the memories faded, he looked at his son much more gently.

Recognizing his father's shift, Davis's labored breaths began to slow as well. The fear and fury draining from Davis's face left a trail of icy sweat on his skin. Max watched the tension leech from his son's neck. Davis's knuckles slowly unfurled like the petals of a poisoned bloom. The volatile breath that moments before had rattled in Davis's lungs surrendered with a deep sigh.

Max had seen the same feral dog in Davis's reaction before. It was a chilling reflection of his own childhood staring back at him through a cracked lens. The boy was a terrifying blend of himself and Ellen, a cocktail neither of them had truly ever fully acknowledged, let alone accepted.

Under the dim glow of his bedroom light, Davis's face shifted toward his feet. The watery sheen in his eyes, reflecting the light, broke through Max's aggression like nails. He saw not just the son who had just exploded, but a frightened boy drowning in a maelstrom of inherited inferiority. The emotion that covered him was a pungent tide, leaving a residue of bone-deep regret in its wake.

"Are you really going to do that to me?" Davis asked the question like a challenge.

"C'mon, buddy, I'll get you some water," his father whispered with soft encouragement, feeling like a monster. The curve of his smile, a slow, deliberate thing, mirrored the gentle arc of his outstretched arm. Davis, now seemingly oblivious to the tension that had been present only moments before, slipped past him and raced to Ellen as if drawn by an invisible thread.

In the kitchen, Max clinked ice into a glass. The sound was rigid against the kind tone of Ellen's voice in the other room. He watched his wife and son from the sink, as water was poured over the cubes. The last waves of guilt passed through him before he joined his family in the dining room schoolhouse. He handed the drink to his son, who smiled and reached for it eagerly.

Davis was now calm and sure, attentively responding to Ellen's words. He didn't challenge her. He didn't bristle. Instead, he listened with a quiet focus on her. She spoke of fractions, of verbs; her voice was soothing and infused with the comforting rhythm of expectation, not accusation.

Max leaned hard against the wall in the corner. The roughness of the textured plaster grounded him. He felt a deep, quiet satisfaction settling in him. He felt like father of the year but didn't need to say it aloud. The sunlit room, the quiet conversation, and the sight of his son engaged and respectful because of his intervention: this was it. This was parenting. Surely, Ellen would be impressed enough to see his point of view.

The feeling of victory died the instant Davis raised his glass as if preparing to present a toast. A vengeful sneer, forming a cruel, predatory curl on the boy's upper lip, was a foreshadowing of carnage to come. Max saw something unfolding but was frozen in place with confusion.

In a slow, calculated act of destruction, their son turned his wrist. The computer's sudden death was accompanied by a sickening crackle, a dynamic burst of blue light, and the chemical stench of frying electronics. The acrid smell of Max's unexpected failure overpowered all of it.

Ellen screamed, filling the space. She lunged, her fingers frantic, yanking the laptop's cord from the wall. Her effort was in vain. The damage was done.

Technology buzzed and smoked until it sat lifeless. Its screen matched the cold, uncaring darkness in Davis's eyes. His face did not move from an impassive mask of indifference.

Davis lightly placed his empty glass down on the table with the precision of a surgeon. The softness of it echoed the indented emptiness in Max's gut. Each of his son's footfalls was a measured beat of his triumphal march as he meandered back to his room like nothing had happened.

Upon reaching his destination, Davis turned to survey his parents before he gently closed his bedroom door with a whispering click.

The numbness that followed defined the intensity of the moment. It pressed down on Max, crushing him beneath the weight of his failure. Ellen's stunned gaze, despondent, pleaded for explanation, for forgiveness, for anything but the bleak reality staring them both in the face.

Max could only bow his head. The weight of his son's unbridled malice bore into him like a sword. Shame grew inside him... not just with the lingering bouquet of burnt circuits, but with incontestable powerlessness.

Max stared at the dark screen in disbelief. He whispered to the room. "Why in the hell did you do that?"

Chapter 4: The Prodigy

Rumbles of thunder drove through Max. There was a deep tremor in his mind, in sync with the crowd's loud applause as his son scored again. Ellen's hand tightly gripped his. It was a silent comfort following the shared agony they had both felt just the morning before. Watching Davis now, all of it was forgiven.

His boy was dominating the game, consuming the field, and leaving absolute wreckage in his wake. The scent of freshly cut grass mingled with the exertion of the crowd. The environment amplified the excitement brewing inside Max. He watched as Davis, a blur of motion in his crimson jersey, was demolition unleashed.

The fear in the eyes of the boy's opponents was obscene, a chilling energy that sent goose bumps across his mother's flesh. He moved with brutal precision, a spiraling collection of brawn and bone; each feint was an instinctual maneuver. Every turn he made on the field demonstrated a challenge to physics. The leather of the ball, slick with dew, seemed to whisper secrets only he could understand. The crowd gasped a collective breath that felt like a detonation.

Time warped as Davis bore down on the goal. The impact of his shot, a thunderclap, sent a shockwave through the stadium. It was a declaration of his skill, a violent punctuation mark on his mastery of the game.

Max felt a lump of pride in his throat so potent it bordered on pain. In his son, he saw a reflection of his own untamed spirit, a spirit he'd both nurtured and feared.

Ellen saw something else. She embraced the fragility beneath his talent, her years of sacrifice and unwavering dedication had cultivated the warrior on the pitch. Their smiles were bittersweet, fortified with the knowledge that this skill carried its own burden, its own price. Their joy was a powerful thing, balanced on the sharp edge of Davis's extraordinary athletic genius. In these moments, he was transformed. The troubled kid who had faced challenges became a star.

His every move on the field was efficient, driven by an inner motivation that fueled his happiness. This was his element; his reason for being. Max and Ellen witnessed his transformation at every game with awe and trepidation. The boastful cheers that emanated from Max were reflections of genuine emotion stirred by Davis's performance. Ellen felt her fears melt away as she watched him control the game.

Davis was a fog of red hue, a hunter in pursuit of his prey. The ball seemed to obey his every command, responding to the understanding that existed between them. His opponents froze in his presence. Their panic was plain. With each dodge and turn, Davis displayed a divine grace, which they could not match.

The crowd watched intently. They knew they were witnessing a powerhouse. Each time Davis approached the goal, time seemed to slow. The impact of his final score was a catalyst for lengthy applause throughout both sides of the stadium. Even the players and coaches from the opposing team stood reverent on the field, bringing their hands together in recognition of his power and potential.

From the stands, his parents' joy was undeniable. It was a bookend to the extraordinary future their son was destined for. Davis threw his arms in the air to accent his team's victory. His teammates surrounded him, blanketing him in a testosterone-filled cocoon, a crescendo to his stellar performance.

Ellen's protective instincts surged. She'd heard the whispers, the mutterings of jealous parents who couldn't appreciate her son's natural ability. A smile curved her lips as she realized their words were rooted in awe, not malice. She understood them more than they could ever know.

"He is exceptional," she affirmed with a whisper, not needing to convince anyone that their son's success was not something to apologize for.

With a wave, she caught Davis's attention. He beamed up at her, and they shared a quick, silent connection. Davis jogged toward the sidelines where Max and Ellen stood. The noise from the crowd subsided, but the energy remained, buzzing like an electric current. Davis, still in his element, exuded a post-game glow.

He moved with the same secure poise toward his parents as he did on the pitch. His face was alight with pride, relief, and a lingering adrenaline rush. The leather ball was securely tucked under his arm, a personal demonstration of his dedication. He would never abandon it.

Max and Ellen darted to meet their son. They knew the challenges he'd faced, the struggles that had added to his resilience, and now, witnessing his elation, their hearts swelled with a love so profound it was cathartic.

The family's departure from the stadium was met with waves, shouts, high-fives, congratulatory pats on the back, and whispered accolades. Davis strutted forward, his shoulders back, his head held high.

Max and Ellen exchanged a glance. They knew the road hadn't always been easy, but moments like these made every battle worth it. The stadium lights glared behind them, a reminder of the heights their son had reached and the promise of much brighter days to come.

Max, Ellen, and Davis trudged through fans and families toward the exit. Their path led them to the equally active parking lot, where familiar faces awaited them at the car. Manny, Irene, and their daughter, Gretchen, stood by the blue sedan, their presence was a comforting constant in the whirlwind of the evening's events.

At the sight of the Day trio, Irene's cheerleading instincts from her college days emerged. It seemed like grasshoppers had possessed her legs. She leaped into the air, her blonde curls bounced with each enthusiastic skyward spring.

"You did so good, Day-Day!" she shouted. Her voice carried above the din. She ignored the eyeroll he delivered in response to her greeting. Her enthusiasm recognized the extraordinary work Davis had displayed on the field and she wasn't going to allow his attitude to diminish them.

Manny, ever the counter to his wife's enthusiasm, stood by with a salesman's smile on his face. His tall, broad frame filled out his suit. Bushy blond hair added a touch of whimsy to his otherwise stern appearance. Though his demeanor was more subdued than Irene's, the pride in his eyes was undeniable as he, too, processed the experience he had just been a witness to.

Davis moved to greet their friends with uncharacteristic politeness. He couldn't help but show off a little by spinning the ball in his hands in the process. Max and Ellen followed him with praise which appeared mildly patronizing.

They acknowledged that moments like these were hard-earned for them, too. Yet, witnessing another triumph, with the support of friends, helped them realize their value. The two couples shared a deep bond, beginning in college. Their support and camaraderie remained unshakable.

Irene's excitement remained constant as she continued to jump up and down. Manny looked on with a touch of embarrassment at his wife's childish behavior.

As the families converged, a chorus of congratulations and well-wishes continued to fill the space, each member playing their own unique part in this harmony of flattery. Davis, still riding the high of his stellar performance, engaged with his parents and their friends with a sense of confidence. The reality of his achievements seemed to settle comfortably on his shoulders, and his face shone with satisfaction.

Davis's focus, almost mechanically, shifted to his other passion. With quick, agile movements, he excused himself and tossed the soccer ball into the back seat of the car, making a beeline for his cell phone.

Social media was his second area of focused dominance; a realm he was determined to conquer with the same passion he felt for his sport. Image and influence were everything to him. He had cultivated his online presence with extreme care, presenting an ideal narrative to the world of a life filled with triumph, affluence, and success.

Each addition, each uploaded photo, was a move in the game he played to ascend the online social ladder. He held an unwavering goal to become a social media influencer. His thumb hovered over the screen, ready to unlock a world of likes, comments, and adoration from his growing group of followers.

The phone lit up his face in conflict with the fading stadium lights that twinkled above, celestial reminders of his brilliance. Davis's online image reflected his loyal ambition. It was a projection of the confidence he had gained through his good looks and athletic achievements.

Every post, every caption, was an intentional move in his quest for dominance of life, a collection of select moments designed to inspire and captivate his audience. Unbeknownst to Davis, his parents understood the power of his online presence and the potential it held for their son's future. They knew the challenges he had faced and the sacrifices they had made as a family. They couldn't help but feel a sense of security as they saw him navigate this new realm with the same passion he displayed on the soccer field.

The rush of foot traffic from the stadium bled onto the parking lot, momentarily swallowing the small group as Manny clapped a hand, thick as a blacksmith's, on Davis's shoulder.

Manny's throat worked, a dry rasp preceding his words. "Day, you played... one hell of a game... If you really apply yourself, you could really be something." He squeezed Davis's shoulder. It was a gesture meant to convey encouragement, but the weight of it felt more like a possessive grip.

Davis didn't immediately look up from his phone, a sleek obsidian rectangle glowing faintly in the gloom. When he finally did, his glance, cold and sharp as icicles, impaled Manny. The pause that followed was a mere beat before he spoke. His voice dripped with practiced disdain.

"I am something, already," he drawled. Each word was a carefully aimed dart. "Don't make a fool of yourself by groveling like a peasant," he replied with an arrogant huff.

Ellen's sigh plummeted through the tense silence and Davis's icy tone. She didn't even look at her son. Her voice was flat but still accented with a weary impatience, "Davis, that wasn't funny."

He didn't bother to make eye contact. A mumbled, "That's good. I wasn't trying to be," drifted from him as he walked away. His retreat was as sharp and cold as the way he'd dismissed Manny. He turned and melted into the gathering dusk.

Davis's 13-year-old eyes widened as he glanced at the screen, the thrill of the game now intertwined with the excitement of his digital domain.

"Hey, Gretch! Check this out," he exclaimed, his voice alive with excitement.

Gretchen's heart raced as she approached Davis, her eyes sparked with mischief and adoration. Her gap-toothed grin, tomboyish charm, and long blonde hair casually pulled into a lazy ponytail did little to mask her intensity. The metronomic echo of his every gesture and tone evidenced how much he inspired her.

Davis had a magnetic quality, drawing people in with his fearlessness and strength, and Gretchen was no exception.

She loved how he took charge and always seemed to be willing to take the blame. This was very different from her more reserved, avoidant nature. Together, they were a dynamic combination; their opposite personalities created a perfect balance. Davis, bold and assertive, pushed Gretchen to step out of her shell. He encouraged her to welcome new adventures. Her cautiousness sometimes kept him grounded.

As he delved into his digital domain, she observed him with nothing short of fascination. Every like and comment fueled his ego. He relished the influencer status he was working toward. Gretchen yearned for a similar designation under his masterful tutelage. She saw his potential and wanted to join him in his arena as an equal force to be reckoned with.

Gretchen, always in tune with his interests, followed his lead eagerly. Her eyes remained glued to his phone. She studied his technique. In her eyes, they were a team, embarking on a pursuit of virtual fame.

Davis encouraged her support, "Remember that prank we pulled on Travis? I just posted the video before the game, and it's already at 5,000 views! It may go viral!"

Gretchen's shriek of delight pierced the nearing dusk. It was an appropriate complement to Davis's laughter. Their shared love for playing jokes on their friends and the thrill of online engagement united them in this not-so-private venture.

The two friends scurried further away from the ears of their parents, shuffling their sneakers on the concrete to draw as much attention to themselves as possible. Davis's thumb continued to dance across the screen as they walked, replying to comments and fueling the engagement and maximizing the validation he, so desperately, needed.

Once the two were out of sight, Max's mood began to shift, his eyes discreetly surveyed the area before speaking. When he was confident young ears weren't listening, he offered a quiet apology to Manny, attributing his son's behavior to a new phase of adolescence.

"I don't know where the peasant stuff came from," he said with an apologetic tone in his voice. "It's his way of pushing boundaries, I guess"

Manny stood silently, contemplating the rudeness of Davis's natural lack of consideration. Irene jumped in to assure her friends that there was no need to apologize, hoping to divert a stream of negativity. She shared her own struggles with their daughter, Gretchen, and her changing behavior. The intent was to show commonality; however, her tone carried an implied accusation. It hinted at a belief that Davis's influence might be a factor, without stating it directly.

"We're going through something similar with Gretchen," she said, her voice trailing off as she cleared her throat. "It's a challenging phase, but we'll get through it. I really wish I knew where she is getting the attitude from."

Max and Ellen exchanged looks; parenting styles were very different between the two families. They understood the complexities of raising children and the solidarity that came with navigating uncharted territories together.

The parking lot, now practically empty after the bustling game, seemed to mimic the retreat of their thoughts and concerns. An awkward silence loomed until Ellen's hands clapped, shattering the building tension with an abrupt change of subject.

"So, Florida!" she boomed, a grin splitting her face, the words a sunbeam slicing through grey clouds. Relief washed over the group; postures softened; hesitant grins blossomed on faces previously strained with serious consideration.

With a sharp intake of breath, Manny Stiles, his eyes already scanning the travel plans he spent weeks on, declared their hastened departure. "Three days early," he proclaimed. "We're hitting the road. This old steed favors the asphalt to the clouds." A wave of nervous giggles washed over the group. Max couldn't mask the strong desire to tease him, balanced just behind his closed teeth. Bad experiences with chiding for this very topic silenced any threat of trying. Manny's fear of flying was a sore subject everyone had learned to avoid.

Manny noticed Max's restraint with an appreciative glance before taking a firm, resolute posture.

A vibrant discussion materialized about their cherished seaside haven, a stately house nestled directly on West Palm Beach's sun-kissed coast. The imagined aroma, a potent blend of briny sea breeze, exotic perfumes, and the subtle sweetness of hibiscus blossoms, was a driving force in Irene's contribution.

The Florida warmth, a blissful escape from the daily grind of their Midwestern existence, seemed almost religious. It promised to be a temporary reprieve already began to feel. The adults' voices, fueled by anticipatory planning, shrouded the post-game parking lot distractions. Ideas for joint activities were tossed around: surf lessons for the kids, sunset cocktails for the adults, evenings filled with laughter, and shared stories around a bonfire crackling under a sky ablaze with stars.

Amidst the promise of sunshine and sand, the stresses of raising and enduring their children seemed to soften. The conversation hummed with the anticipation of a fantastic ten days of fun and freedom.

Ellen's eyes, glittering with determination, met Max's broad grin. Across the group, Irene's restless energy and Manny's, endearing, nerdy personality added variety to the group dynamic.

Max looked forward to the ocean's calming embrace, a much-needed escape from the pressures of their lives. Irene painted vibrant images of past vacations. Her genuine laughter and heartfelt recollections enhanced the anticipation of their upcoming trip.

Orange hues from the burgeoning sunset reminded the adults that time was pressing forward. Irene morphed into a general rallying her troops. With a shrill, motherly call, she summoned Gretchen and Davis.

"Hey, you two! Where are you? Time to go!" She peered across the emptying lot and crossed her arms impatiently waiting for a response that never came.

After a few moments, the pair emerged and slowly made their way back to their parents. Before heading to the car, Gretchen spun Davis around and planted an exaggerated kiss on his cheek before rushing away to her place in the Stiles' car, giggling.

It was a childish gesture that elicited an instant reaction. Davis's fierce stare and dissatisfied response, "Arrrgh...Yuck!", echoed through the parking lot. Gretchen's intrusion was a violation of his personal space that sent him storming to his seat. He ripped the back door of the car open and shut it behind him with a forceful slam. He made no effort to conceal his anger; in fact, he was intent on emphasizing it.

Gretchen's laughter, as sharp as shards of glass, ran him through.

Chapter 5: Gretchen

Florida hovered in Gretchen's thoughts, stirring sun-drenched beaches and the faces unseen for years. Going back felt less like a vacation and more akin to an act of reentry, like an astronaut adjusting to gravity after a long spell away. The familiar sun and beaches couldn't dispel the quiet unease. It was the idea of fitting herself back into that old mold, knowing it had likely hardened in her absence, and the rhythm of days slightly suspended from real life, that unsettled her now. This return to something that no longer fit quite right was the true source of her discomfort.

Within this wash of sun and forgotten voices, one presence resonated with a distinct and almost insistent clarity: Davis. His voice, sharp and unfiltered, came back with ease. He had always rushed to speak first, cut people off without meaning to, and filled the air with whatever thought entered his head. He had been bold, reckless, and hard to ignore. Somehow, he had also been the one person who made her feel like she belonged, even when he was making everything about himself. There had been something magnetic about him. Infuriating and impossible, but familiar. And now, with the trip only days away, she couldn't stop wondering what it would be like to see him again.

Of course, her own wondering was a one-sided affair, a silent conversation with a ghost of who he used to be. Three years had passed without a word. He hadn't reached out, not even once. No text. No call. No vague apology for the time or distance. It hadn't surprised her, but it had stayed with her anyway. She hadn't expected much, but the silence still managed to land somewhere deep. It was the absence of effort that stuck. The way someone so loud could go quiet when it counted.

She lay still beneath the covers, her eyes open to the dim light filtering into the room. The quiet settled in, dense and unmoving, shaped by the knowledge that it wouldn't last. Soon, she would be back there. Surrounded by people who thought they knew her.

The upcoming trip pressed against her with a pressure she couldn't ignore. Each breath felt off-rhythm, as though simply existing in the days leading up to it violated the quiet agreement she had made with herself not to look back. Gretchen could still remember the rough texture of the Florida sand pressing into her fingers, the way melted ice cream had turned sticky on her skin, collecting grit and heat beneath the sun. Those days lived on in her memory, vivid and persistent, shaped by feelings that no longer felt familiar or important.

She remembered the rush of being near him. Davis had always drawn people in. His laughter cracked through the air like lightning, yet she had leaned toward it without meaning to, pulled by something reckless and electric. For a long time, that noise had pushed everything else to the edges until nothing beyond him felt worth noticing. But beneath the attraction, there was a quieter tension. The anger had come slowly. It built over time, sharpened by neglect, by his distance, by the years he had chosen not to look back. Their vibrant past now felt tainted by the long, echoing silence that had followed over these unattended years.

She was angry with him. Three years of his silence had settled into her. She had been the only one left to feel it. However, the truth had never softened. She still wanted a response from him. A glance. A sign that he remembered who she was, or at least who she had been. The attraction hadn't faded. If anything, it had deepened into a feeling she no longer trusted. It had tangled itself in guilt and the need to be seen. It wasn't innocent. It wasn't sweet. It was a hunger built from distance, neglect, and the quiet space where their friendship used to live.

The chill overtook everything. It crept beneath her skin and sank into her muscles, stiffening her arms and locking her jaw until even breathing felt like a trespass. The thought of facing Davis, of standing in front of him and meeting his eyes, twisted her stomach in slow, nauseating turns. His judgment always came too fast, too direct, with no room to deflect. He wouldn't just see the girl he grew up with. He would see how she was now different, and somehow less than.

Davis wasn't the only one. The Days would see it, too. His parents hadn't seen her in years, but she could already imagine the way they might look at her. Not unkindly. Not cruelly. Simply softly, in a way that made her want to turn away. She didn't want their concern. She didn't want to be met with silence stretched too thin or eyes that tried too hard not to stare. Even imagined pity felt unbearable. It made her feel exposed like they already knew every inch of what she had failed to hide.

Her feelings for Davis had changed in his absence, and they didn't make sense, not even to her. She didn't think of him as a childhood companion anymore. She tried not to think about these ideas much, knowing how much they complicated things. They had grown quietly over the long silence between them, rooted in her own need to feel seen. They lingered at the edge of everything she thought she had put behind her.

She wanted to escape it. All of it. Despite her attempts to avert them, her thoughts ricocheted through her mind, searching for a door that didn't exist. She wanted to run. She wanted to disappear. She wanted to lose herself in any place where no one would look at her. The idea of entering that space, of being seen by them and having nowhere to hide, froze her in place. She feared what they might recognize. And worse, she feared seeing it, too.

Her history spread through her veins. The bedroom around her was quiet and still, the day just beginning. She could still see him. She could feel him. The memory of his presence brushed against her mind, as vivid as if he were still standing there. His curly black hair, always untamed, framed a face that seemed to linger in both worlds: beautiful yet unreachable. His eyes stayed locked in her thoughts, steady and dark, cutting through the quiet even now. Although she hadn't seen him in years, his online posts made it impossible to forget him. He never disappeared completely. She never stopped watching.

His selfies commanded attention. Thousands of followers celebrated his every move, every accomplishment, every natural grin. The comments poured in, a chorus of admiration for his athleticism, his confidence, and his polished persona. But to her, he wasn't just a figure on a screen. The way he carried himself with the strength he exuded, reaching past his surface. It unsettled her and left her searching for something more solid to hold onto. There was a presence about him, one that drew her in even when she didn't want to follow. His smile held power in its simplicity. It was confident, unshaken, and impossible to look away from. It hung around in her thoughts long after it faded from the screen, leaving her wondering how something so seemingly light could carry such weight in her mind.

It was a cruel irony. His beauty concealed a temperament as unpredictable as the wind. Everything about him invited attention. He was the embodiment of what the world admired in men, but beneath that surface lived volatility she had never learned how to ignore. His boyish charm worked in tandem with something far more unsettling. There was a recklessness in him, a flicker behind his eyes that suggested limits were only suggestions. That blend of charm and carelessness, confidence and impulse, refused to stay quiet in her mind.

He wasn't safe. Not emotionally. Not socially. Not in the way people meant when they described someone as kind. But there was something about his immaturity, the way it brushed against cruelty, that kept her tethered. He had crossed lines before. Said things. Done things. Moments that should have repelled her only drew her deeper. The appeal didn't soften with sense or distance.

It grew teeth. And in the darkness, as her breath caught the edge of his name, she couldn't stop herself.

The memory of him, so potent and unsettling, began to bleed into the present quiet of her room. It was a strange alchemy, this echo of a past self-intertwined with the woman she was now becoming. The intensity of her focus on him, on his image and the complicated magnetism he exerted, felt like a final reckoning with that earlier chapter of her life.

"Perfect," she whispered. The word hovered in the air, stripped of peace. It didn't sound like admiration. It sounded like surrender. Morning light crept into her room, brushing across the sheets and calling her into the day ahead. She didn't move.

As the morning pressed forward, Gretchen found herself thinking about the changes in her since those early pre-teen years. Gone was the tomboy frame she used to call her own. Sitting up in bed, she became aware of the gentle weight of her breasts and the quiet shape her body had taken on. The curves along her sides and the way her hips transitioned into her waist felt natural now.

She had grown into herself. Her body made more sense to her than it used to. There was a kind of stillness in noticing it, a calm understanding that hadn't always been there. But along with that awareness came doubt. She wasn't the girl he remembered. The last time he saw her, she was narrow-shouldered, sunburnt, always loud. Back then, she was just one of the children. Now, she wasn't. Her body no longer let her blend into the background. She was a woman now.

There was a power to him she couldn't explain. It had settled in quietly, without permission, and refused to leave. She liked him. She wanted him to notice her. To look at her and see someone he could want. She tried not to care. She tried to keep it to herself. But it stayed there, waiting.

"Too bad. He probably won't feel the same way about me."

She recalled his face, the clean angles and the careless charm, and the way his laughter had drawn her in. Trusting him had come easily. She hadn't noticed the tension behind that charm back then. Max and Ellen would be there, too. And Gretchen knew their concern would be the hardest part.

As she dressed, her thoughts turned to him again. She could see the way he moved in the short clips he posted—always in motion, always performing. Even his still photos had energy like he was caught mid-laugh or mid-thought. Lately, that version of him had taken over the one she remembered. His feed stayed full of polished moments and athletic victories. Everything he showed the world looked simple. Why would he ever look at her after everything that happened?

She hated how careless he seemed. The calm, the beauty. None of it matched what was inside. That dichotomy stayed with her. She had stopped trying to make sense of it, but it lingered anyway. It made her wonder what people saw when they looked at her.

Gretchen's relationship with the Day family had always been layered. Davis, especially, had once felt more like a brother than anything else. That made her attraction to him harder to sit with, even if it came without warning, and she refused to let go.

Despite the shame she carries now and the memories that still surface when she lets her guard down, the upcoming vacation felt like an opening. A chance to see him again. Maybe even a reason to believe she could be more than what had been done to her.

As the vacation approached, Gretchen kept thinking about how much time had passed. The people she would see, the memories they shared, none of it felt as far away as it should have. Everything about those years still felt unfinished. Pieces were left scattered, waiting to be understood.

And still, Davis was there. Already preoccupying her. The memory of him formed a quiet tangle of feeling she couldn't unwind. She wanted to make sense of it, to know if it had always been there or if the years apart had given it life. The uncertainty made her ache, a restless hum she couldn't quite ignore.

Max and Ellen, with their knowing looks and quiet compassion, represented a different threat, one that unsettled her more than anger ever could. As she dressed, she couldn't get her worries out of her mind. She knew that facing Davis and his parents would force her to confront the rape she had kept buried for years. With each passing moment, Gretchen felt a shift within herself, a quiet strength she hadn't known in years. It felt like time to confront the past. Maybe it would be the first step toward feeling like herself again.

She had carried the consequences and pain of her rape for years, tucked deep, never ignored but rarely named. The trauma, distress, and dread that followed completely overwhelmed her, clenching her heart in its grip. It had lived with her, shaped her, and defined too much of how she knew others saw her. But she never wanted to be identified as a victim. And lately, something inside had begun to move. The fear was still there, but so was the urge to do more than just survive. She needed to get out of the house so she could begin to heal. She needed the air and the space, the feeling of her own limbs carrying her somewhere freely. The walls had been closing in, pressed by a tenderness that had begun to feel more like surveillance than care.

Her parents meant well. Their careful questions, their soft tones, and their eagerness to accommodate had become uncomfortable and almost patronizing. They hovered without realizing it. Every offer of comfort, every cautious glance, reminded her of what she had endured. It kept her in it. Their kindness felt more like a vigil than a refuge, as if they were still waiting for her to shatter. She needed room to feel normal.

She knew the devastating truth, the one that could dismantle everything she had spent years building. A secret lived just beneath the surface, waiting to destroy what little peace she had managed to create. Her parents were lucky, she thought. Blissfully unaware. They didn't know the full story. They didn't know the choice she'd made or the depth of what had been done to her. The details still violated every instinct of decency, every fiber of her being.

A shiver tore through her spine. Her chest tightened, her limbs suddenly were too light and too heavy at once. "Davis can't know about Ethan," she whispered, the words paper-thin and already falling apart as she spoke them. They offered no comfort. No protection. Only the reminder of how close everything was to unraveling.

The truth surged through her, unstoppable. It filled her throat, pressed against her skin, and made her stomach twist as if her body wanted to reject it entirely.

Ethan, the golden boy. The other star. He wasn't a victim. He played his role, and he did it willingly. And she, out of necessity, played hers. Their lives were tangled now, fused by choices she couldn't undo. Her innocence was the price of trust.

The sick churn in her gut was rage, tangled with the sting of betrayal and the sharp memory of being exposed while he protected himself. She felt stripped bare, blamed, and used. There was no softness in what lived inside her. The certainty that she had been violated, betrayed, and left to carry it alone was all that remained.

She slipped her backpack over one shoulder and adjusted the strap, the motion automatic. The hallway was quiet as she walked toward the door. She grabbed her keys from the hook and turned the deadbolt. The familiar scrape gave way to soft light as she opened the door and stepped outside.

The morning air met her with a soft chill. It wasn't cold, not really. It just hadn't warmed up yet. Light filtered through the trees, brushing the steps in uneven streaks. She closed the door behind her and locked it. The bolt slid into place with a sound she had heard a thousand times. Today, it landed differently. Ordinary.

Davis was everywhere in her world. She saw him every day, at least on her screen. His face, his body, the way he moved across fields and through crowds. She knew what he looked like, maybe too well. That thought stayed with her, steady and unfinished.

She knew his body as well as the grid he curated. Broad shoulders, bronzed skin, that perfect balance of muscle and lean. Every shirtless post was a performance, and it worked. She noticed. Everyone seemed to. There was no hiding the fact that he was stunning. Every part of him was sharpened, defined, and built to be seen. His captions, his stories, the way he laughed at his own jokes. There was a boyishness that hadn't gone anywhere. A self-importance that clung to everything he touched. That contradiction drew her in more than anything. He was beautiful, reckless, and completely unaware of how transparent he could be. And she hated how much that still pulled her.

She considered the similarities between Davis and Ethan. The posture. The build. The confidence that seemed baked into every step. They both had the same way of filling a space, of moving like the world had already said yes to them. Davis's body language, his grin, and the subtle arrogance in his eyes.

She had seen all of it before. Ethan had carried those same qualities. The connection between the two stood stationary in her mind like a warning. She didn't know if this was intended to push her away or pull her in closer.

The pressure of her life felt endless. It was always there, waiting. Holding onto it made it easier to explain and carry. She knew the truth about what had happened with Ethan. She knew what she had done and what he had forced her into. She hadn't wanted it. She hadn't planned it. She would never have stepped into the role of a victim if he hadn't made her one.

The experience had altered everything. It lived in her, reshaping how she moved, how she thought, how she understood herself. It violated her sense of right and wrong and stained everything she was supposed to be. She felt it in the way she carried herself, in the way others looked at her without knowing what to say. People called her a "great young woman," as if the words could make her whole again. The words felt small. Polished. Dismissive. As if being great could cancel out what had happened to her, as though excellence erased damage. She never corrected them, but she never forgot them either. It was easier for everyone to believe she had turned out fine.

The morning moved around her, careless and bright, as Gretchen's anxiety bloomed. She felt like a fraud. The kindness everyone praised was a mask, polished and practiced, hiding the darkness she still didn't know how to name. She wondered how long she could comfortably wear it.

Chapter 6: The Trip

Twenty hours. That's how long Irene had been in the economy rental car Manny had chosen; each mile was pushing her closer to Florida, as each bump in the road was a fresh wave of irritation. Her finger traced a crack in the worn vinyl of the dashboard. She found it funny how a little imperfection could hold her attention. She followed it slowly, letting the rough edge guide her thoughts the way the road hadn't. As they rattled over the Georgia border, the heat pressed in through the windows. When Manny announced they were getting close, she didn't feel relief, only restlessness.

Butterfly Universe. The image of fluttering wings and wildflowers clashed with the crawl of the seeming eternity of the drive. She caught her daughter's reflection as she glanced in the rearview mirror, mesmerized, with a blur of frantic fingers drumming a staccato rhythm against her phone. That phone, constant and glowing, was Gretchen's tether to a world Irene no longer understood. She longed, hopelessly, to reach her daughter in the same way. Gretchen hadn't looked up in hours. She hadn't truly looked at her in even longer.

She thought of the beach house, unchanged in her memory, though it had been three years since they'd last been there. The last time Gretchen had breathed that salty air, she had been a child. Her laughter had echoed in the open spaces, carried by the breeze, bright and unfiltered. That was before Ethan. Before the silence, Gretchen shielded herself. Before Irene had learned to stop asking questions she didn't want the answers to. Time had chipped away at their closeness until only familiar shapes of what once had been remained.

In the car, silence filled the space. Gretchen breathed slowly, unmoved by the hush her parents couldn't seem to break. She watched the road pass, intermittently, and thought about what she might say. Nothing meaningful came to mind. Scrolling through Davis's recent posts had paused. He hadn't updated his status for hours. The app was still open, but her attention had shifted inward.

Her father sat stoic, with his hands firmly positioned at ten and two o'clock. Manny's posture was stiff in a way she had come to expect. The miles rolled by, mechanically, for him. For Gretchen, Davis was a passenger, unseen but undeniably present.

She opened the window, letting the wind cut across her face. It didn't change anything. She preferred the stillness when it belonged to her. She could feel them both glancing toward her now and then, waiting for a signal or an opening. She remained silent, content to keep the moment exactly where it was.

"You okay, honey?" Irene's voice barely carried a fragile whisper against the roaring stagnancy in the car.

"What? Oh, yeah. Fine." Gretchen didn't look up. Her response was hollow, flattened by distraction and stripped of warmth.

Manny's voice cut through the tension, too loud, too polished. "Of course, she's fine. Why wouldn't she be? Let's go!" The salesman's cheer coated his words, a slick gloss over the glimmer in his eye that always felt a shade too sharp. His performance grated against Irene's nerves, the way saccharine icing only draws attention to the bitterness beneath.

Then, the quiet settled again as they finally stopped. It was getting harder for her to ignore what she had been trying not to feel. The air outside pressed against them, warm and humid. Irene stepped out last, the atmosphere folding around her. The conservatory, Butterfly Universe, stood before them, bright and inviting, an unexpected oasis carved into the otherwise mundane stretch of Florida roadside.

The glass structure was massive, with curved panes catching the sunlight and scattering it across the pavement in shifting patterns. Inside, the air changed immediately. Humid and fragrant, it wrapped around them with a softness that eased the edges of Irene's tension. Tropical plants lined every walkway; their leaves glossy and oversized, some shaped like fans, others like fingers reaching up through the light. A soft mist lingered near the ground, catching in Irene's hair as they stepped past the threshold.

Above them, the ceiling stretched, a dome of clear glass that bathed the entire space in natural light. Sunlight poured through, illuminating every corner, turning the leaves translucent and catching in the wings of butterflies as they moved through the air. It felt borderless, unconfined, as if the roof itself had been replaced with sky.

Water trickled from hidden pumps, flowing gently down the sculpted sides of faux rock formations. The sound, subtle but persistent, blended with the soft movement of wings and the occasional murmur of other visitors. Flowering vines curled up metal trellises, their blossoms vivid in violet, gold, and crimson, planted to draw the butterflies close. Dozens of species drifted and darted overhead, their flight paths fluid, weaving through the air with grace. There was peace here, carefully arranged and full of motion.

Gretchen raised her phone and snapped a photo of a Blue Morpho as it settled on a vibrant bloom. Irene, still adjusting to the brilliant light and color, spotted a cluster of Monarchs feeding nearby. Their orange and black wings moved in a slow rhythm; each one marked with a lattice of delicate veins. She found herself watching them longer than expected, drawn in by their steadiness.

Manny, his cheerfulness now quieted by awe, stood before a cluster of Paper Kite butterflies. Their translucent wings shimmered where the sunlight struck them, fragile shapes suspended in slow motion. Around him, the rest of the conservatory unfolded in layers of color and movement. Vivid reds and yellows burst against the dense green backdrop, each wingbeat painting the space with momentary brilliance. The Grecian Shoemaker danced high above, its distinct eyespots flashing as it circled the canopy.

A lone Queen floated past, its wide wings moving with unhurried grace. The sight carried regality, as though the entire space had been built to honor its flight.

As they continued through the conservatory, the tension that had traveled in with them began to ease. Nothing had been resolved, but for a moment, the color, motion, and calm allowed them to exhale. It was a stillness they had not known for some time, and Irene felt it stretch between them without demand.

Gretchen felt it more acutely than she expected. The natural beauty pressed in on her. The butterflies, delicate in their flight and sporadic in their movement, reminded her of her own fragility.

She thought of the secrets she carried and the effort it took to hold herself together. The butterflies moved with the same quiet deception, cloaked in vibrant color while hiding something raw and breakable beneath. Their brief, radiant existence mirrored her own sense of impermanence and the dread that her past might surface without warning.

Gretchen's pulse quickened, though her face stayed composed. She moved through the conservatory with an extended index finger, offering herself as a landing place for the Blue Morpho. Their wings shimmered as they hovered and twisted through shafts of light, impossibly bright against the green. She had locked onto a single image: A butterfly resting on her finger. The photo lived in her mind already, pulled from fairytales she had memorized without meaning to. If it landed, it would mean she was chosen. Touched by grace. Marked as different in a way no one could argue with. She followed the curve of the path and kept her eyes on the butterflies.

She couldn't explain why it mattered so much. The image itself meant something. Holding the moment. Owning it. In a place that felt unreal in its peace, she craved proof that she had been seen. That beauty had come to her. She kept walking. Her feet barely disturbed the stone beneath her, each step a quiet offering to the stillness she refused to break.

Then Irene's voice cut through the quiet.

"Gretchen. Look to your left."

Gretchen turned slowly, uncertain about whether her mother had actually seen anything at all. She half-expected emptiness, another disappointment. But there it was, motionless on her shoulder. The Blue Morpho's wings fanned wide, luminous, and steady. It perched on her as if it had always belonged there.

She froze in place. She didn't dare move. Up close, its beauty held her. The wings shimmered with a softness that looked impossible to describe. She wondered how it could possibly carry its own body. Her chest tightened as she stared, gripped by the quiet tension of being chosen, even for a moment, by something that beautiful.

Irene stood beneath the vaulted glass above them, the conservatory glowing in soft, refracted light. A rare moment of stillness had settled between her and Gretchen, quiet and fragile, shaped by years of silence and missed connection. Irene's camera hovered just below her eye, her finger trembling above the shutter button. The scene before her was precise, her daughter holding herself still, the Blue Morpho resting on her shoulder like a question not yet asked. Irene remained still, afraid to break the balance, afraid that even her breath might send it away.

A subtle flick of the butterfly's wings interrupted the anticipation. It shifted, shimmered, and lifted. The moment dissolved as quickly as it had formed. The cobalt blur disappeared into the canopy above, lost among the branches and light. Irene pressed the shutter too late. The click echoed, empty, a reflex chasing what had already moved on.

She lowered the camera slowly. Her hand hovered for a moment, suspended in disappointment. The photograph would show Gretchen with her shoulder turned, her hair brushing her cheek, and light streaking across her sleeve. The butterfly would be gone. What had made the moment matter slipped through her grasp in the space between instinct and intention.

Gretchen remained where she stood. Her arms dropped to her sides, and her chin tilted slightly, not in defeat but in acknowledgment. She looked toward the place where the butterfly had disappeared, eyes focused and unreadable. The stillness around her deepened. She had wanted the image. Wanted the weight of it. And now it belonged to the air.

Irene stepped closer, leaving just enough space between them for the silence to settle without pressing. She didn't reach for her daughter. There was no gesture to offer that wouldn't shrink the moment. Instead, she stood beside her, sharing the quiet.

They stayed like that, surrounded by the shifting light and the soft hum of subtle fans. The world beyond the conservatory faded, replaced by a sense of nothingness that neither of them trusted, but both refused to step out of. The silence between them no longer felt like distance. It felt like the beginning of a recognition, resting gently in the space they had both been afraid to enter.

They remained in place, surrounded by color, movement, and the soft murmur of water trailing through the exhibit. Butterflies drifted overhead and passed close to their shoulders, dipping through columns of filtered sunlight and weaving into the dense green. Wings shimmered in layers of blue, gold, and rust, each color bending slightly with the angle of the light. The stillness between Irene and Gretchen pressed closer than any movement around them. Irene kept her focus on her daughter, tracking each change in her expression and posture.

A pressure gathered in Irene's chest. She watched the line of Gretchen's jaw, the tension at the base of her neck, the quiet way her arms rested at her sides. Nothing about her seemed shaped for an audience. The posture was private, closed off, and made from instinct. Irene recognized it. There had been years when she had moved the same way when reaching had felt dangerous, and stillness had been the only way to endure.

She shifted her weight slightly, turning just enough to face her daughter without drawing attention to herself. No words came. Nothing inside her asked to speak. Presence was all she could manage and all she believed Gretchen would accept.

Around them, the landscape moved with its own rhythm. Wings lifted and vanished into shadow. Blossoms opened above the walkway, bright against the backdrop, their petals thin and almost translucent at the tips. Sunlight poured through the glass and bent along the floor in fractured ribbons. The space remained as it was, holding what it held.

The path narrowed at the back of the greenhouse, ending at a curved wooden arch and a sign painted in pale green: The Life Cycle of a Butterfly. Beyond it, the light cooled. The space was lower, more angular, and fit with display cases that stretched from waist height to the ceiling. Pale tile replaced the gravel path. A row of ceiling fixtures cast a steady wash of light across the room, their reflections shifting faintly across the polished surfaces.

Inside, enclosures lined the walls, each sealed and labeled with printed cards. The lighting was colder here, more direct. There was no narration or music, only the occasional scuff of a shoe or the whisper of a parent pointing out a name. Gretchen moved toward a long central case and stopped.

Dozens of chrysalises hung from a wooden frame, suspended in clean rows by thin wires. Some remained unmoving, pale green and matte under the light. Others twitched, small pulses stretching the cocoons in irregular bursts. One near the center shifted more than the rest. The casing tightened, then relaxed, then flexed again in uneven waves. She watched the motion and tried to find the boundary between what had emerged and what still remained inside.

A seam split. A shape pushed outward. A folded wing slid free, wet and darker than she expected, clinging to itself as it trembled in place. It looked like effort. She stayed where she was and continued watching.

Nearby, a child asked if the butterfly was going to be pretty. A woman answered with a soft, confident reply as if the outcome had already been decided. The sound drifted off as they moved along. Gretchen stayed focused on the case.

The butterfly's legs reached for the wooden beam beneath it but slid each time it tried to hold. A second wing followed, curled and dragging, no stronger than the first. The shape rested unevenly, unbalanced, and incomplete. It adjusted slightly, legs trembling, still unsure how to hold its place. Gretchen watched with steady focus. There was no beauty in the motion, no grace, just a fragile insistence on remaining upright. She knew it for what it was. It was the same invisible work she performed every day, keeping her posture smooth, her voice even, and her expression intact. No one noticed that part. No one ever did

Gretchen blinked and stepped back. Her eyes lingered on the exhibit a moment longer before she turned to follow her parents toward the exit. The space around her still buzzed with warmth and motion, but the focus that had held her in place was gone. Whatever she had wanted there, she carried now.

The Stiles family moved slowly toward the exit, following the final curve of the walkway past the last few habitats. The butterflies moved less now. Most perched on broad leaves or floated near the ceiling in loose, drifting patterns. Their earlier bursts of color had softened beneath the fading light. The brightness that had filled the building when they first arrived had diminished. Nothing shimmered the way it had at the start.

Irene glanced at Gretchen. "What a place, huh? So much life... It felt almost like we were walking through a living painting."

Gretchen didn't respond, her eyes fixed ahead. Irene waited, hoping for a glance, a word, anything that might have suggested she'd been heard. Nothing came. The moment sat between them, untouched and unmoving. Irene gave a soft sigh but didn't press further. She adjusted her pace and fell in behind her daughter, unsure whether she had tried to connect or simply filled the silence with noise. Either way, it was over. She followed the gap between them, still intact.

The sliding doors opened, and the heat met them head-on. The parking lot stretched ahead, sun-bleached and motionless. The last of the light lay flat across the pavement, broken only by the long shadows of palm trees leaning over the sidewalk. A sprinkler ticked in the distance, its arc slow and even, watering grass that already looked beyond help.

The car's surface was still warm. The seats stung against their legs until the engine started, and the air conditioner began to cool the cab. Irene adjusted the rearview mirror without meeting her own reflection. The moment had passed. Whatever hint of closeness she thought might take shape had already flattened. Gretchen had let her in just enough to notice the distance, and then was gone again.

Gretchen stared out the window, her mind still caught in the wings and light, the blur of color she had held for only a moment. She tried to hold onto the feeling to make sense of what had passed, though it resisted any shape she gave it. She finally spoke without turning her head, and her voice was steady.

"I am a butterfly."

Manny glanced sideways at her, his voice soft and reassuring. "Of course you are. You're beautiful, delicate, and have a free spirit."

A slight smile touched her lips as she lowered her eyes to the phone in her lap. The glow bathed her face in a familiar light. Her post had already landed. The comments had begun. She could picture exactly how it would be received: soft, introspective, carefully wounded. The kind of thing people called brave.

In the time that followed between this place and the beach house, she held the truth easily. She hadn't meant any of it the way her father thought she did.

Let him believe it.

She preferred it that way.

Chapter 7: The Beach House

Ellen's cheerful voice carried forward from the front seat, nudging the others to abandon the car and face the rain. The downpour had grown steadier, each drop hitting with more consistency than the last.

"Do you two want to brave it? I can't sit here any longer. I'm getting antsy!"

Her hand hovered near the door handle, fingers drumming against the armrest. Max gave a small nod, his eyes still on the windshield where rain streamed in quick, broken paths. The house stood ahead, sprawling and low against the rain. Pale sandstone gleamed beneath the water; its hue deepened by the downpour. The stonework's detail appeared sharper now. Every seam, every angle stood out beneath the steady wash. Tall arched windows stretched across the front, their glass streaked and glinting. Columns framed the entrance, broad and symmetrical. A curved walkway snaked through the manicured lawn, leading to heavy wooden doors protected by a shallow overhang.

In the back seat, Davis showed no sign of interest. He remained absorbed in his own world, the light from the screen flickering faintly across his features. His expression didn't change. His fingers tapped with mechanical rhythm. Some private thread unfolded beneath his thumbs. The screen held him.

Ellen turned and reached back, tapping his knee with playful exaggeration.

"Earth to Davis!"

The sound of his name seemed to physically prick Davis, a reaction too habitual to fully register. Annoyance flickered across his face as his eyes lifted from his hands. The outside world returned in fragments. The soft tap of rain on the roof. The fog pressed against the windows. Beyond it all, the house waited, its windows streaked with water, its silhouette muted by the storm. He stared at it for a moment, unmoved.

Ellen and Max moved in quiet agreement. Max turned the key and cut the engine. The faint whir of the air conditioning faded, replaced by the steady cadence of rain on the roof. Ellen pulled at her sleeve, then smoothed the fabric across her lap. A brief laugh slipped out, too small to break the mood but sharp enough to acknowledge it.

"Well," she said, looking ahead, "it's not going to stop just because we are looking at it."

Max rested both hands on the steering wheel and blew a long breath through his nose. "Figures. The second we park, it decides to get serious." His tone was flat, worn by travel and the dull disappointment of weather getting the last word.

He reached toward the door, resting his fingers on the handle. They hung there, lightly curled, caught in a moment that didn't quite demand movement yet. Ellen leaned back in her seat with her arms crossed. Her fingers traced the inside of her elbow, the way they sometimes did when her mind was elsewhere, quietly waiting for Max to move first.

When Max looked over, Davis was still lost in his digital paradise. His eighteen-year-old son sat in the same position he had when they pulled into the drive, shoulders slouched, head bowed over his phone. The screen cast a faint glow across his features, highlighting the sharp lines of his cheek and the edge of his jaw. His thumbs moved with ease, tapping through the feed.

Ellen's hand impatiently brushed the door handle, then rested against her lap. She turned to Davis, watching him quietly. Her eyes softened as she took him in. He sat, aware of her presence but still distant. She felt a rush of love for him, the same emotion that always rose when she saw him. She didn't need anything more at the time. His presence, his quiet being, was enough.

"Davis, remember what we talked about when you see her," she reminded him.

Davis's fingers stopped, and his eyes immediately met Ellen's. His jaw and neck tightened; every part of him was still. His breath came in shallow bursts, fast and erratic. His whole body screamed with rage. The anger surged through him, tightening his chest. His face flushed red, teeth clenched, and eyes narrowed. The phone was in his hand, and the next thing Ellen heard was the sound of it slamming onto his leg with force. The car seemed to shake with the impact. Davis surged forward, his body jerking with the violence of his release.

"God!" Davis shouted. His voice was raw and jagged. "I know! Just... shut up! Yeah, I get it! You don't have to keep repeating it like I'm an idiot!" His body jerked. The rage stayed, coursing through him like a storm. "I understand! I'm not stupid! I heard you the first time!" His breath was ragged. His chest heaved. "What do you think I'm gonna say? 'Hey, Gretch, sorry you got raped, want to catch some rays?' Who does that? Jesus Christ!"

The last words came out as a choked, heavy boom. The syllables cut through the quiet with blistering fury. The temperature in the car rose with the heat of his ire. The sound of the rain faded behind the echo of his words.

The tension grew with Max's correction, a visceral, threatening growl, like the sudden crack of a leather whip.

"Don't you dare use Jesus's name like a cuss word," he snapped, his words were loud, sharp, and unforgiving. The Day household held this as an inviolable truth. Davis knew better than to cross it but didn't care.

The boy swallowed. His hands flattened against his thighs as he leaned back into the seat. His body remained tense, but the storm inside him was stopped by his father's confrontation. He had gone too far. He stared at his lap. Racing, irrational thoughts scrambled as he struggled to regain control. The anger still simmered, but it no longer felt urgent or overwhelming. He watched his parents move in a blur; their combined energy was sharply at odds with his stillness.

Ellen, masking her own discomfort, decided to act. With a feigned lighthearted tone, she sang, "It doesn't look like it's going to stop. Are you ready to get wet?"

She had given up. She swung the door open and leaped into the downpour. Her enthusiasm was contagious. Max followed suit. They gathered their luggage, giggling as the rain pelted them, determined to press on. Davis, however, remained stretched across the bench seat. He ignored the activity around him as his parents hurried toward the house. The gap between his stillness and their energetic movement was unmistakable. Annoyance radiated from him as he watched their futile attempt to escape the downpour.

Ellen and Max, driven by their eagerness to reach the house, braved the soaking rain. Their clothes clung to their bodies. Water soaked their faces in streams as it flowed from their hair, but they hardly seemed to notice. The short distance to the house felt like an adventure; their laughter rose above the sound of the downpour. The luggage, held above their heads as makeshift umbrellas, became almost an afterthought as they moved quickly. Their energy was infectious, in spite of the storm.

Davis stayed where he was, stretched out in the back seat with his luggage beneath his head. He didn't move. His body remained still; his attention fixed on the glowing display of his phone. The world around him seemed to blur into the background. His outburst felt distant, as if it had never existed, completely wiped from his mind as he retreated into a space of his own.

The insistent drumming of the rain against the huge windows created a specific atmosphere upon their arrival. As Max and Ellen stepped in, the sleek lines of the beach house seemed to absorb some of that persistent rhythm. The house was a study in modern design.

It was a single-story structure with an open layout featuring large wood-framed windows that offered sweeping views of the ocean. Inside, the space was minimal but elegant. A low, soft gray linen sofa anchored the living room, paired with a sculptural armchair made from reclaimed wood. A polished stone coffee table sat at the center. Neutral hues of white, taupe, and gray blended with natural wood accents throughout, creating a warm, inviting oasis.

Art was minimal. A few abstract pieces were mounted on the walls in muted tones that complemented the surrounding decor. Light, textured rugs softened the space, adding a layer of comfort to the otherwise open feel. The kitchen, with its sleek marble countertops and simple cabinetry, seamlessly blended with the living area. Every detail, from the carefully chosen furniture to the open design, contributed to the clean, luxurious feel. Some things remained unchanged over the years: the furnishings, the uninterrupted view framed by the large windows, and the tranquil presence of the ocean beyond.

As they settled into the house, their eyes showed the pride and satisfaction of creating a place that truly felt their own. Ellen moved through the rooms, deciding where their belongings would go. Each choice reflected her care, shaping the space to match what they had built together. She ran her fingers along the smooth surfaces as if imprinting her presence into the very walls, making it feel like home once more.

Max stood still for a moment, taking in the home around him. It reflected everything he had worked for. The light pouring through the windows, the openness of the space, the view of the ocean, and everything else spoke to his sense of accomplishment. This house was a mark of what he'd done, a place to finally rest and take pride in his achievements.

As Ellen and Max settled into their temporary home, the rain poured down, transforming the beach house into a private refuge. The storm had stretched on for what felt like hours, but eventually, it relented. A calm followed as if the world outside had exhaled. Ellen, always aware of the undercurrents within their family, turned to Max with a concerned look. She knew how easily tension built between them, and how the smallest incident could shift the mood.

"Do you think he's alright out there?" she asked, her voice carrying subtle anxiety. It was a simple question, one that needed an answer, but the weight of it lingered on her as she considered Davis's isolation and anticipated her husband's reaction.

Max glanced out the window at the still car, his expression unreadable. He took a step back from the window, running a hand through his hair. He stood for a moment, his focus drifting, before he muttered, "Probably just needs some time alone." Max moved toward the luggage by the door, picked up a bag and absently checked it. "Stiles' family should be here soon," he remarked, changing the subject.

"I talked to Irene. They stopped by a butterfly exhibit on their way and should be here around eight. She sends her love and apologies for the delay." Ellen paused for a moment after speaking. She ran her fingers over the counter's surface absently. She looked at Max with the weight of her thoughts fueling her expression.

After a long pause, she spoke, her voice quieter than usual, almost hesitant. "Max... I'm really worried about Davis." She leaned against the counter, her hands pressed flat against the surface as if she needed something solid to hold her together. "His bipolar diagnosis... it's been harder to manage lately. His temper... it's getting worse as he gets older." She released a forced breath, looking down for a moment, collecting her thoughts. When she met his eyes again, the concern was clear in her expression. "And his motivation? I don't know what's going on, but he just doesn't seem to care about anything anymore except for soccer and that damned phone." She paused to check Max's reaction. Her voice warbled slightly as she added, "What if this doesn't change? What if he doesn't figure it out?"

Max glanced at her, then back to the window. His eyes were fixed outside, but he wasn't really seeing anything. He exhaled sharply, tightening his jaw as his focus shifted inward. He stood still for a moment, processing her words in silence before walking across the room. He moved to sit on the couch, taking a seat at the edge. He rested his hands loosely by his sides as he exhaled again, trying to release the tension that had begun to settle in his chest. He did not like this conversation.

"Are we really doing this again right now?" Max asked, his voice low and flat, indicating his rising frustration. His response wasn't meant to invite discussion but rather to shut it down.

Ellen remained at the counter with her hands pressed onto the edge. The tension climbed through her arms and settled in her chest. She closed her eyes briefly, trying to find the words. When she spoke, her voice carried more force than before.

"You weren't the one who had to finish his coursework. You didn't sit at the table every night trying to drag him through assignments he flat-out refused to do."

Max stayed on the couch, unmoved. He crossed his arms defensively. His eyes remained fixed on a spot ahead of him.

"I was working, Ellen," he said. His voice stayed calm, with a strong undercurrent of impatience.

She turned on him, and her voice rose with frustration. "Yeah. You were working. And I was raising a kid who wouldn't talk to me unless he needed something." She swallowed hard, trying to keep her voice from cracking. "You think I wanted to do his schoolwork? You think I didn't want to scream half the time?" She paused for a moment. "I kept us afloat while he fell apart."

Max finally looked at her with his hands pressed against his knees. Something tense flickered across his face. He leaned forward, his voice tight and direct.

"And now what? You want to keep holding him up forever?"

She pushed away from the counter and crossed the room. Her steps were quick and uneven, each one driven by everything she'd been carrying for far too long.

"He wasn't ready. I put out every fire he started. The emails. The meetings. The neighbors." She gestured sharply as she spoke, her frustration spilling over. "Every time he acted out, I covered for him. What else was I supposed to do?"

"You're still doing it," Max said, his voice low but firm. "He's not a boy anymore." He rested his elbows on his knees, his hands loosely clasped. "You need to stop acting like it's all on you."

She looked at him, her mind tangled with everything she didn't have the energy to explain. The fight had drained out of her, but nothing felt resolved. She sat beside him, tensely. Her silence carried more than words would have, anyway.

She begrudgingly rested her head against his shoulder. Max stayed still for a moment and didn't move his arms from his sides. Then he ran his fingers gently through her hair. Her jaw began to relax, and her eyes closed as she leaned in closer.

Suddenly, the front door swung open. The moment between them broke. Davis stepped inside. His face was drawn and tense. Frustration played on his shoulders. It was built and carried in from the car. He didn't look at either of them. His steps were hard and restless, and the fragile calm in the room collapsed under his presence.

"Oh, the king has arrived," Max fawned, a gleam in his eye as Davis finally lumbered in. The disgust on his son's face clung to everything, spreading through the room like smoke.

"You didn't bring my stuff in?" he snarled, the words sliced from his mouth with all the edge he'd been carrying. His entire posture radiated contempt, the bitterness in him worn plainly across his face. Max remained seated, watching him closely.

"No, Day-Day. You don't have servants yet. And don't even think of blaming your mother. I had to wrestle a bear to keep her from walking back out."

Davis let out a roar that tore through the room, jarring against the walls of the rented house.

"ARRGGGHHHH! How many times do I have to tell you to stop calling me that?! It's retarded! Who does that to a kid? Give him a last name for a first name and then call him Day-Day like some kind of... retard."

Ellen sprang from the couch. Color rose in her face, and her expression dripped with fury. Her words came without hesitation. They were cut from the center of her anger.

"The r-word, Davis. You know better."

"ARRGGGHHHH!" The second outburst also came without hesitation. It was louder and more violent than the first. It pushed out of him, loud and shaking with rage. The volume cracked through the room, stripping away anything that had been held back.

Max rose like a warning. His arm shot out with his pointed finger locked on the door.

"Go get your shit from the car. Bring it in. And try, just try, to act like a halfway decent human being for ten days... NOW!" His message was clear. He was done speaking.

Davis froze. Every muscle in him remained braced, but nothing moved. He stood exactly where Max had left him, fury collected in his body until he shook. The fire hadn't gone out. It stayed behind his face, radiant and trapped, where no one could reach it. He didn't speak. He didn't flinch. He simply remained there, locked in place by the command that still echoed through the room.

Max's anger, rarely revealed, was a force of nature, and Davis knew it.

He glared through his father, and the room fell silent. Every ounce of anger in him flared, vivid and alive. His emotions took form without sound. It was more violent than anything he could've said out loud. His eyes stayed locked on Max, daring him to utter another word. He stood in place waiting for it.

The challenge burned behind his eyes, etched across every inch of his face. His presence alone made it land. His anger coursed and radiated outward with untamed ferocity. The moment hovered on the edge, and Davis was the one holding it there, ready to see it break.

Then, he simply turned. He planted his foot and barreled out through the door, his body taut with the force of his anger. His steps cracked against the tile as he stormed away. Without hesitation, he hurled the heavy door closed behind him. The slam landed with a thunderous crash that rattled the house. The mirror in the foyer tore from its hook and crashed to the floor. Shards of glass were scattered in all directions, catching the dim light in erratic, jagged flashes.

In the aftermath, the house felt strangely hollow. The broken glass glinted on the tile, each piece reflecting the light unevenly. The stillness that followed pressed down on the space, clinging to the edges of the walls and floor.

Max and Ellen watched the carnage unfold in a grim, detached trance. The aftershocks of the explosion resonated in the room's quiet. Their faces were outlined by the stress of the moment, betrayed by the familiar weariness that came with raising a boy like Davis.

Then, Davis reappeared.

The furious set of his jaw and the rigid lines around his eyes were gone, replaced by a slump that stripped him of everything he'd walked out with. Ellen stood still, her hands faintly trembling, her eyes fixed on her son. Her hope for the vacation, threatened moments before with shouting and irrational power plays, returned like a breath held too long. The stink of confrontation departed and left behind only the faint, lingering whiff of lemon polish. Max, still seated, kept his eyes on Davis; the tension in his face had yet to retreat.

Davis pushed the door open with his shoulder and stepped inside, dragging his suitcase behind him. The wheels thudded and rattled unevenly across the tile, catching on the edge of the rug as he moved through the entry without slowing. He bumped into the side table, knocking over a lamp. He didn't apologize or even look up. His every motion was slightly too forceful, too careless. He wasn't angry anymore, but it seemed he still wanted the room to feel it.

"Where's my room?" he asked.

Max stood beside the couch, arms crossed, eyes fixed on Davis like he was waiting for the next collision. The boy moved through the room without aim, suitcase clipping corners, bumping into furniture, leaving a trail of small impacts. Max felt more than heard.

"Davis, watch what you're doing," he said. "It's where it always is."

Davis didn't answer. He adjusted his grip on the handle and kept moving. The message was clear. He had heard it. He just didn't care enough to respond.

"It isn't always anywhere," Davis muttered, dragging the suitcase a few more feet. "Last two years, I was in the one by the bathroom."

Ellen shifted slightly on the couch, her hands smoothed the fabric beside her. "True," she said cautiously. "I think it's best if you take the other one and let Gretchen have the one she's used to." She glanced toward Davis, measuring his reaction. "Besides, you know it's best for girls to be closer to the bathroom."

Davis stopped walking and turned toward her. He blinked, then narrowed his eyes slightly.

"That makes absolutely no sense. Why do girls need to be closer to the bathroom?"

He stayed where he was, waiting for an answer.

"Well, it's because... um..." She blew out a quiet breath and gave a small laugh, holding up her hands in surrender. "You know something? You're right. It doesn't make any sense at all. I don't know."

"They need to be closer because there's less distance to travel when you gotta go," Max said, stepping forward slightly as he spoke, his voice pitched just loud enough to claim space. He nudged Ellen's knee with his and gave her a look, waiting to see if she'd play along.

Ellen turned to him with exaggerated innocence, her eyes wide as if she were genuinely confused. "What are you talking about?"

"Less distance than boys... you know."

Max lifted his hands and spaced them apart, forming a crude, confident measurement midair. He tilted his head slightly as he held the pose, making a point of checking the distance like he was sizing something real. The spacing wasn't small. He made sure it wasn't. He didn't say the words, but his silence made them louder.

Ellen looked at his hands, then back at his face. A laugh escaped, light and sudden, and she sat up straighter, clearly enjoying herself. Her voice carried a mock innocence, but her grin gave her away.

"Depends on the boy, I guess," she said. "Or the girl these days."

She gave a small nod toward Davis as she said it, like she was tossing him the line just to watch him squirm.

Davis, halfway through the room, shook his head and let out a loud gasp as though the stupidity of the moment had knocked the wind out of him. His face twisted with theatrical disgust. He groaned loudly, threw up one hand as though swatting the whole moment away, and turned without a word.

"Oh my friggin' god," he muttered, swinging his bag over one shoulder and storming down the hall as if the conversation had physically injured him.

"Whatever," he called out. "I'm taking the room I had last year. It's not my problem that they didn't come down. Snooze, you lose."

Max pressed his lips together, trying to contain a laugh. His shoulders bounced once with the effort, the smirk already creeping out despite him.

"Okay. Whatever you want. If you need to be closer to the bathroom..."

Davis didn't miss a beat.

"I definitely don't need to be closer to the bathroom, you sickos," he snapped, the insult landing like a slap. His face flushed with real offense, cutting past the banter. "ARGHHH! Fine! I'll take the friggin' crappy room." He spun around, shoulders rigid, and stomped off with all the indignation of someone who had just been seriously wounded.

Ellen raised her voice, gently steering the mood back to center. The edge of amusement faded, replaced by the easy cadence of routine authority.

"And when you get done, you need to clean up the mess you made, slamming out of here like a lunatic. You knocked the mirror off the wall."

"I did not. I just got here," Davis shouted back from deeper in the house, the words pitched high with bratty defiance. He hurled the denial without hesitation, letting it echo behind him as a parting shot. "You probably knocked it down. I'm going to the beach."

Ellen stood with a sigh, her movements jerky as she brushed at her pants, the kind of pointless gesture meant more to release tension than remove lint. She yanked the closet door open with more force than necessary, the motion sharp, unspoken annoyance trailing behind her, charged and unresolved. Each step was clipped and brisk, her mouth set in a firm line that dared interruption.

"Here we go again," she muttered, her voice tinged with irritation, not surprise.

Max watched her with a measured expression, his arms folding loosely across his chest. He wasn't angry, but the question pressed with intention.

"What are you doing?"

"Cleaning up the seven years of bad luck, I guess," she said. "We can't have the Stiles walking into a minefield."

She opened the closet, retrieved the broom and dustpan, and headed for the broken glass. Her movements were brisk and practiced, more out of habit than temper.

"You have got to give him a chance to do things," Max said, planting his feet and crossing his arms again. His voice stayed calm, but the edge behind it was unmistakable. His eyes narrowed slightly as he watched her move. The patience was thinning, even if he didn't say so outright.

Ellen kept sweeping, but her shoulders tensed, the broom tapping unevenly against the tile.

"And when exactly does that happen?" Her voice cracked slightly, not from weakness but from the restraint it took to keep from shouting. "I will not. I mean, if it isn't picked up, I'll think about it until it is. Her hands gripped the broom tighter, her next words rushing out like something unsustainable. "Even if he did clean it, I'd just follow around behind him to do it over because…"

Max shifted his stance, his voice firmer now.

"Honey, that's the problem. You say, 'I'm not doing this,' and then immediately do what you said you weren't going to do. What is he supposed to think?"

Ellen halted mid-sweep, her grip tightening on the broom handle as she straightened. Her shoulders squared, eyes locked on him with sharp precision, the tension in her stance pushing forward with defiance.

"So, this is my fault? You are seriously saying this is my fault?"

Max took a breath and shifted back, his stance softening as he reached for safer ground.

"I've been right there with you the whole—"

Ellen talked over him, her voice slicing through his excuse with pointed fury.

"Don't feed me that horse manure," she snapped, her tone edged with disbelief. Her eyes narrowed, chin lifted just slightly, preparing for the next blow. "You've been there; sure, you have. You've been there to smooth it over, to be a buddy... the good cop... the rational one always set against the crazy witch of a mother who has the nerve to expect an adult to act like an adult or a teenager to act like a teenager or show a slice of responsibility or respect."

Max raised his hands, palms forward, not to defend himself, but to ease the building disagreement between them.

"See? Look what is happening. You're letting this get to you. Just let him clean it up. He will do it. He will. You just gotta give him a chance."

Ellen lowered the broom to her side with a quick, clipped motion, the handle tapping the floor as she steadied it against her leg.

"You are still blaming me."

Max stepped in carefully, arms opening in a gesture meant to soften, to regroup.

Ellen didn't move. She shook her head, the laugh that escaped landing without thought, empty of amusement.

"Don't patronize me. I'm not the villain. The Stiles will be here any time. This is not a hill I'm willing to die on. Either help me clean or don't. If you're not helping, get the heck out of the way." She turned her back on him as she spoke, sweeping glass into the pan with short, forceful strokes.

Max knelt and started gathering the larger shards with careful hands.

"Okay, okay. I'm not going to try to stop you. I know better. I love you. I'll take this down to the dumpster, then run by the store and grab a bottle of wine. We need it. Everything's going to be fine. I'm sorry. Really, I'm sorry."

Ellen gave a small nod, her hands still busy with the broom.

"I'm sorry, too. I'm just stressed. Just no Pinot Grigio... the wine."

"Ah, gotcha. Be right back."

"Better get a few."

"Yep. No argument here. Twist my arm."

Max stepped out the front door, glancing back once with the hint of a grin still tugging at his mouth. He lingered a second longer than necessary, the energy in the house finally beginning to settle. A trace of warmth slipped into his expression as he eased the door closed behind him, careful not to let it slam.

The air outside greeted him with open arms, balmy and bright, brushing past his shoulders as though greeting an old friend. He rolled his neck once and exhaled, stepping down onto the path with a bounce that hadn't been there minutes ago.

He reached the bottom of the steps and paused, then turned to look back at the house. A flicker of affection crossed his face—faint but real. He gave a small nod, the motion quiet and sure, a private promise made in silence.

He pulled the front door shut with quiet reverence, the latch catching cleanly in the frame. Then he was gone.

Ellen stood alone in the quiet that followed. The broom rested against the counter, forgotten. She walked into the kitchen and placed a hand on the cool edge of the sink, her eyes drifting toward the window.

"I am happy," she whispered. Her own words surprised her.

Chapter 8: Fear

Seeking refuge in happy memories, Ellen felt a sense of peace begin to settle over her, a welcome balm to her frayed nerves. A glass of cold water soothed her parched throat and calmed the unrest in her stomach. Her eyes drank in the serenity of her surroundings, and her mind wandered to happier times. It had been too long since she had seen her friends and laughed with them. She yearned for a return of those days and the joy they brought. Especially, she missed Irene and the bond they shared. The anticipation of the upcoming reunion brought a smile to her face. She knew that soon she would be enveloped in the warmth of their company, reminiscing about past adventures and creating new, cherished memories. The thought of it all filled her with a sense of contentment and hope. The tension that had gripped her earlier now seemed a vague memory. With a renewed sense of calm and a heart full of expectation, Ellen stepped forward, ready to hold onto the future and all the happiness it promised.

The plush throw rug yielded softly under her feet, a welcomed change from the agitated drumming of her earlier anxieties.

Transient sunlight, slanting through the living room window, illuminated dust in shades of gold as it passed through the room around her. She moved as if underwater, each breath slow, each step deliberate. Then, her focus snapped into place.

Davis.

Bare-chested, he stood rigid as a statue, his skin slick with sweat, catching the early evening light. His eyes were narrowed, dark pools reflecting nothing but simmering anger that radiated from him like heat from a furnace. The developed muscles in his biceps were writhed, a silent storm brewing beneath the surface. In his hands, three pairs of bright, absurdly patterned swimming trunks lay limp and accusing. He presented them to her, one pair at a time, the movement agonizingly slow. A drawn-out, exaggerated exhale punctuated each item displayed.

"What...are... these?" His voice was a low snarl, each syllable stout with menace. The question was a javelin, poised and pointed at her, a violent threat twisting the sunlight into something harsh and ugly.

Ellen's calm exterior, carefully cultivated moments ago, began to crack under the threatening tone of Davis's building anger. "I don't have time for this, Davis," she said, her hand still wrapped around the glass, cool against her skin. Her thumb traced the rim, slowly and rhythmically, as if smoothing tension into the curve. The condensation left a print on her palm, and she didn't bother to wipe it away. She set the glass down beside her with a quiet knock, sending a clear message that she was done. Davis's intensity remained. His eyes were dark and fixed on her, holding the moment still. The muscles in his arms stayed flexed; the swimming trunks formed a crumpled mess in his fists. Whatever words he wanted to say were lost in the intensity surrounding them. He didn't speak. He didn't need to.

The energy around him did it for him, closing in with every passing second. A tension gathered between them, pulling the room tight and brittle. Ellen's breath shortened as a cold tremor slid down her spine. She knew that look. His eyes didn't waver; heat burned behind them, close and fierce. Ellen's spine straightened. She anchored herself in the rehearsed quiet she had learned to wear. Her gaze held his steady, the flicker behind her ribs sealed in place. She reached for a sliver of light in the charged air and let a small, nervous laugh break the stillness. "They're swimming trunks, Davis. What do you think they are, Christmas stockings?" She offered the words like a lifeline, hoping the tease might tug him back toward ease rather than fury.

For a breath, the room paused around her question. Then the nylon in his fists crackled as his fingers cinched tighter, and heat rushed from him, swallowing the thin bridge she had tried to build. Her laugh vanished; her shoulders dipped, and her fingertips tightened on the counter's edge, steadying herself as the silence confirmed she had misread the moment.

"I know they are swimming shorts," he snapped, his voice sharp and biting. The fabric in his hands might as well have been a threat to the reputation he had worked so hard to cultivate. It burned against his palms, useless and unwanted. But more than that, it proved what he had feared the second he saw them. She may have heard him, but the meaning was discarded before it ever touched her. He had pointed out the right ones. Gone out of his way to make sure she knew. And still, she stood there as though everything he said had already been erased. The air between them tightened. The frustration had been with him for years, but now it pressed harder, edged with resentment that never dulled.

"I was clear. I told you what I needed. I gave you every single detail." The words surged through the pressure building in his chest, each one more bitter than the last. "You said you'd handle it. You looked me in the eye and said you had it covered." He needed more than calm. What he wanted couldn't be found in reason. He needed her to register it. To feel what he felt. Everything else had been pushed out by the fury. What he held in his hands now was cheap, basic, and wrong. It confirmed how easily his words could be ignored.

He gripped the bundle without release, unwilling to let it drop. There was no room left for grace. Every breath had been pushed out. Softness had been erased. "What part of that did you not understand?" The words landed hard, exactly as intended. He had no intention of explaining himself. There was nothing left to clarify. He wanted her to know she had done this on purpose. The words tore free, instinctive and uncontrolled. He shouted when holding it became impossible. Now, she stood with complete dismissal as though his outrage had never made contact. Her eyes flicked for the briefest second. It was a passing response. She caught it fast. Nothing else gave her away.

Ellen's eyes scanned the kitchen briefly, only a moment of uncertainty, but she quickly regained her composure. She knew this was a make-or-break decision, and she refused to back down. "I heard you, Davis," she replied calmly despite the turmoil within. "But sometimes, we have to make do with what we have." Her tone held a dismissive challenge, an assertion of her own strength.

He stared at her hard without moving. She experienced a rush of what felt so much like hate that it made her emotions collapse inwardly. Davis did not blink; his eyes were twin lasers burning into Ellen's as if searching for a chink in her armor or a weakness he could exploit. The discomfort between them created waves of unwanted memories... of their volatile shared history. It was a standoff, a test of fortitude, and neither was willing to yield. A primal instinct, honed by years of battlefield motherhood, slammed into gear. She switched her approach.

"Try them on," she said with a playful pout, intending to lighten the mood, her words soft as pillows. "They'll be fine. And if they're not, we'll fix it... We'll see what we can do."

The instant, but subtle, easing in her son's posture was a fragile bloom of relief. After the storm of his earlier outburst, even this small concession felt like a win. His instigation gave way to a slow, grudging acceptance. The fear that had clung to her spine for the last five minutes loosened its grip, retreating barely enough to let her breathe again. Whether the moment carried real surrender or only a tactical withdrawal, she couldn't say.

Hope surged in her chest for a beat. Even that rise seemed risky, a dangerous indulgence. Dodged a bullet, she thought, grim satisfaction pulsing beneath her ribs. Her hands tensed briefly at her sides, the nerves catching in her fingers. Memory, pressure, and the phantom ache of fights she'd had to win without looking like she'd fought at all. She studied the change in him. The smile Davis gave was too precise, held long enough to appear natural. She recognized it for what it was. A shimmering mask draped over a storm. Still, she mirrored it, knowing too well that optimism wasn't a feeling. It was a tactic.

Her shield had been polished over years of carefully navigating his moods, adjusting course every time the wind shifted. "Okay, I'll try them on," Davis said, voice wound in that familiar blend of resistance and reluctant humor. "But I'm telling you, they're going to be awful." There was a flash of humble compassion in his eyes. It felt like a quiet acknowledgment that he was backing down. She accepted it, satisfied with the outcome, even if she didn't trust it completely. He turned and disappeared into the hallway, leaving behind a calm that felt earned. Ellen held her ground, steady and resolved, knowing this round belonged to her.

Davis stepped in front of the mirror with quiet pride. The win he anticipated lingered in his chest. Every part of him felt sharper, more aligned. He had taken control, and for once, the moment belonged to him. The shorts scraped against his thighs as he slid them on, their polyester fabric rough and unyielding. They were everything he'd feared: generic, lifeless, wrong. The fit betrayed the body he'd carved from sweat and discipline. The waistband sagged. The length fell awkwardly, neither short enough to show off his quads nor long enough to be fashionable. The shorts were clumsily designed to completely mask his package. His followers needed to see the lush life he had promised. The entire look would destroy everything he had built.

He stared into the glass, catching the insult head-on. The boy, looking back at him, shoulders squared, stomach flat, chiseled, deserved better than this. Years of effort, curated image, and every ounce of confidence built on making sure he never looked poor. He flexed his fists once, then let them fall loose as he stepped back from the mirror. The fabric clung in all the wrong places, every seam a reminder of how little she had listened. He would show her. He'd walk out there, let her see exactly what she had picked, and wait for her to flinch. An urge moved through his fingers, a signal to begin.

He yanked at the waistband with just enough pressure to strain the stitching, letting the fabric resist before giving way. His movements turned jagged, each one propelled by urgency that eclipsed frustration. Each tug, each adjustment, was designed to frame her reply. He planned her answer in full view. Her choice echoed the version of him she wanted to see. This wasn't about shorts. This was her handwriting on his life, and he felt it down to the bone. The performance needed no script. He emerged from the hallway with perfect pacing, a processional act tailored to hold attention. His feet dragged across the tile, arms loose at his sides, his expression twisted into a sweetness that dared her to call it real. The shorts sagged just enough to sell the failure, swaying with every practiced step. She noticed, exactly as she was meant to. That was the point.

"See?" he said, his voice casual and bright, painted to disarm. He motioned toward the uneven hems, the forced rip near the seam, the shift of fabric that stripped away his edge. "Terrible, right?" Ellen's eyes stayed on him, held just long enough to register control. She followed the motion of his hand, the exaggerated lean of his posture, the grin that hung too easily across his face. She saw the show and offered no resistance. Her breath slowed. The pause before her reply was small, deliberate.

When she finally spoke, her tone stayed light, tempered with experience. It held the weight of a mother who had played this game before and knew how to keep the next move hers. "They'll be fine, Davis," she said, her voice trimmed with resolve. "We can't afford four-hundred-fifty-dollar swim trunks… I mean shorts. You know that." She kept her posture easy, one hand resting against the edge of the table like she might push off it at any moment. Her calmness was a ruse, a practiced response to chaos. She waited for him to let it go. He didn't. He stepped in, close enough for her to see the slight sheen above his brow.

His hands hovered midair for a second, then dropped, caught between flailing and restraint. "Mom, these swim shorts will ruin me online," he pleaded, the edges frayed. "Everyone will see me in these…" His hand lifted and dropped again, no longer sure whether he was showing her the shorts or himself.

"Who is everyone, Davis?" Her tone was consistently curt. "Gretchen? That false version of you you've built online isn't real." She crossed her arms, elbows sharp, holding her ground. "You don't have a job, and you expect me to spend four hundred and fifty dollars on swim shorts? Your real friends don't care. Manny and Irene aren't buying designer bikinis for Gretchen." She shook her head once, slow. "You need to snap back and deal with it." Her words fired from her mouth like a bullet, hitting home.

Davis didn't move, but something jostled in him. The shift came fast, unplanned. He had expected her to fold. Instead, she held firm, and it knocked the wind out of him.

His posture didn't change, but the charge behind it had. "You told me to try them on and said if they didn't work, you'd get the ones I wanted. You said that. You are a liar." The words hit, sharp and immediate, tearing through the air. His voice cracked, raw with the weight of everything he'd kept buried. Davis didn't hold back. His body jerked forward, stiff with the effort to contain all the heat he was trying to hold inside.

"I did not say that, Davis. I said we'll see what we can do." Ellen's voice rose, a rare show of defense. She watched as Davis's fists clenched tighter around the waistband of the swimming trunks, the cheap fabric bunching under the strain. This was not how this was supposed to go. Davis's breath hastened, his eyes were feral as he searched for an escape or a target for his anger.

His gaze landed on the trunks around his waist, and he gave them a violent shake. "These are a joke! You might as well have bought me a pair of cutoff jeans! I can't be seen in these. You know that, right?" His voice rose in pitch. His words danced with dismissiveness and anger.

Ellen's heart sank as she realized the depth of her son's distress. "Davis, calm down," she said, her voice flat but her mind racing. "I know you're disappointed, but we can't always get what we want. I'm sorry, but that's the reality of our situation."

Her words, meant to soothe, seemed to bounce off him, leaving his distress untouched. A strange sound rumbled from his throat, a sound she'd never heard before. His body tensed, every line of him began radiating a contained fury. His eyes became vacant, and he stood before her, a stranger.

A flash of rapid movement came suddenly. The shriek of tearing fabric, a sound like flesh splitting, clawed at Ellen's ears. The scent of sweat and something feral, something animal, filled her nostrils. This wasn't her son; this was a creature spawned from a nightmare, its eyes burning with a cold, primal fire she'd never glimpsed in the boy she'd raised. Shreds of the shorts rained down on her like a blizzard of prismatic shrapnel as Davis, a cyclone of irrationality and power, tore them apart and threw them at her in pieces. His face, devoid of expression, held a terrifying blankness.

He stood before her, naked and shivering. His clothing was ripped to shreds. Pieces of fabric marked her panicked retreat in a ragged trail behind her. She stumbled backward. Her chest was tightened with fear. His unnaturally hairless body, slick with sweat, stood fully exposed before her. The sight was untamed and terrifying in its power. She felt dirty. This was not the boy she had raised. This was a man disguised as a boy. His presence was an assault on her, on the mother she thought she was. His skin glistened with sweat, a grotesque mockery of innocence as he stood there, an embodiment of broken control.

The violence of the moment took her breath away as if the very air had been ripped from her lungs. "Davis! God, stop! You are scaring me!" she screamed, but her words were overpowered by his deafening roars.

He sprang onto the couch, an unhinged force of destruction, flinging the cushions as if they were toys. Each violent toss was a crack of lightning, a strike that sent a jolt of terror through her. The brutal power of him that she had never seen, the force in his movements, were realities she wasn't prepared for.

It cut deeper than the violence; it stripped her of everything she thought she understood about him. Tears streamed down her face, hot acid, as she pleaded, her voice a whisper against the madness taking hold of him. She flinched away from him, from the savage glint in his eyes. The sting of a zipper, a cruel bite against her cheek, was nothing compared to the chilling knowledge that this creature, this untamed beast, was her son.

A throw pillow, impacting her like a brick, sent her sprawling to the tile floor. He towered over her, a looming shadow, his panting breath a wild growl, the charge of his rage vibrating in the air. The weight of his body, the promise of violence in his eyes, pinned her in place. Helplessness, cold and absolute, seeped into her bones. He was going to kill her.

A helpless scream ripped through Ellen; a sound born not of lungs but of panic too raw to shape. She launched herself to her feet, unleashed, every fiber of her body burning with adrenaline. "Davis!" she shrieked, the word a jagged splinter of lead shattering the misplaced silence. "You are terrifying me! Stop this now!"

His eyes, wild and feverish, were the only things that moved. He froze, a grotesque, his breath was ragged. A guttural snarl escaped him. "Scared? You're scared?" he shouted, his entire body vibrating with fury. His chest heaved with each breath; muscles clenched so tight they looked ready to snap. "I'm the one who'll look like an idiot. I'm the one who'll lose everything!" Spit flew from his mouth. His fists pounded against his bare thighs as he shouted again. "I'm the one. Not you. I am the one! Do you hear me, woman?" He lurched forward suddenly, eyes blazing, the veins in his neck standing out as he roared. His voice tore from his throat, raw, shredded, violent, and the sound of it scraped through the room, jagged and wild. Ellen slowly stood up, the force inside her building with every inch she rose.

Fear still burned in her, but it no longer led. Her voice didn't shake. It cut through the air with startling clarity. "You're right," she hissed, her words laced with disapproval. "You do look like an idiot. You are chasing a woman, chasing your own mother around the house. NAKED! Look at yourself! Go on, look at yourself!" One step forward closed the space between them. She jabbed her finger toward his chest, his stomach, his bare legs, and his exposed genitals, forcing his eyes downward. Control was hers now. Every word that followed landed with force.

He stood frozen, breathing hard, his chest rising and falling as the weight of what he had done began to land. His body held in place, but everything inside him had started to fall. Years of clandestine ritual, a critical, self-mutilating pilgrimage, had led him to this: the tanned, toned flesh his mother could now see, the reality of her witnessing his exposed body, manipulated to appear like that of a child. His eyes fixed on the trembling flesh of his penis, the shame pulsing through him with unbearable heat. This was the cold, exacting horror of a boy laid bare by the force of his own unraveling.

Whatever surged up in that moment didn't belong to him. It ran through him, alien and uninvited. Hot tears tracked paths through the dust on his skin. He reached for his mother, desperate, grasping lunge, but she recoiled. Her rigid movement was as sharp as honed metal.

She didn't budge. She remained exactly where she was, watching him. When she spoke, her voice carried no fear. It only offered judgment, sharpened to a point. "Who, Davis? Who in this room would be labeled a psychopath if someone came in right now? Who?" She waited. Davis's whimper was swallowed by the sound of his own cries. Humiliation tightened around him, skin to skin, offering no escape. He dropped onto the cushion-less sofa, legs folding beneath him as if struck. Both arms wrapped across his lap in a frantic, clumsy effort to shield what was left of himself from view. His back was hunched. His shoulders curled inward. He had no words.

Eventually, he bent forward, trying to disappear behind his own limbs. "I... I'm not... a..." he croaked, the word "psychopath" a strangled whisper, buried under the collapse of everything he thought he was. His face sank into his hands, and he stayed there, motionless, as if any movement might shatter him completely.

Ellen spoke with a clinical, caring firmness. "Go to your room. Get dressed. This is unacceptable." Her tone allowed no room for discussion. "We'll deal with it when you're in a position to do so." He stood slowly, unfolding from the couch, one arm dropping fast, the other drawn tight against his body. His hands scrambled between his legs, frantic and shaking. Panic surged through him. He grappled to cover himself, to pull everything behind his grip. A tremble passed through his legs as the shame rooted deeply. The first touch of tile against his feet sent a jolt through him, and he lurched forward, shoulders drawn in, trying to get away from the eyes behind him. The hallway offered nothing but emptiness. Each step pushed his body into awareness of how much of himself he had revealed, of what he had done, of how little he had managed to hide. His steps barely made a sound. He didn't stop.

He didn't slow. His only thought was escape. The front door opened with a dry groan, a sound that split the room down its center. Max stepped into the frame, holding two bottles of wine in one hand, their necks clinking together in the quiet. He froze at the sight of the torn-up furniture, the cushions scattered across the floor, the room stripped of order. His eyes jumped from Ellen's disheveled frame to his naked son, then back again as if searching for an explanation that refused to exist.

He looked to Ellen, reaching for clarity, drawn to her as the only fixed point in the room. Her hand rose sharply, without a glance, cutting off his breath before it left his mouth. The force of that motion knocked the question out of him. He froze, eyes wide, hands half-lifted in helpless confusion. Max's mouth opened, but nothing came. He stared across the room at Davis, trying to form a thought strong enough to carry. His eyes dropped briefly to his son's hands, to the way his body curled around itself like a wound. The sight hollowed him.

Davis kept his back to them as he walked. Even without turning, he felt Max watching, frozen in place, clutching the bottles, not breathing. The tension behind him pressed into his skin like heat. Davis kept moving, holding himself together with each step. He walked through the hallway, arms drawn close, head still down. The tile beneath his feet carried each step forward without pause. He didn't rush, but he didn't linger. The moment did not follow him out.

"...Go!" The word tore out of Ellen with commanding resolve, the only thing she could give him in the moment.

Davis disappeared, and with him, the last thread she'd held together. Ellen stood in the wreckage of it all, holding on for one more second. Then she turned to Max and reached for him. Her breath came fast. The tears followed hard. She grabbed hold of him with both hands, pressing herself into him like she couldn't bear another second on her own.

Max wrapped his arms around her without hesitation. He didn't ask what happened. He didn't try to speak. He just held her. Her sobs came harder the longer he stayed silent, and when she could finally breathe through them, she spoke. "Help me clean this up," she said, her voice was desperate and overflowing with everything she could no longer carry alone.

Chapter 9: Evening Tide

As dusk deepened, a sweep of headlights seemed to coax the sandstone beach house into being. Its details were accented with the warm, temporary light washing over it. Max and Ellen stood, peering out the windows, their wide smiles were a soft mask for the easy weariness that had begun to soften the edges of the evening around them. Yet, a vibrant current of excitement surged through Ellen, refusing to be contained.

From the rented sedan, before the engine had even fully settled, Irene was the first to move. The second the car stopped, she threw open her door, her face alight with anticipation as she stepped into the humid night. Her excitement spilled out in every movement. She smoothed her blouse and scanned the house, her eyes flicking toward the entryway with barely contained urgency. Her pace quickened without thinking. She practically bounced as she circled the car.

Gretchen stepped out more cautiously, pausing beside the open door before joining the others. She tugged at the hem of her top and ran her fingers through her hair, brushing it over one shoulder. Her eyes moved carefully across the glowing windows and sculpted landscaping, already aware of how she might look stepping into a place like this. She adjusted the strap on her duffel and followed Irene, walking slightly behind.

Manny stayed in the car a beat longer. He exhaled through pursed lips, shoulders slumped. The long drive still clung to him. After twenty hours behind the wheel, his joints felt locked in place. He opened his door with a groan and stood slowly, stretching just enough to ease the pressure on his back. Then he made his way to the trunk, hoisted out the heaviest suitcase, and let it thud gently onto the smooth pavers. One by one, he lined the rest beside it, steady and methodical, even as the stiffness in his limbs lingered. Irene doubled back to grab two of the lighter bags, and Gretchen wheeled her own behind her without a word. Together, they moved toward the front entrance, the luggage rolling quietly beside them as the glow of the house pulled them in.

Ellen didn't wait. She rushed toward the door, propelled by the sound of familiar voices outside and the rush of everything she'd been holding in. The anticipation in her expression was unmistakable, bright, and overflowing. In one swift motion, she flung open the massive oak door, releasing a wave of salty ocean air and the warm, humid Florida night. Their exhaustion visibly melted away as the welcoming glow of the house enveloped them, a beacon of warmth and comfort against the inky expanse of the ocean.

Ellen's triumphant cry shattered the remaining quiet. "Davis! They're here! Finally! Come on out!" The heavy door swung shut behind them, and the house, moments before hushed and still, exploded into a joyous maelstrom. Laughter, the scrape of luggage, and the rhythmic pounding of feet created a perfect storm of a happy reunion.

Manny rubbed his temples and murmured. "This place… It's amazing; it's exactly like I remembered it." His voice barely rising above the soft din as he stepped farther into the room, eyes scanning the space with quiet recognition.

Ellen, racing to grab a bottle of wine, smiled as she transformed into the perfect hostess. She carefully placed it in a prepared ice bucket and began arranging glasses around it on a whimsical beach-themed tray. "I'm sure we could all use this." She practically sang.

Irene, breathing deeply, let the moment settle in before whispering, "Thank you, Ellen." The strain of the day slipped off her shoulders, and the house itself radiated with a warmth that matched their happiness. The day's harshness, the rain, the battles, and the long journey melted away in the shared laughter and stories.

Davis walked in, showcasing confidence, his presence filling the room. He entered like he belonged, wearing an unbuttoned linen shirt, leather sandals, and a brand-new, form-fitting, designer swimsuit that displayed his physique. His smile was bright and genuine.

"Hey, guys," he beamed with a wave, his voice warm and inviting. "Hope the trip treated you well. It's quite a drive, isn't it?" He gestured expansively and settled into his chair, relaxed but undeniably in command. The room crackled with anticipation. He filled the space with natural gravity, every glance and gesture inviting attention.

Irene, unable to contain herself, launched into his arms. She pulled back with a soft laugh, turning slowly as if reacquainting herself with a place she'd only ever seen in dreams. Her eyes moved from wall to ceiling to the familiar faces around her, absorbing it all with wonder. "I just now realized how much I needed this vacation." The house, the people, everything... it was exactly what she hadn't known she was missing.

After settling onto the comfortable sofas and chairs, Manny took the opportunity to pour the wine, generous for some, while providing smaller portions for the teenagers.

The house stirred with life; old memories, jokes, and friendships flowed freely. The sun dipped below the horizon, painting the sky in vibrant, warm hues. The rhythmic crash of the waves provided a perfect background to their joy. Davis moved with a relaxed energy, heightening his parents' shared vision for the days ahead. The exhaustion of their journey vanished, replaced by the comfort of their closeness.

Gretchen and Davis settled onto the floor near the coffee table. Wine glasses balanced carefully between their knees. Their posture easy, relaxed; the casual sprawl of people who felt safe enough to let their guards down. The adults lounged nearby, some perched on the couch, others leaning into the cushions, the mood loose and familiar.

Irene lifted her glass, her smile bright. "And there were butterflies just everywhere. You guys really need to go there."

She laughed lightly, her voice weaving through the room's gentle noise. "One landed right on Gretchen. I mean, right on her shoulder. I tried to get a picture, but as soon as I was about to hit the button, it went off... ha ha. Missed the boat on that one. Didn't I, Gretchen?"

Gretchen laughed, shaking her head. "It was funny because the whole time, I was trying to get one to land on my finger. Like a fairy tale or something. I musta looked crazy with my finger out like this." She mimed it, holding out her hand, and the others chuckled. "Right when I gave up, there it was. Using me as a rest stop. Sitting on my shoulder on its own terms. The second we did something it didn't approve of, that was it. I was dead to it. My feelings didn't matter. Boo hoo! It was a pretty cool experience, though. You guys should totally go there."

Irene smiled warmly, resting back against the cushions. "Great start to—"

Manny cut in, voice low and fond. "A family vacation. It has been too long. You know. Life happens. Time off is harder and harder to get. The daily grind. You know how it is."

Davis stood, shifting his weight easily, his glass of wine still in hand. He glanced toward Ellen with a boyish grin that softened his strong features. "Hey, Ma. Can we go walking around for a while? I feel cooped."

Ellen lowered her glass, her arms crossing, unsettled. "I don't know. It's dark. Gretchen just got here a while ago. Been a long drive and..."

Gretchen shifted beside him, brushing her hands along the carpet idly. "No, it's fine. I'd like to get out for a minute, too. Stretch. Chill out a little."

Ellen pressed her lips together, watching Gretchen closely. "I'm not sure if that's a good idea."

Manny waved a hand dismissively from the couch. "Oh, let them go. They are practically adults."

Max, who had been quiet, spoke up with a casual warning. "Stay out of the ocean. It's darker in the water than you think."

Ellen shot him a wary look, her voice tense. "Max. I don't think—"

Max smiled lazily. "It is fine, dear. Loosen the apron strings a little."

Irene chuckled and lifted her glass again, her voice teasing. "Let them go. Who wants to stick around the parents all night?"

Ellen exhaled sharply, then nodded with reluctance, her shoulders stiff. "Only for a while. Do you hear me?"

Davis and Gretchen exchanged a grin and moved toward the door.

Ellen sat up straighter, her voice following them sharply. "Nuh-uh. Wine stays here, kiddos. You may be practically an adult, but the law in Florida is still twenty-one."

Gretchen laughed softly, setting her glass down carefully.

Davis mimed the tipping of an invisible hat. "Yes, ma'am."

The screen door clicked shut behind them as they stepped into the night. Moonlight coated the path ahead while the rolling rhythm of the ocean welcomed them forward. Their footsteps sank into the damp sand as the surf moved in harmony with them. The night stretched around their forms like a shelter, and for a while, it felt like enough. As they strolled across their rented plot of beach, the surf moved in harmony with them. A breeze brushed over them, carrying the warmth of the house behind and the salt of the sea ahead.

Their conversation drifted quietly upon the gentle sea air, leaving behind only the promise of renewed friendship.

Chapter 10: New Light

Indigo bled into the darkening sky. The crescent moon, chipped and low on the horizon, hovered above the beach. Silver light skimmed across Gretchen's face, catching the strands of sun-bleached hair drifting across her shoulders. She sat upright, though her body betrayed the effort. Her shoulders sagged. The quiet tranquility around her wasn't satisfying. She sat, expectant, held in place by more than his presence. A flicker passed over her mouth, not quite a smile. Davis didn't notice it, anyway. Behind her, the beach house glowed with amber light.

She and Davis sat close together yet somewhat apart, both of them sunken slightly into the cool sand. It pressed against their legs, shifting with every minor movement. He leaned forward with his phone balanced on a knee. He held it tightly as if it was part of him. Davis's fingers traced the screen in sharp, agitated lines. Each swipe produced a faint, repetitive rhythm that tangled with the hush of the waves. The gentle percussion carried on unnoticed. It moved through the air, then vanished with the wind and the sounds drifting up from the nearby houses.

He looked up briefly to Gretchen before returning his full attention to the screen. The movement felt casual and unconscious. The beach around them waited. Florida seemed to hesitate as if listening with them to the sounds that drifted through the dark. Laughter floated from other homes, arriving in fragments, swallowed by the tide. Wind pressed against the sand, sculpting and undoing spirals in slow motion.

Davis angled his phone with the ocean behind him, the screen glowing faintly as he scrolled through filters. He took the shot without smiling. His thumb lingered at the edge of the screen, waiting for the right moment to make it real. Beside him, Gretchen drew one knee closer and let her arm fall over it, her eyes locked on the way the screen highlighted his features. She felt her stare holding too long before returning to the waves. They were two teenagers on the sand. A familiarity existed between them as they experienced the moment like strangers.

The moon rose higher as the evening marched forward, casting a pale wash over the teenagers. Gretchen rubbed her arms as she caught a slight chill from the evening wind sweeping across the tide. She closed her eyes and let it move through her.

Somewhere beyond them, the surf roared and retreated, never settling. Gretchen leaned back slightly, letting the breeze press against her chest while Davis traced lines in the sand with a fingertip. His attention was split between the pattern forming beneath him and the awkward presence beside him that he did not know how to address. Their shared past tugged at them. It hovered at the edge of the moment.

Davis continued, absorbed in the plan he was carving into the grains. Gretchen watched him work, letting the peace wrap around her. Her fingers brushed the edge of her shirt, then hovered as if unsure where to place them. She leaned forward, then back again. Searching for something to do, she cleared her throat quietly and lifted her hand to get his attention. "Can I sit by you?"

After a contemplative pause, he blinked incredulously. His brow creased, followed by the muscle at the corner of his mouth twitching with mild irritation. His index finger left the sand before pausing and returning to the exact same spot, continuing the design as if nothing had been said. His voice then came slowly, articulating each word with a sarcasm he did not bother to conceal. "You... are... sitting by me."

He wasn't wrong. Davis had always been blunt, but the closeness he recognized hadn't shielded her from the chill rising off the waves. She let out a quiet chuckle, more breath than sound, and rose to her feet. Sand clung to her calves and the backs of her thighs. She swept it away with quick swipes of her palms, then folded her arms tight across her chest, hands rubbing warmth into her skin where goosebumps had already surfaced.

"I mean," she clarified, her voice barely audible above the environment, "it's a little windy."

Davis offered a shrug of invitation with a lazy roll of his shoulders that clearly conveyed disinterest more than welcome. His fingers traveled through the sand, carving long lines that spiraled outward from a central point. His shirt shifted with the motion, catching a glint of moonlight in its folds, briefly exposing the tension in his neck and the stillness in his jaw. Whatever he was tracing held more of his focus than she did.

The edge of her shirt brushed against her shorts as she sat beside him. Her knees left shallow impressions that filled slowly with the shifting grains. She slid over, settling her hip near his, narrowing the space between them while maintaining just enough distance. She leaned forward and lifted her hand. It hovered a breath above his shoulder, then landed with care. The shirt pulled beneath her palm, stretched tight where he hadn't moved.

He jerked beneath her touch. The sudden movement broke the pattern he'd been drawing, and he sighed with disgust.

Her fingers sank deeper into his skin as she tilted her head closer, with blonde locks veiling one side of her face. She watched him through the wispy curtain it formed. She traced the slope of his cheekbone and the line of his jaw with her eyes, drawn to what he wouldn't offer freely. A tremble passed through her fingers, delicate and alive. It carried through the point of contact, a current sparked by wanting more than she could ask for. Her hand stayed, resting in the curve of his shoulder, deepening the contact.

She didn't pull away. Her fingers adjusted slightly against him, just enough to show she meant no harm. When she spoke, her voice was careful, almost tender. A smile ghosted at the edge of her lips, not bold enough to claim the moment but enough to meet his recoil with something gentler. Her thumb brushed the seam of his sleeve near his collar.

"Don't worry, Day. I just need you to block the wind. I promise you are safe."

Davis stopped what he was doing and stared at her. The closeness pressed against his composure, lessening the distance he had worked to keep intact since she arrived. A twitch ran down the arm he'd used to draw, a leftover reaction with nowhere to go. He sat motionless, waiting for the discomfort to pass, but it stayed. He didn't want to speak, yet he also didn't want to sit there in silence. His thoughts spun through topics he didn't care about, reaching for anything easy. Nothing landed. The pressure rose swiftly, demanding an outlet. He provided one: "So... how has school been?" It was a good start because he didn't care about the answer.

Gretchen didn't respond right away. She let the question sit, then brushed her hair back with a slow flip and sank her toes into the sand, pushing them down until the grains spilled over. She dusted the grit from her thigh and straightened her back, planting both hands behind her in the sand to brace herself. "School has been... manageable." She spaced the words with care; each one placed just far enough apart to feel disingenuous. Then she laughed. It hit sharp and sudden, cutting the moment clean. She tipped her head with mock surprise. "School?" she repeated, dragging it out with an edge that sparkled enough to taunt. "Is that really what you want to talk about? After all this time?"

"Uh... yeah... What else? I figured you had enough butterflies." The words dropped flat between them, spoken with the same stillness he'd held since the question left his mouth. He offered the line the way someone might hand over a receipt. Flat. Forgettable. Slid across the counter without thought.

Gretchen giggled. It escaped before she could stop it, just enough to pass for ease. She adjusted her position and pressed the sand beneath her heel. "Well, that actually was pretty cool. I figured you'd want to talk about the monkey in the room. That's all."

A guffaw broke from Davis as he sprang to his feet, a smug grin stretching across his face. He threw his arms wide and shouted, "There's a monkey in the room? Where?" The words tumbled out between fits of laughter, each syllable heavy with mockery.

Gretchen stared up at him, startled. Laughter peeled off him in waves, loud at first, then thinning without warning. He focused on her face as her expression changed. The warmth she carried a moment ago folded in on itself. She looked at him like he had slapped the air out of her. He regretted how far he'd taken it, even if he couldn't understand why she didn't find it as hilarious as he did.

Something inside him stalled. For a breath, he saw the girl who used to trust him without flinching. She was hurting, and he was the cause. It mattered. "You meant elephant, I think." He tried to pull it back with a smirk, but it stuck halfway, more habit than expression. He dropped down beside her. "So what's your monkey?" The words reached for levity after his pause, but the spark had gone out. "It doesn't matter, Gretch. It can be a monkey if you want." He knew what it was, anyway.

His grin felt far-fetched, a grotesque imposter of loyalty. He knew. He knew exactly what her "Monkey" was. His parents had told him in hushed tones, made him promise not to bring it up. He had hoped she wouldn't, but here he was.

Gretchen rolled her eyes again before meeting his. The lightness between them faded. The tension inside her spilled into motion. Restlessness crept in, leaving her with nowhere to go. When she spoke, the words came unfiltered, heavy with the truth she had held from him too long. It carried the ache of someone who had kept quiet because she refused to be reduced to a simple target of someone else's sympathy.

"Seriously? You think I'm that naive. You know, Davis. Everyone does. You… know! My age doesn't equate to stupidity." She leaned toward him as she spoke, each phrase pressed forward with controlled emotion. Frustration simmered beneath every word, driven by the weight of everything she had been forced to carry alone. She reached for the edge of her sleeve, then let go before finishing the gesture. "I was twelve." The words arrived numbly as if her voice hadn't gotten the message her heart was trying to send. "My boyfriend at the time, someone I trusted, hurt me."

She paused long enough to be seen. She noticed how the cruel joy on his face from teasing her had evaporated. It seemed like he was actually seeing her now instead of her imperfections. "I lost everything that day. My innocence, my sense of safety, and the girl I was." The wind snapped through, flinging strands across her face, underscoring everything she had just laid bare.

"My parents tried to protect me from the shame and judgment. I moved to a different school, a different town. I had to run away from my own life, leaving the pieces for someone else to sweep up." Her voice dipped but didn't waver. "And you, my best friend, were nowhere. No calls, no messages, not even a whisper of concern. It was like you wanted to forget that I existed."

Davis moved toward her, drawn forward by the gravity of hearing her pain directly rather than through his parents. The performance had drained from his face. What remained was genuine attention, etched with compassion that he did not recognize. He absorbed it all and stayed with her in the experience. Her pain held him there.

"I survived, but it changed me, and I'll never be the same again." She watched those words land between them. Her tone softened. "But I'm not saying it to hurt you. I just needed you to know."

Davis's lips parted, but the words waited. When they came, they came without polish.

"I... I'm sorry, Gretchen. I never meant to make you feel that way. Everyone around me told me to give you space. They said you'd come to me when you were ready. But you never did. It was a mistake not to reach out. I should have tried harder." He paused, struggling against the knot building in his throat. "We've been friends longer than anyone else. And I let you down. I screw up a lot. I don't want to make it about me. But I should have been there."

Gretchen simply nodded and pressed her hand to his back.

"I know it wasn't easy for you," she said, her voice no longer trembling. "And you're right. Everyone told me to take my time and that it was okay not to feel like I had to talk to people about it. I understand. But it still hurt that you weren't there."

"I needed my friend, and you were gone." She spoke with remorse. The sound filtered through the truth and remained. The sound moved through the truth and lingered. A tremble reached the edge of her mouth. She caught it with a steady breath.

Tears burned, then receded, quelled by a pure, unyielding intention. Memories drifted through her like smoke, leaving no residue. Her eyes produced a faraway look, lost to a past that bled into the present. A relentless surge of optimism wrestled despair to a standstill until her mind cleared, snapping her focus forward. The road ahead began to open as the door to yesterday slammed firmly shut.

She shook her head and allowed a nervous laugh to overtake her for a moment. "I survived, though. I had to rebuild myself and find a new sense of strength. It changed me, but I'm still here."

Davis caught himself staring at the sea. Guilt crept in as he realized he had broken eye contact when she needed him most. Conflict pulled at his center. The urge to withdraw pressed against the choice to stay. He stayed because she deserved that much.

"I can't even try to understand what you went through," he said quietly. "But I'm here now, and I'm not going anywhere. We can start over if you want. I promise to be a better friend." He offered her a pensive smile, his eyes hopeful. "And if you ever want to talk about the monkey... or the elephant... in the room, I'm cool with it."

He expected a response. A laugh. A shift. Gretchen watched him with patience. Something deeper moved between them. His fingers drifted toward his artwork lying beside him. He searched for comfort in the shapes he had created but had quickly lost meaning. Anxiety rose. Words scattered. He pressed his palm across the sand and swept the lines away.

Unable to control the impulse, he broke the silence.

"Do I know him... Do I know the guy?" he asked as he searched Gretchen's face for clues. She nodded a hesitant affirmation.

"Ethan," she said softly. A spark of recognition passed through Davis.

"Ethan... the one who was always getting into trouble? Your boyfriend, Ethan?" he asked, relaxed now in the wrong way, with unintended rudeness.

Gretchen projected a small, melancholy smile. "Yes, that's him," she said. Her voice held, but the strain showed in the space after.

He struck the sand with the side of his fist as he spoke. His intent was stripped of performance. "I'll kill him."

Gretchen reached toward him. Her hand met his back. "You can't kill him, Day," she said, her laugh catching on the thrill of being defended. "He's in juvie, and he'll be there for a while. He won't be able to hurt anyone else."

A tear slid down her cheek. She didn't wipe it. His hand rose, brushing it away with his thumb. The moisture caught him off guard. He dropped his hand like it had contacted something live.

"I'm sorry, Gretchen," he said, his voice unsteady. "I wish I could help. He should never have done that."

Gretchen nodded. Her fingers curled slowly into the sand. The motion was quiet, instinctive, giving her a moment to settle. Her eyes lowered, lashes brushing downward as she blinked against the silence.

When she spoke again, her voice softened, her breath carefully spaced. "He's underage," she said. "He'll be out soon, and he'll get to live his life like nothing happened." Her voice thinned. The next words took longer to reach. "It's not fair… He… he…" Her lips parted, but the rest caught. Her eyes shone, and her breath faltered. "He hit me, Davis."

Davis moved without thinking. One arm reached around her waist before the other found its place across her back. The hug came all at once, too fast and without grace. His shoulder pressed into hers at an awkward angle. One of her curls caught against his shirt. He didn't adjust it. His grip tightened, uneven and unfamiliar but firm. He held on, not because it felt right, but because it was the only thing he could do that didn't feel wrong.

Gretchen's shoulders trembled as she buried herself against him. "It's not fair," she whispered. "It's hard when he'll be out there, living like nothing happened."

He held her and stared ahead, watching the tide pull against the shore. The grief wasn't his, but it hovered between them. His hands brushed at his designer swimming shorts in aimless strokes. Then he let her go and clapped his hands together once. The sound broke the moment apart with a shock.

Davis's face beamed a smile broad enough to mute the moon. "How about we don't talk about it anymore?" The suggestion didn't rise. It settled with a silent affirmation, which was both unexpected and greatly needed. "You're here with us now. You're beautiful. Safe."

Gretchen stepped toward him, arms outstretched in friendship. Davis instinctively took a small step back, his hands lifting, a subtle gesture acknowledging the need for space between them. Gretchen stopped and nodded her head. She understood him. "I know I am. Took me a long time to figure that out. Thank you, Davis. I really mean it. By the way, you are, too."

Davis couldn't find the words to match the moment, so he said the first thing that came to mind. "We should start hanging out again when we get back. I've missed you."

Her eyes lingered on him for a moment longer than he expected. Then, she looked away, offering a smile. "We definitely should. I've missed you, too."

Before he could respond, Irene's voice called from the beach house, clear and familiar. They both turned toward the light spilling from the open door, where Irene stood, looking out at them. "Hey, you two, it's getting late! The beach will still be there tomorrow. Time to come in."

Davis extended his hand to her, offering assistance. Gretchen paused for a moment, delivering a smile before accepting his hand. He helped her up and released her, making certain to not hold contact for any longer than absolutely necessary. The two of them walked toward the house, side by side, but it didn't feel like it usually did. Davis kept his eyes focused ahead on the darkened house. Gretchen kept hers on him.

Chapter 11: Echoes of Neverland

The mechanical ticks of the clock burrowed into Ellen's consciousness. Each sound arrived with surgical precision, clean and exact, a sound designed to leave no room for rest. The pattern didn't change. It gnawed. It knew her. She felt confined. Her mind ran in circles of fear, anger, and betrayal. The cadence of her husband's peaceful, sleeping breath beside her only intensified the tension building within her.

She didn't understand how he could remain so calm while she had to fight to merely stay still. The cycle of conflicting ideas had taken residence in her mind since retiring to bed, a repeating chorus of echoes with no foreseeable end. Ellen's thoughts raced as she lay awake; the clock seemed to enjoy taunting her, second by annoying second. She found herself growing angry at the clock as if it were an enemy. She turned on her side to try to find comfort in a different position before finally giving up.

"Screw it," she whispered with contempt. She knew the true source of her unrest lay within herself. It was a situation she had faced many times before when dealing with Davis, but tonight, her emotions pressed harder with each thought. The glowing red numbers of the clock stared back at her, unblinking.

"See if you can sleep now, you useless bitch," the clock seemed to taunt, its voice her own, filled with loathing she barely recognized.

Ellen's concentration shifted back and forth between the clock and her husband, feeling alone and trapped in a riddle that only she could decipher. The urge to act, to do something drastic, was building. She sat up in bed with her flag of surrender unfurled. Her body reluctantly lagged behind her racing thoughts. She knew that if she stayed in bed, the temptation to wake her husband with a violent knee to the groin would become all but irresistible. "That'll wake him up," she thought, a small, satisfied smile playing at the corners of her mouth.

Instead, she slid her legs over the edge of the mattress and shuffled into the living room to reset. As Ellen stepped into the hall, an angst-ridden sigh pierced the silence, its source seemingly rooted in the very heart of humanity's woes. She immediately noticed the blue light of a cell phone bathing the living room in an eerie glow, casting an otherworldly light on the scene. She paused, frowning at the bare feet protruding over the edge of the upscale sofa. With a mix of curiosity and resolve, she approached, hoping the owner of them, Davis, was not preparing for round two. Her rationality wrestled with her scorn as she hoped to find a sleeping asshole, unaware of her presence.

The phone's glow led her on a path of discovery, each step a cautious venture into the unknown. Ellen's attention shot between the glowing phone and the shadowy, motionless figure on the sofa. With each quiet step, she drew closer, preparing herself for whatever awaited her. The phone became a beacon, drawing her in. Taking a deep breath, Ellen accepted the reality that she had encountered a wide-awake asshole. Davis's fingers racing across the screen answered the riddle. "Let's do this," she thought.

She cleared her throat softly, barely more than a breath.

"What are you doing up? It is 3:00 AM."

Davis turned his head toward her slowly, the pale glow of the phone screen fading from his features. His face was tired, hollow around the eyes.

"I can't sleep."

She held her arms tightly against herself, bracing inwardly. Although she already knew the answer, she felt compelled to ask him, "Did you take your meds?"

He pushed himself up with reluctance, letting the phone slip onto the cushion beside him. "No. I don't like drugs."

Ellen approached him, her steps soft but steady, stopping an arm's reach from the couch. "Davis, they help you. Don't you see?"

He shook his head. His voice carried a thin edge of irritation. "They really don't do anything. I don't like drugs, okay? I'm just thinking about today."

She moved carefully, lowering herself into the chair across from him. Her body folded with visible weariness, her hands resting loosely on her knees.

An exasperated breath escaped her, "Okay. Fine. We talked about it earlier already. Please don't worry about it anymore." She let her voice soften even further. "Just pay attention to your temper from now on, Davis. You are not three. No more tantrums. That's all."

Davis dropped his gaze to his hands, turning them over as if they might hold information he had previously missed. "Not about that. I am really sorry about that, by the way. I really am. It's embarrassing. You know that I don't act like that."

She stayed quiet, waiting, letting him have the space to say what he needed to say.

"I was thinking about Gretch," he said, his voice barely louder than a whisper.

Without hesitation, Ellen rose and crossed the room. She sat down beside him on the couch, and in one smooth, instinctive motion, she slid her arm around his shoulders, pulling him gently into her.

Davis leaned into her naturally, his fight slipping away as her arm settled around him.

"Oh, honey. Everything is going to be alright. She has a lot of support. She has been through a lot but look how good she is doing. Just be a friend. That is all you need to do."

He pressed closer, letting his head tip against her side. "I will. I am. She said that she has grown up a lot. She has. It made me just think that I have not. She is like an adult."

She brushed her hand slowly through his hair, the movement comforting, practiced. "You will. Boys take a little longer to mature. It is science."

Davis closed his eyes for a moment, his breathing easing into the stillness between them. "I don't want to grow up. I just want it to be like this forever."

A quiet smile touched her mouth, one stitched from old memories. "My little Peter Pan. Remember that story when you were little? He was your hero. You said you wanted to be just like him... except with parents."

He opened his eyes again but did not lift his head. His voice came soft, almost tentative, clinging to a hope he did not want to let go of. "What's wrong with it?" He paused and looked at his mother for a response, which didn't arrive, before continuing, "I could stay with you forever. I do not want to get a job and live a pointless life with no fun. Live by rules that limit me. Lose my dreams."

Her hand remained resting against his head, steady and warm. His mother encouraged him, "Oh, Davis. We do not lose our dreams. They just change. They get more colorful. Sometimes, there are good ones and bad ones, but in the end, it is all wonderful... Most of the time."

She let the words drift into the soft dark of the room. "You'll see."

He moved slightly under her arm, pulling back just enough to see her face. "No. I won't. I already have my dreams. I don't need any more color. I feel like adding some will just ruin them... smudge them... I don't see anything but bad coming from that."

Ellen dropped her hand gently to his arm, giving it a quiet, reassuring squeeze. "I don't know what to say other than, you'll see."

She rose slowly from the couch, her body stiff with the hour. She took a few steps toward the hallway, her fingers grazing the back of the sofa as she paused. "The funny thing about dreams is we don't take them with us... They take us with them."

She lingered, her outline faint in the low light. "Well, Kiddo... you ready to go to bed?"

Davis pulled the blanket tighter around his chest. "I think I am just going to stay out here."

Ellen leaned in lightly, her voice gentle but steady. "I wish you would not. People are going to be getting up in a few hours, and you know how grumpy you are when you get woken up."

A tired smirk emerged on Davis's face.

She offered an aching smile, burdened by a love that could not keep him where he wanted to be. "Alright. You are too big for me to carry anyway. Remember your promise in the morning."

"I remember it now. Night, Mom. I love you," Davis returned with an innocent smile.

Turning slightly, she spoke over her shoulder. "Night, baby. I love you, too. More than you know."

Ellen took a few more slow steps toward the hallway but did not disappear completely. She pivoted so she could still see him, close enough to hear him when he spoke again.

"I know a lot", he mumbled, "I am bad. I know I am, but you love me anyway," Davis said in a slow tenor tone.

She stopped in her tracks and listened.

"You are not bad, Davis. Don't say that. Do you think that? You are the kindest, sweetest, most caring boy in the world. You just have a hard time expressing it sometimes. Everything is just extreme for you; it seems like. Things are either the best or the worst. Nothing in between. There are bad days, but that does not make you bad."

Davis tucked the blanket closer around him, cocooning himself in the small warmth it offered. "Maybe. I live in the moment. That is good... right?"

Ellen tilted her head thoughtfully, her voice thick with fatigue but filled with affection. "Sometimes... That is much more philosophy than my brain can handle at this hour. Just get some sleep, okay?"

Her son watched her with reverence until she finished speaking. He extended his arms widely, an offer of a hug which she eagerly accepted. As she turned to leave, Davis's whispered admission, "Maybe," struck her. This moment was special. He trusted her with his deepest honesty. He allowed her to visit inside his head for a moment.

With a cleansed heart, she retraced her steps back to her bedroom to join Max, her mind no longer swirling with conflicting emotions. The once-tormenting tick of the clock was now inconsequential.

Ellen's earlier resentments and inner turmoil had, in a brief conversation with her son, been replaced by a profound sense of understanding. She became determined to help him navigate the turbulent waters of his own self-value. As she crawled back into bed, exhausted, the sleep that eluded her earlier now became a seemingly distant memory.

Chapter 12: The Last Night

The salt-infused wind tore at Gretchen's hair, wisping it across her face as she laughed. Her time with Davis was wonderful. A gripping dread filled her with the thought of going back to the Midwest when things were going so well. Ten days. Ten damned days weren't enough to exhume a friendship choked by years of festering pain and her own stubborn inferences.

Davis.

His eyes were shaded like a storm and carried a tension that clung to his every expression. A forced casual charm always clung to his presence like a costume barely concealing the turmoil she sensed beneath. She wanted to break through and know him. She felt it in her gut. What she saw on social media was superficial. She wanted more than what he freely offered to everyone else.

The hot sand, searing through the soles of her bare feet, was molten glass. It served to balance the icy loneliness she had experienced over the past few years. The taste of salt bit at her lips. The sting ran through every glance and unspoken question between them.

They spent days together, tearing into each other's fears and feeding on support like famished beasts gnawing on bones. His tales were of the battles he never stopped fighting. The evidence was etched onto his face like a roadmap of scars.

Each furrowed brow was a reaction to a perception of life wrestled from the jaws of symbolic and repeated death. He fascinated her. His eyes held that same darkness she had seen in the ocean. It never revealed the dangerous undercurrent beneath the picturesque surface. Hers, flecked with gold trapped in sunlight, burned with a fierce desperation that masked an experience so profound it threatened to completely shatter her.

Their pasts clawed at them from within. Each breath carried a fragment of what had been. Scars formed beneath the surface, not to be seen, but to shape them. The two bonded over the course of days. Their friendship was a patchwork of what they remembered, what they were facing, and what they couldn't yet imagine.

The sandcastles they built were obscene monuments to a bond resurrected from the bones of perceived betrayal, a pathetic attempt to stitch together a tapestry of the past. Each turret stood, shaped with care, pointing at the open sky. The moats mirrored the space between them. Nothing they built could hold. Their laughter twisted. It cracked and collapsed into a sound that didn't belong on the beach. Years of pain surged to the surface and slipped out before either of them could stop it. The ocean didn't care. The sky didn't either. Still, the feeling followed them.

Davis's camera, a cold, unblinking eye, captured only the meticulously crafted façade he created for his public. His toothy smiles were brittle lies, barely concealing the tremor in his hands. His posts provided fleeting glimpses of a connection as fragile as a moth's wing in a hurricane.

He saw the transient evidence of pain in Gretchen's eyes. Her unconscious movements spoke of a shadow of a girl who had been destroyed, a girl he refused to allow to be hurt again. He felt his past failure and refused to repeat it. She had been through enough.

They carried too much because some things can never stay buried. Their bond was a twisted intimacy, a merry-go-round riding on the edge of inferiority. The absence of romance between them was a cavernous Utopia. It thrived in the undercurrent of their rekindled friendship, which was all either of them claimed to want.

The sun slammed against their skins as it retreated, a brutal parody of their comfortable peace. The last sliver bled into the Gulf, painting the turquoise water the bruised purple of a ripe plum. Small piles of seaweed, abandoned by the evening tide, lay scattered on the beach. Davis sprawled in a faded lounger, barely registering the spectacle with his usual intensity. His phone, a glowing symbol in his slack hand, consumed him. His thumb, a ninja among yellow belts, scrolled endlessly.

Gretchen watched him, the setting sun casting long shadows that stretched and distorted his relaxed form. Her body read it before her mind did. She'd seen this before, the withdrawal, the vacant stare. This time, she intended to intercept it before he was lost for the evening. A tentative, "Day? You, okay?" escaped her lips, a whisper swallowed by the rush of the evening breeze and changing tide.

He didn't react. The rhythmic tap-tap-tap of his thumb against the glass continued, a metronome counting down the moments. Gretchen's patience, usually boundless, snapped.

"Davis! What's wrong?" Her voice was sharper this time and cut through the ocean's rush.

He finally paused to look at her, complete with a mild expression of annoyance she had come to recognize quickly. The blankness in his eyes, a vast, unsettling expanse, both thrilled and bored her. He was there. At least, a part of him was.

Her voice, in that moment, was a jackhammer against his already frayed nerves. He enjoyed his alone time in spite of also enjoying the time spent with others. He sat up and kicked at a discarded plastic bottle. It produced a hollow, skittering sound-skip as it marked its path across the sand.

Around them, a kaleidoscope of brightly colored towels and sun-drenched bodies pulsed with a chaotic energy. People were everywhere. A scowl invaded his forehead while he sifted through the meager collection of photos on his phone. He evaluated a few blurry shots of Gretchen, mostly obscured by other tourists, before he deleted them.

"Not enough pictures," he muttered, the words flowing from his mouth, hitting her with accusatory ease.

Gretchen, ever optimistic, offered a bright smile. "We can take some more now."

His jaw tightened instantly. His eyes, usually warm and playful with her, now held the cold, hard flash of steel. He gestured wildly at the throng of people, a sea of limbs and laughter stretching to the horizon. "Look at this!" he snapped, his voice not remotely a whisper. It cancelled the ocean's thunder. He threw his arms in the air and twisted his torso, pointing out the environment. "It's a freakin' zoo! This isn't... this doesn't look anything even close to a private beach."

Gretchen giggled. Her laughter was light and teasing. It danced irritatingly through him. She posed for him on her lounger, spaced directly across from his. She gracefully flipped a lock of blonde hair over her shoulder. It was a ploy to soften his mood. It may have been futile, but it was the solution she had at that moment. "But, silly, it's not a private beach." She cheerfully corrected him.

Davis stared past her without seeing her. Then, as if a switch had flipped, his focus sharpened, landing on the curve of her smile. He sat up slowly. A soothing ghost of softness played on his lips. His voice, when he spoke, was low and carefully modulated, tainted with light explanatory humor that hinted at something deeper.

"Yeah, but it's gotta look private," he explained, the words revealing his carefully crafted intention. This was a deception he needed to verify the very illusion he created for his followers. He paused, his eyes searching hers, waiting. Then, with the charming arrogance that had become his unique trademark, he firmly clarified his position, "I can't be… that guy. The guy on a friggin' public beach."

Her incredulous facial expression that followed his words was off-putting to him. Gretchen's smile faded and was replaced by a look of disappointment. A feeling of sadness crept through her. She understood, suddenly, the purpose of his effort, the point of his online persona. With a serious but caring tone, she asked the unaskable question which had been plaguing her for days. "Why can't you just be who you are?" His lack of response stopped her.

He simply stared at her, hard with disbelief.

She whispered with careful sincerity, "Do you not like yourself?"

With a raucous laugh, Davis shook his head. "What? No… I'm sorry… I mean… What?" He could hardly believe the words as he heard them. He stretched his arms across the horizon and remained seated. He stretched them widely like he was trying to hold the whole of Florida in his span. He threw his head back before folding his arms around his torso and proclaiming, "Of course I like myself! I am unique. I'm going to do amazing things. I'm going to be friggin' famous."

She looked at him with an expression of awe he hadn't seen from her since they were kids.

"You obviously don't know me very well. I love myself. Everybody knows that. I just need to make sure that everyone sees what I am going to be, not what they think I am now. The future… Publicity! I don't want any evidence that can be used against me later, that's all." He reclined again, smugly and looked at her with a broad grin and a cocked eyebrow. He folded his hands confidently behind his head.

"Oh," Gretchen said with the dramatic, playful pout of a starlet. She lifted her index finger to point at him, surveying him. "Do you think I am ugly or something?" she asked slowly, quietly, fearfully, pensively.

He responded with a careful effort not to appear insensitive, "Huh? Where did that come from?" She stood and moved toward him. He promptly looked elsewhere, searching for something else to anchor to. The way she moved made him uncomfortable. She was getting too close. Too bold. Too certain.

Despite his efforts, his eyes were drawn to the curve of her breasts and the smoothness of her hips. He turned away with intention.

She drew him back. "I'm being serious right now, Day!" she pleaded. "I am obviously flirting with you. Every time I do, you friend-zone me." She twirled around him like a dancer, remaining in his direct line of sight. "Am I not glamorous and A-list enough for the soon-to-be-famous Davis Day?" she teased as she sat next to him, without permission.

Davis instinctively scooted over to allow some space between her hip and his. He was annoyed. Gretchen, you are beautiful. You already know that. You are probably the most glamorous person on the beach."

As the palm trees swayed in the evening breeze, their gentle rustle provided a melodic backdrop to the unfolding moment. Her eyes, akin to the shadows cast by the trees, moved languidly over him, soaking in every detail with a painter's precision. The late-day sun's warm caress on his skin echoed the soothing touch of the fading light on the sand.

In a whisper that floated like a breeze, Gretchen's words intertwined with the natural cadence around them, adding a touch of playful admiration to the tranquil setting. Her voice, soft and alluring, weaved through the air like the palm fronds swaying above, creating an unusually charged atmosphere. Davis shifted uncomfortably as he tried to make sense of the moment.

Her focus remained on him. Her fingers daringly traced the outline of his ridiculously expensive, perfectly tailored swimming suit. She purred, "Aside from you… those shorts… your white teeth… that perfect tan…" Her eyes lingered on the sun-kissed gleam of his skin. Her hand skimmed the taut curve of his hip. "And that incredibly juicy soccer ass…"

The touch, feather-light yet undeniably bold, sent a jolt through him. He felt the tickle of her hand against his body. His eyes became wide with a mixture of disbelief and something that looked suspiciously like terror before they darted to meet hers. His expression slackened. He held his breath for a moment. His words had been knocked loose before they formed. The question in his eyes, however, remained: Is this really happening?

She judged his expression, brought her hands to her lap, and flatly asked, "After all of this time, you really only see me as a friend?"

Innocently, Davis paused, searching for the right words to convey what he was feeling. He dragged a hand over his face and then let it fall beside him. He bent forward, looking at the sand between them like it might explain what she meant. He sighed. It left him like a secret let slip as he responded, "But... we are friends, ... right?"

She scrambled to her feet with a frantic movement that revealed her frustration. A wave of conflicting emotions crashed over her, leaving her gasping. He sat on the edge of the seat with an impassive look on his face, creating a marked disparity between his understanding and the storm raging in hers.

She could only speak in choked, humiliated sobs. "Yes, Davis... we are," she forced out, the words much more effortful and resigned than a few moments before. Her acknowledgment, colored with unresolved rejection, clearly confused Davis as he tried to figure her out. "I'm so sorry, Davis," she breathed, her voice cracking. "I... I always thought..." Her voice trailed off with tears blurring her vision. She noticed him blankly staring at her.

The silence stretched, thick and throttling, punctuated only by the ragged rasp of her breathing. A single tear escaped, then another, and then a torrent. She let them fall freely as she spoke. "I know... you see me as...a..." She swallowed the word whore, allowing it to remain unsaid yet present between them. She waited, attempting to regain control. Her hand rose to her throat to stifle the emotion. "I'm not one," she insisted, her voice barely a breath.

"But... I understand." She forced a brittle smile, a fragile mask that cracked the second she turned away. "It's... it's fine. I'd probably feel the same," she managed to compose herself, leaving her voice flat and devoid of conviction or feeling.

An impatience descended, weighty and quashing, a leaden plate pressing down on her. She waited, her breath catching in her lungs, for an argument, a fight, something. Nothing came from him.

The silence threatened to swallow her whole. Finally, with a sigh that seemed to carry the weight of the world, she straightened. The gesture was stiff and mechanical. Her voice was firm and staccato. "Let's go back to the house," she announced, turning on her heel, her voice flat, devoid of any emotion. The words spoken were clipped, narrow, and delivered with the same detached tone she might use to state the current time. She walked away, leaving the wreckage of her shattered hopes behind. A lone seagull cried; its call was swallowed by the whisper of the tide.

Davis stood and slowly moved toward her. He maintained enough control to conceal the undertow of his boiling discomfort. His voice, a subdued crash usually reserved for banter, resonated with a strange, tender firmness. "Gretch, you know that none of that is true. Come here." He reached out to her, extending his arms, gesturing for a hug.

Gretchen paused but remained stubbornly rooted to her spot. She refused to move.

He didn't speak again. Instead, he approached her without hesitation. The sand, still warm from the day's heat, yielded slightly under his weight. He stepped into her space and closed his arms around her. "It's...weird for me," he stammered, the words not coming to him easily. "I always thought...we'd be more than...that," he said. It was a blatant lie he hoped would bridge the awkwardness between them. "I thought about it, anyway. You and me. You just...caught me off guard. You know? It sort of came out of nowhere."

She smiled over the shoulder of his embrace, where he couldn't see it. A slow curve built across her face, releasing a broad grin. She eased herself from his hold, after a moment, and reached for his hand.

"Follow me," she said, her voice a silken command, her hand closed tightly around his with a grip that didn't loosen. Confusion again etched itself onto Davis's face, like it belonged there, but he followed her with curiosity, anyway, as she led him across the landscape.

"Where are we going?" he asked with a tint of aggression, his voice barely heard against the growing twilight.

"You'll see," she sang. She didn't answer him directly but used his hand to lead him toward the water and then across the beach. Each wave of the ocean seemed to propel her forward. He stayed a step behind her as they crossed the terrain without a word. Davis hated surprises but didn't bother to tell her. She had already chosen the path, and he wanted to avoid navigating through any more of her weird emotions.

Chapter 13: Death of a Boy

Sand moved beneath Davis's feet as he followed her blindly, a gritty prelude to the smooth sandstone slabs ahead. The shift from sand to stone was sudden. He stumbled, catching the edge of a tile on his big toe. Pain darted through his leg. Gretchen's hand, small but surprisingly strong, tightened briefly to steady him. Each step he took after that echoed with resentment, clearly evidenced through his gritted teeth. The rising moon glowed like a coin in the sky, casting long shadows on the path. Rental beach chairs lay vacantly scattered across the beach. The entire vacation had felt like a sandcastle on shifting ground to Davis.

Gretchen's blonde hair shimmered in the twilight, framing a face too innocent to trust. She curved her lips subtly and turned her chin with a knowing tilt. He caught the way her eyes, bright and wide, missed nothing yet showed the game she was playing. He saw her now, a discriminating variation from his own image. His hair was damp with sweat and clinging to his neck. He was tired. The shape of his eyes was narrowed from the frustration of being in the position he found himself in.

He pictured himself, instead, slicing through the inky water on a sleek yacht, the wind whipping through his hair. The mental picture was cinematic, a cruel taunt against the reality of the unstable tiles below him. He didn't own a yacht, or even a rowboat, but the fantasy was a carefully crafted Instagram post, a strenuously maintained lie.

Gretchen stopped abruptly. The destination had been reached. Davis crashed into her, biting his tongue in the process. She yanked her hand free, leaving his palm empty. With an elaborate flourish, she presented a luxury Cabana standing before her. Davis, unimpressed, retained the negative emotions racing through his mind. His jaw tightened while a slight earthquake rumbled in his chest.

Ignoring her gesture, Davis curtly demanded an answer, "Why'd you stop all of a sudden?" The question swung between them like a metronome, more noticeable than the moon itself. The innocent pretense in Gretchen's eyes dropped just a fraction, hinting at a glimpse of someone much older and wiser before she spoke. He waited impatiently with his attention fixed on her. A silent challenge was posed in the shifting moonlight. He did not want to be here.

She spun to face him with an impish grin as she again pointed out the cabana at the very end of the path. Her arms were outstretched as though she was a game-show model handing over a prize. Gretchen's happiness widened her mouth while she displayed the opulence of the beige tent-like structure that stood out against the darkening sky. Its canvas walls billowed gently in the evening breeze, inviting them inside.

The cabana was spacious, with a high ceiling that created a sense of openness. Soft, warm lighting illuminated the interior, creating a cozy and inviting ambiance. Plush cushions and comforters adorned the space, their neutral tones complementing the tropical exterior. A small table stood in one corner, usually bearing a tray of exotic fruits and a chilled bottle of champagne, but not at this hour. Davis hesitated, his eyes narrowing as he took in the scene. Despite the class of the cabana, his mind remained focused on the yacht that had eluded him.

"These aren't free," he said, with matter-of-fact authority. "You have to rent them. Besides, they are expensive, and we already have a whole beach house. We should go back." He gestured vaguely in the direction they had come, his bare chest rising and falling with suppressed discomfort.

Unfazed by his reluctance, Gretchen stepped forward, her movements graceful and purposeful. She ran her fingers along the smooth canvas, her blonde locks shimmering in the moonlight.

"Oh, come on, Davis," she said, her voice a persuasive draw. "Where's your sense of adventure? We can't pass up an opportunity like this. Just think, it would be an excellent post. Nobody knows it's after hours." Her eyes sparkled with a different light. They were hard for him to read.

Moonlight, fractured by the woven canvas roof, shadowed Davis's skin in shifting patterns. His phone hummed as he directed it, a steady rhythm against the soft thud of his thumbs on the screen. Each click was a small victory captured on his image roll: the intricate knotwork of the cabana's interior, the water shimmering beyond, the lazy drift of palm fronds against the impossibly dark sky. His focus was intense, even in the dim light, as he scanned the photos. A satisfied smile etched across his face. His arms flexed with excitement as he continued, the phone never left his hand.

"Friggin' good idea, Gretch," he muttered, his voice hiding an arrogant excitement partially exacerbated by simmering paranoia of being caught trespassing. "These'll be killer."

A gentle brush across his broad shoulder stopped him mid-stride while walking toward the exit. He didn't turn around. The feeling of light pressure against his skin, the unexpected touch of a hand lingering just long enough to make him subtly aware of its owner before it receded, confused him. His breath stopped. A bracing transformation of his posture emerged as if he had just felt the force of a powerful wind.

"Relax! Live like a celebrity", she half-whispered and pulled at his arm, guiding him to sit on the edge of the white, high-end bed. The sheets, a fiery inferno against him, scorched Davis's skin as she eased him onto it. He sank into the feather-soft down; the plushness was a deceptive comfort against his mild distress. She gently straddled him. Her weight settled on his stomach, a slow, anchored press. His abs tightened beneath her. The pressure was a weight against his spine as she shifted. Her every gesture was immersed in a confidence meant to be felt. The heat radiating from her body was palpable, an ember against the tender flesh of his abdomen.

Her heavy breath stirred the sensitive skin of his chest. He caught the smell of vanilla, followed by a sharpness that didn't belong. Looking down at him, her smile was a riddle in the dim light of the room. The shadowed space, an erotic mix of silk sheets and darkened corners, whispered of intimacy and something else far more instinctually present.

"How does this feel?" Her voice was a purr in the silence of the room. The agreement of friendship plagued him, questioning his miscalculated expectations. Davis's dark hair, slicked back with sweat, caught the weak light. His deep brown eyes were shadowed with something else entirely. It was a flicker of apprehension masked by a thin, strained smile. His robust frame remained locked beneath her, all tension and no breath. From this angle, her breasts appeared impossibly large and were exaggerated by the low light.

"This is the life, right?" she breathed, her voice a teasing caress. He managed a hoax of a smile, the strength in his jaw working against the silent scream clawing its way out of his throat. Time slowed inside him.

The lamplight cast long shadows across the rumpled sheets, highlighting the dust particles dancing in the stillness. Her fingers, feather-light at first, traced the contours of his abdomen. A chill, sharp and unexpected, jolted through him, a ripple of pleasure and disorientation that spread outwards, a warm explosion blooming on his skin. Then, her touch deepened with a firmer pressure, kneading the tension from his pectorals.

Knots of stress slowly unraveled beneath her skilled hands. He quailed with a barely noticeable tremor, feeling absolute surrender to her control. A breath held in his throat, followed by a controlled gasp escaping as her fingers teased, then gently pinched his nipples. They hardened in response.

His involuntary laughter, breathless and surprised, broke through his stunned silence. "Stop tickling me," he protested, the defiance in his voice softening, with a jovial exasperation remaining. He watched her, captivated by the way the dim light animated her.

This is not happening! The thought echoed through his mind, yet his eyes, once wary, held a different perspective: part approving, part hopeful, and the largest part was desperate to escape. His self-concept bounced in rapid cycles. He wanted to say something to stop it. Anything. The pressure in his chest rendered him mute. This experience is not one he wanted, or was it? His silence was more potent than anything he could say.

Her persistence stung his eyes as he wrestled against her, and a shriek of laughter tore from his throat. Her fingers, like icy spiders, danced across his ribs, each pass left traces on his skin of an astonishingly pleasurable assault.

"Yes! Right," he panted, forced between rounds of ungovernable laughter. "This is the life! Stop...tickling...me!" The plea was a half-hearted protest to the delicious torture. His laughter faded, leaving an audible vacancy as he looked at her through tender eyes.

She stopped. Her expression became soft. Davis braced himself when her smile morphed into something much more terrifying.

Her light, intrusive touch invaded just below the thin elastic waistband of his swimming shorts. Her boldness sent him into a private panic. The luxury structure, heated throughout the day by the harsh sun, suddenly felt cold beneath him. His body, traitorous, responded in a way that made his stomach wrench.

"This is good," he mumbled, the honest words feeling like lies. Relief flooded him as her fingers retreated, only to be dissolved immediately by the firm pressure of her hand on him. Her arm reached behind her back, then formed a bold grip around the evidence of his arousal beneath its spandex fortress.

An uncomfortable blush set fire to his cheeks. He had experienced this grip many times before when he was alone, stealthily hidden under his blankets, but this was different. The heat of her skin pressing against his sent frenzied electricity through his nerve endings. Every graze, every stroke through the fabric was intense. His breath was syncopated with every movement she made. The sound of the waves crashing against the shore became a muffled trumpet in his ears.

"You do think I'm pretty." She giggled as she erotically and slowly stood and stood over him. She surveyed his body and noted the evidence pressing outward against the fabric of his shorts. Another ripple of laughter released from behind the ramparts of her lips as she slinked around him. She posed for him, a silhouette against the moonlit canvas. Her eyes were unabashedly fixed on his erection. Shame bloomed hot on his skin.

He watched helplessly as she traced the unmistakable outline of the growing, moist stain formed on his ridiculously expensive shorts with her finger. The wetness was a crown on the significant monument of his internal mortification.

"Can I...look at it?" she breathed, her fingers gently tugging again at his shorts. His hands clamped down on them like lightning, a vise around his own boundaries. The struggle was brief. A silent ballet played out against the rhythmic crash of waves. Then, as quickly as it began, the friendly conflict ended with him retaining the last trace of modesty he could still claim.

She retreated; a gentle expression of understanding replaced any hint of past challenge. Respect glowed in her eyes. He inhaled a choppy breath, sounding like a drumroll in the hush of the evening.

"We...we should go," he quickly blurted out, the words flowing like rain. His voice was a mixture of relief and lingering fear. The salt air around him suddenly felt asphyxiating.

"Take off your shorts, I want to see it," she coyly demanded, the words a sexy taunt, a ripple in the warm air, smelling of coconut oil and sea.

She removed her bikini top, a compromise to complement her directive. The arc of her hand was graceful. She moved with a slow unveiling of her full, firm breasts, the glow of the cabana catching the peaks, turning them the color of ripe peaches. His expression carried confusion as he met her stare. The sudden, unexpected intake of his breath mirrored the pounding of his own heart. Oh God, the thought battering him, a double-edged blade forged of obligation and blistered desire.

"What?... Out here?... Outside... I—" He started, the words halting, stopped by the undertow of her smile. "We shouldn't..." His voice lacked the conviction he craved.

Before he could finish them, she chuckled, a sound as bright as the sun glinting off the water, her fingers entwining with his, pulling his arms far above his head. He held his breath. Her fingers fumbled at his waistband, and he instinctively reached to the fabric, again, to deflect the inevitable. Her grin returned, providing a visual challenge that both soothed and ignited him.

"No," she whispered like a nurse, her touch trickling across his arm. "No, keep them there. Don't worry. I just want to look at you.... That's all. There's absolutely nothing to be ashamed of. You are a big boy."

Her words were a wall of confidence against his rising anxiety. They left him insecure and breathless. With a long, slow exhale, he obeyed, arms raised, his skin prickling with vulnerability and wonder under her powerful spell. The vast, shimmering expanse of the ocean seemed to hold its breath with him.

He took a moment. "Okay", he begrudgingly agreed. Davis's innocent demeanor, usually so confident, was suddenly dismissed as Gretchen's slender fingers slid his expensive shorts down his legs; his embarrassment was amplified by the sharp, staccato smack of his rigid flesh springing against his torso like a rubber band. Another blush colored his cheeks.

She dropped to the floor in a colorful pool, leaving him fully exposed under the dim light. His erection, freed from its confinement, shook like a trapped bird. He saw it standing like a tower, unblemished by the tainted fauna and flora of adulthood. A fear raged within him. He wanted to bolt, to disappear, yet he stayed rooted, mesmerized by Gretchen's sixteen-year-old intensity. "We don't have to do this," he mumbled, the words as valuable as dust.

Gretchen's beaming reply held the slow confidence of someone who knew she'd already won. "We don't have to do anything we don't want to. But this... this is right... It's what we want. It's not like it's forced or anything." The statement, though spoken softly, ended his reluctance. She knew, from experience, what force was. He did not want her to add to her trauma by rejecting her attention. A surrendering smile grew on his face, chasing away his shame.

"No," he whispered with reassurance, "It's not forced."

Her touch was feather-light as she cupped him, her fingers tracing rhythmic patterns along his length. His back arched involuntarily, and he moaned softly.

"I'm not scared, are you?" she asked, her eyes glinting with the expectation of his reply.

"No," he mouthed, the lie was a thin veil over the turmoil within. His words were difficult to form. An internal struggle was building between his superficial breaths. He suddenly felt the warmth of her mouth on his skin. Her softness pressed against the hardness of him, and for a moment, nothing made sense.

He watched her with fascination. The image of her bent over him, violating every expectation he'd formed about their friendship, slowly seared into his consciousness. Was she enjoying this?

He thought of locker room banter, of the crude descriptions, of his own disgusted reactions to the stories recounted by teammates. Then he felt something else, a profound trust for her, a real connection that transcended everything he'd ever known.

Gretchen's hand continued to move against him. As the smooth skin of his body met her lips, his past dissolved around him. He was beyond exposure, beyond fear. He was lost in the terrifying and intoxicating truth of this moment. Then, he felt it happening. Slight tremors manifested from his core and spread through his body until they became convulsions.

The sensitivity of his nerves exploded under the stimulation of her touch. He wanted out. He had changed his mind. He wanted to speak but couldn't. All he could form were primal grunts. He was frozen.

Neverland screamed as he stopped breathing. He was fighting a losing war. His hips moved, almost involuntarily, and a dizzying uncertainty overtook him. He felt numb and lost as Gretchen sat up and watched him squirm as she cannibalized the boy he'd never wanted to give up.

From this moment forward, he had changed. She casually stood up, donned her bikini top, and lovingly patted him on his thigh.

"The boy is dead," he thought, before he slowly rose to put on his shorts and leave the cabana. It became both a mausoleum and a place of birth. He felt a loss as he crossed the threshold into the waiting evening. They walked back to the house together without speaking, abandoning the only identity he had ever known.

Chapter 14: Travis

Davis was a lifetime away from the unassuming boy he had always understood himself to be. His carefree traits were replaced with a quieter reason that now defined him. Months had passed since the humid embrace of the beach, and Florida was now a faint memory. Here, the late afternoon sun beat down on the Midwest soccer field he had known as his second home for as long as he could remember.

Davis sat, poised on the sideline bench, taking in the familiar scent of the suburbs and trampled earth. He focused his camera on his best friend, who moved the ball with powerful energy. Alone on the field, Travis's every step tore at the turf, hitting harder than the last. He adjusted his angle, carving wider arcs and adding unnecessary flair to each move. He often checked the direction of Davis's lens between passes and made a point to show off when he knew it mattered.

He'd pop the ball up when he didn't need to, creating a brief, performative pause before catching it again on the bridge of his foot. It wasn't about the drill; it was about being seen. Travis wasn't looking for directions. He just moved.

Travis was a lean, muscular seventeen-year-old. The school soccer uniform, crisp white with deep navy accents, clung to him where sweat soaked through from his vigorous performance. Light brown hair was plastered to his forehead, slick with perspiration. He launched into a series of dizzying heel-to-toe flicks. Each movement was a controlled explosion of energy, a blur of white and blue against a grassy backdrop. He kept himself in Davis's frame, reveling in the attention. He felt the burn in his thighs and the familiar ache in his calves, but he would never show it. Adrenaline masked it all.

Almost there. Almost good enough. He stole a glance at Davis, documenting his every move with his camera. Davis's smug face with his trademark, all-knowing smirk was all the encouragement Travis needed. He pushed himself harder. He produced a rapid-fire sequence of stepovers, the soccer ball glued to his instep. His breath expanded his torso as he successfully maintained control. His green eyes remained locked onto the ball, burning with intensity.

He could feel the presence of Davis's judgment. It was an intense pressure that drove him, fueling an irrational need for approval. *He's better than me. Everyone knows it.* The ball danced, resisting gravity with every flick. As a final, almost careless flourish, he performed a superfluous backflip before the ball settled precisely at his feet, in perfect position. He looked up and bowed. Davis's uncommitted whistle, devoid of any overt praise, was more potent than any cheering crowd.

"Is that it?" Davis asked flatly with a cocked eyebrow. "This is so short, it's not even worth posting."

Hell no! On cue, Travis returned the ball to motion without hesitating. He rainbow-flicked it, lifting high in the air before dropping, into perfect position, near his left foot. The rhythm of his movements matched his driving heartbeat. Sweat blurred his vision, but he remained fixed on the ball. It mattered.

His muscles burned hotter, but he covered it well and did his job. Every flick, every touch, demanded attention. He wasn't just showing off anymore; he was performing. He increased his pace to challenge his threshold, unwilling to break the connection he earned. Davis was watching. That was everything. The burn in his thighs and calves became meaningless, compared to the pounding in his chest, but he ignored them all. Every second of good footage he could provide was his mission.

Much like Davis, the ball was an extension of himself, obedient to his every whim. It was a weapon he wielded with increasing perfection. This is for them, for the doubters, for Davis, for me; he willed himself to excel. Each trick felt smoother, each glance at Davis brought more reassurance, though his foundation of insecurity never truly disappeared.

As he executed a perfectly timed elastic, he glanced to see an almost invisible smile playing on Davis's lips. Travis felt a jolt of energy. It was a victory in his ongoing struggle for recognition. He knew it wasn't a true appreciation of his skill, but a genuine acknowledgment of his persistence. He would never have Davis's natural talent, never going to possess his effortless grace or untouchable coolness. It didn't matter. In the moment, he knew he was enough.

His final offering, a daring sombrero, left him panting. The ball spun slowly, managed with competency, evidence of his undying dedication to the game they both loved. He finished his routine and stared at Davis, waiting. The sun outlined Davis in a silhouette, highlighting the sharp angles of his jaw and the intensity in his discriminating eyes. It wasn't enough, not really. But for Travis, in the heat-haze of exhaustion, it kept him grounded. He knew the real work started now, the endless pursuit of a perfection he may never truly achieve. Travis glanced over as Davis studied the play.

He watched Travis with intensity. His work was practically flawless. He could do better, but this was about Travis. The way Travis moved, the control in every trick, made it feel sharper, more fluid. Davis had seen him push before, but this time, there was confidence in each movement.

Davis began to grin, but he wiped it away quickly. There was no need to give too much away. This was just another day, another repetition. But when Travis finished and looked at him, Davis felt admiration. Travis was performing for him.

For a moment, Davis almost smirked, watching the effort Travis put into it. Despite this, they both knew who was always in control and who was the only one on the field with a massive audience. Travis was creating confidence, and Davis was creating social media content.

"Okay…okay… stop, Travis!" he called, a silly edge defining his voice. He slammed his fist into his thigh, the impact echoing the anticipation coursing through him. "Badass?... Epic doesn't even begin to cover it!"

Travis grinned with a wide flash of teeth. He exhaled slowly, then grabbed the hem of his jersey to lift it from his torso. He desperately needed to cool off. The muscles in his chest still twitched from exertion as he sat beside his buddy on the bench. The metal radiated heat through his shorts, creating a slight burning sensation on the backs of his thighs.

Davis's thumbs, agile as spiders, danced across the screen in a blur of motion. He paused to think; an amiable excitement existed between the boys, and his contemplative silence was broken only by the far-off hum of traffic. Then, he shoved the phone toward Travis.

"Caption? Think this works?" Travis evaluated the text, his expression unreadable. He assessed it before he slowly shook his head with disappointment.

"Nah, man. That's... weak," he groaned with careful reticence.

A shiver reverberated in Davis's gut, aligned with Travis's criticism. He typed intently before turning the phone back toward him.

"Now?" he asked, sarcastically.

Travis leaned back in, smirking with the satisfaction of pushing Davis's buttons. "Got game? ... Duh." His response dripped with deeper criticism. He enjoyed challenging his best friend's fragile patience. His tone was condemning, but the gleam in his eye hinted at levity. Davis was taken aback, but he laughed anyway, deciding whether to be receptive or confrontational.

"Shut the frig up, Travis! It's marketing. It's edgy. It'll grab attention. You know?... Got Milk?... Remember?" He jabbed a finger at Travis, daring him to deny the power of the iconic slogan. Travis chuckled, waving his hand dismissively. A broad smile consumed his face.

"Okay, okay. Maybe it's not completely awful," he agreed, slapping Davis on the back with a solid, friendly thump. The two boys exemplified camaraderie, a bond forged in shared ambition and mutual respect, a bond built on shared ambition and the constant push to outdo each other. Davis, teetering on the edge of an explosion, planted himself like a king surveying his domain. His voice, a low growl vibrating with barely contained power, boomed.

Davis accepted the perceived apology with indignation. "I was gonna say, who is pushing three hundred thousand followers? Not you. Not any of your lame-ass friends... Watch this!" The click of the post button was a gunshot at the races. Davis kicked his feet against the metal legs of the bench as he spoke, accenting every word. Each number was announced with an over-articulated theatrical flair. He made no effort to hide the volume or the condescending grin on his face. This was his moment, and Travis was meant to accept his superiority.

"Five... four... three... two... one..." His eyes burned with a need, remaining glued to the display in his hand. He spun the phone around, revealing a blinding flash of notifications. He thrust it a few inches from Travis's nose.

"Ha ha! Eat. That." Davis roared, the sound reverberating. "I made you famous, yet again, you loser. You're very welcome. That was five seconds, five seconds! Name one person ... one... who can pull off thirty-five likes in that time. Huh? Who?" Travis just smiled and nodded, revealing a hint of something deeper than agreement. It was awe. He ran a hand through his short hair, the gesture showing acceptance, inspiration and mild irritation. He shrugged while he processed his response.

"Thirty-five whole people, Davis. Oh, wow! Thank you!... Thank you," he bleated with melodramatic sarcasm while bowing to Davis on the bench. His volume was loud enough to echo across the empty field. The blatancy cut through Davis's volatile energy, creating more intensity than the moment required.

He knew Davis. He understood Davis's hunger, his need to dominate everything he did, the frightening precision with which he manipulated his digital world. And he, in his own way, was just as formidable. The entire display was about power, control, and the thrill of the popularity game. And they were both players in a high-stakes contest, each understanding the rules of their strange, exhilarating partnership. Travis tossed a half-empty water bottle onto the cracked concrete.

He waited long enough to watch Davis bask in his self-constructed pride before delivering a blow. "L.A. Brit-nay gets a million likes for a burp, dude... A burp!" His tone was casual and dismissive, but every word he said carried intended confrontation. Davis leaned back and turned away from him in disbelief.

"She's an influencer, Travis. A big one. She doesn't count. I said... who do you know?" The accusation in his tone was unmistakable. A twitch originating in the corner of Davis's mouth uncovered the insecurity beneath his bravado. Travis allowed the moment to settle before eagerly usurping control of the moment.

He presented facts to counter Davis's accusation. Excited words rushed into the space between them: "We went to school together, man, up to eighth grade. After that, she bolted for California and her Insta-fame." He gathered great satisfaction from Davis's rare speechlessness. It wasn't familiar, but it was real, and it felt good. For once, he had the upper hand. Davis wanted something from him. He could feel the question brewing in his blank expression.

The conversation, all edge and ego, halted. The sound of fingers rapidly tapping on glass screens proved to induce an annoying throb in Davis's temples. The revelation that L.A. Brit-nay followed Travis but not him unnerved him. The confidence that usually defined him slipped. A different feeling crept in to take its place. It was jealousy. For a moment, he was the one being measured. He hated it.

Unable to wait for an offer, he hit Travis gently on the thigh. "You're gonna ask her," Davis's voice was friendly fire. "Look, I sent her a follow request four months ago. Four MONTHS ago! On my birthday! She hasn't accepted it yet! I'm sure she just didn't see it."

He stared at Travis expectantly for a moment before cracking, "What's she doing following you, anyway?" He flexed a bicep, rippling under his tanned skin, displaying a blatant exhibition of his insecurity.

Travis looked up from his phone, bored. "Look, Davis, there's no guarantee she'll listen to me. I'll do it, but this whole thing reeks. It's…shady as hell, and sort of embarrassing."

Davis's Hollywood smile beamed. "Once you mention it, Travis, it's a done deal. She will totally do it. Why wouldn't she? Look at me! There's no way she wouldn't. This is me we're talking about." He ended his statement with another obnoxious flex.

Davis sat motionless before flexing again, this time he tensed his biceps hard enough to make his eyes squint. His confidence was beginning to appear more like desperation. Travis couldn't contain his blatant eye roll, which was delivered with intention. Arguing with him would be futile. He was accustomed to Davis's peculiar nature.

Chapter 15: The Girlfriend

She stepped off the pavement and onto the field, each footfall bending the grass beneath her shoes. Ahead, two figures hunched together on the bench, their shoulders bumped as they leaned toward the same glowing screen. Their laughter drifted back to her in bursts. She didn't call out. She liked watching them like this. They were oblivious, caught in their own world, leaving just enough space for her to slip into it.

They looked good together. Travis held himself with clean lines and an easy lean. Davis was sharper at the edges, always half-ready to pounce. From behind, the contrast between them was striking. She paused a few steps back and let herself absorb the scene. The angle was perfect. The way they sat was relaxed and close, their posture casual, but their presence built to draw eyes.

She spotted them across the field, her pace quickening at the sight. Of course, they were waiting for her. She admired their shared passion for the game. She used to hate the two hours between Travis's last bell and her own, but now, seeing them out here waiting for her, it felt exactly as it should. Travis was sharp and unreadable. Davis was unpredictable and hers. She owned them both in different ways. She lifted her chin, letting the moment crown her.

The three of them fit together with precision. Travis understood the space she took and somehow made room for it. The way he handled Davis was half the reason their bond held together. She watched them like she was watching her own design in motion. Davis pulled things off course. Travis brought it back. She made it matter.

She crept gently toward them, her body moving covertly to keep herself undetectable. Her grin tightened as she closed the distance, ready to pounce. She narrowed the distance between them in perfect, stealthy increments, growing more excited with every inch she stole. She leaned over Davis's shoulder without a word and hovered there, triumphant, letting the moment swell before it shattered. Then, a voice, galled and honed to a razor's edge, cut through their harmony.

"Finally! School's. Fucking. Out!"

She clamped her hands onto Davis's shoulders and screamed it inches from his ear. He shot sideways with a short, startled yelp, nearly slipping off the bench. Travis's arms snapped upward, and the phone shot from his hands and tumbled end over end, almost out of reach, onto the ground behind him. He sat upright fast, planted himself square to the ground, and glared at her. For a split second, the effort it took to hide how much he hated her wasn't enough.

He wiped the distaste clean before she had the chance to register it, but the resentment in Travis's stiffened expression was undeniable.

"You got me again," Travis sang behind a rehearsed mask of tolerance, lifting his arms in surrender. "I swear, it's like you have some kind of sixth sense." He bent backward from the bench to retrieve his phone.

She glanced at the ground and dropped fast to claim it first. Her fingers brushed his in the process. She let the contact linger so he could feel the pause before she picked it up and turned it toward herself. Travis simply sat up and stared at her in disbelief.

"Oh, I do. It's called knowing you two are hopelessly predictable."

She looked at the screen, briefly at first, as she stood. Then, she studied it with more interest. Her eyes thinned to hard lines as her cheeks flushed. Humor morphing into rage was illustrated in her features. She stood motionless, aside from an emerging tremor, visible only in her face.

Her eyes lifted from the screen and locked on him.

"Who's this slut, Davis?" Her tone was infused with disgust; she didn't bother to hide.

Davis tilted his head and laughed out his words with the trademark dismissive arrogance she despised. He lifted a shoulder, an uncommitted shrug, and let it fall. The gesture closed the moment.

"L.A. Brit-nay? She's not a slut. She's a mega-influencer, and she follows me. It's not a big deal... Whatever." It was a lie, but he wore it well. She'd be following him soon enough, anyway. He patted her thigh once, casual as ever, and asked after a meaningful pause, "Jealous, much?" He smirked faintly as if she'd missed the joke; only he understood. He waited, then turned to Travis and smiled.

Gretchen simmered with fury. The steel beneath her softness strengthened with every word she held back. The dangerous calm of her voice didn't go unnoticed by Travis.

Travis crossed his arms. The posture matched hers, though he didn't notice.

Gretchen continued without restraint.

"Only desperate whores parade themselves naked online. I know she's not naked on this, but I know she's doing it. Look at that smile."

Her long fingers, tipped with fresh polish, traced the screen of Travis's phone. She was the only person who could see it, but it didn't matter. Her conclusion had already formed. She didn't need proof. The image was enough. The smile on that girl's face said everything she needed it to say.

"Probably on porn sites, too," she added, continuing to scroll for a moment before tossing the phone in Travis's direction. It landed in his lap with a pointed thud. He released a slight groan to punctuate his irritation, even though it didn't hurt. He picked up his phone and held it like a wounded child.

Davis shrugged as he repeated himself, "Whatever," and swiped his social media app closed. "You ready?" he asked her without feeding into her drama.

"You know it's so disrespectful to be looking at other girls when you have a girlfriend?" she asked him with accusatory determination.

He stood up and laughed, playfully reaching for her. She recoiled and crossed her arms.

"Looking at other girls?" He repeated himself to emphasize his point. "Looking at... other girls. I wasn't looking at other girls."

Gretchen watched his focus move from her to Travis. Staying out of familiar crosshairs, Travis leaned away from them slightly, his hands lifted in a casual shrug, his tone jovial and light.

"I'm staying out of this one. Path of the tiger."

He stopped talking, sat awkwardly, and opened his phone. He increased the brightness with an absent tap, fully immersing himself in his own interests. Beyond that, he had checked out and immersed himself in social media.

She didn't miss her opening. To her, the point was just proven. "See? He knows. It's like cheating." She stared through Travis with an extended hand. "Give me the phone. I'm deleting it."

Travis scoffed as he placed his phone in his pocket. "My phone... not yours. With that being settled, if you guys want to go, we need to do it. Mom needs the car. She's got shit to do tonight." He pivoted like a soldier and ambled toward the parking lot.

The couple watched him retreat and climb into the soccer-mom van. A momentary standoff ensued until the frustration drained from Davis's face.

She noticed his irritation softened when he leaned in for an apologetic kiss. Davis stepped in with a crooked grin, dropping his shoulders as he reached for her waist, just as he always did when he wanted to regain control before she had the chance to say more.

Without warning, Gretchen planted her feet and lifted her arm with precision, drawing it back to slap him across the face with enough force to turn his head. The sound was a resounding clap. His skin flared red where her palm had landed. He stumbled two steps back with his left hand pressed against his cheek and his right hand clenched into a fist that refused to rise. His jaw flexed, and his brows drew together, but he didn't speak. His stare stayed on her like she had just stolen something from him.

"That is fucked up, Day!" she screamed, jabbing a finger toward his chest like she was branding him. "You shouldn't have any girls following you, and you definitely won't have any following you. Carrying girls around in your pocket is…" She muffled and swallowed a scream as he stared at her in complete disbelief.

"FUCKED UP! IT IS TOTALLY FUCKING DISRESPECTFUL! I WILL DESTROY YOU!" Her voice tore out of her like a siren, sharp and high and meant to land hard. With a final shriek, she drew her foot back and kicked the ground, driving dirt and grass onto Davis's shins to solidify her conviction.

Davis just looked at her with a foreign unfamiliarity. She relished his surprise. The sound of Travis's horn broke his trance, catching the couple's attention. Davis immediately returned to assess his shoes. He stepped closer, voice low and almost convincing. "It's not cheating. I only want to be with you."

He then pulled her close and comforted her, another foreign behavior for him. She stopped. A feeling of guilt swept over her. Maybe she was too harsh. No, she wasn't. She refused to let herself be manipulated.

"I know it seems crazy to you, but I'm so broken after everything that has happened. I probably am more jealous than other girls because of it. Please promise you will block the other girls, Day. I can't handle it. I really can't."

Tears streamed down her face as she clung tighter mid-plea, the desperation pushing through her words before the tears followed. "Please, Day," she pouted through a forced sob, clinging tighter as Davis scanned the field, though there was no one watching. She noticed her boyfriend's eyes darting haphazardly to the people around them. He hated judgment and any form of unplanned public attention.

He avoided her eyes and said it with resignation. Brittle lived beneath every word. "I'll block them," he lied. "I promise."

Gretchen squealed and kissed him hard. Her sadness and anger disappeared with a word. The parking lot, an unwelcomed intruder in the moment, bellowed and broke her elation and the sound barrier.

"I'm leaving!"

Travis's threat was not idle. They both knew from experience he meant it. The steely disgust in his bright green eyes was infectious. She grabbed Davis's hand and propelled them both toward Travis's van in a sprint. The two of them took off, a whirlwind of blonde hair and a tower of juvenile masculinity. Their sudden bolt was a twin-barreled shot of adrenaline toward the waiting van.

Chapter 16: Teenage Underground

The rearview mirror reflected Gretchen's manicured blonde hair, bouncing with laughter as she whispered and flirted with Davis. Travis's jaw tightened. The afternoon sun, a ball watching over the woods, cast long shadows across the van's dashboard. He gripped the steering wheel firmly enough to whiten his knuckles. Davis hadn't even glanced at him from the back seat, leaving him feeling like a mule hauling cargo.

The scent of pine and damp earth fought with the faint sweetness of Gretchen's perfume, a nauseating reminder of her presence that grated on his nerves. He parked with a sharp thwack, the sound momentarily disrupting the calmness of the State Park. Before his friends could even unbuckle their seatbelts, he was already out. The gravel tumbled under his sneakers as he stomped ahead. Davis, gleaming with his special brand of arrogance, sauntered behind with a hand casually slung around Gretchen's slender waist. Her innocent smile didn't reach her eyes; Travis saw the calculation behind it.

"Can't wait 'til you get your own car, Day," Travis muttered, his tone grounded with both friendly ribbing and heartfelt resentment. His thumb tapped his index finger as he pressed ahead, a nervous tick he didn't know he had. Davis just grinned a cocky flash of teeth, then winked at Gretchen, who responded with a flutter of eyelashes that was far more frustrating than an argument. They exited the van and briskly walked to catch up with Travis.

As the trio entered the woods, the path wound between towering oaks and maples. The tension slowly dissipated as they moved forward. Not even the heat of the afternoon could permeate the cool shade of the dense forest. The environment had a way of making everything better. Travis continued to lead the way with confidence, despite feeling ignored and used. His frustration, however, was still lingering beneath the surface.

"How much farther?" Gretchen's whine bored through the field of Travis's over-exposed nerves. She dramatically slapped a mosquito on her thigh, accompanied by a brief, high-pitched scream. Travis was not convinced that the bug wasn't a calculated figment of her imagination. "We've been walking for HOURS," she complained.

Travis glanced at his phone with a look of disgust on his face. "It's been less than five minutes." The subtle roll of his eyes was lost on Gretchen but not on Davis, who offered a knowing smirk of acknowledgment. The journey fell silent for a while. Gretchen's moans, punctuated by the crunch of leaves underfoot, provided a soundtrack for their journey.

"My legs are falling off," she bitched, her voice a dramatic whine. Without hesitating, she leaped onto Davis's back with force. He fell forward, sending him sprawling, falling face-first onto the ground. Decaying leaves, pebbles, and dirt coated his lips. A distressed grunt erupted from him. His chest tensed with irritation as he pushed himself up. His demeanor instantly darkened.

Davis turned and shot her a glare, brushing the dirt off his knees. "What the frig was that?! A little warning next time, Good God!" Gretchen looked at him with innocent, apologetic eyes. The anger immediately drained from his face as he looked at her and involuntarily smiled. He reached towards her, picking stray leaves from her hair. Her fingers, long and slender, trailed across his upper body as she comically batted at the viscid foliage clinging to his shirt.

"You have leaves in your hair, too." She murmured, her voice soft and teasing. A sly look danced in her eyes. "And you need to work on your upper body strength. I'm just a girl." Travis groaned and shook his head disapprovingly. He knew this game all too well. Davis, never one to miss a challenge, ever ready for a show, arrogantly peeled off his shirt. His body told the story for him. He was built for the field but was always ready for the stage.

He flexed for no one in particular. "Hop on, then," he said as he passed a playful wink to her. A shriek of pure, unadulterated glee burst from Gretchen. She slapped Davis's firm backside with a resounding smack.

"Giddy-up, horsey!" she squealed, her laughter ripped through the trees. Davis grinned, bracing her legs around his waist, and kept walking. Sunlight, breaking through the canopy, lit their way as they hiked deeper into the woods. Gretchen clung to his back.

She let out another shriek. To Travis, each yelp sounded like a violin string snapping. Davis didn't seem to care. A consistent, satisfied smile was painted on his face; he seemed to like the chaos she created. Travis fought the urge to ignore her but kept turning to look at them as they continued.

Travis was on a tight schedule and simply wanted to get to their friends before he had to get the van back home. She had taken too much time already with her antics. It felt intentional. He was becoming increasingly tired of her high-pitched demands and calculated manipulations to keep Davis's undying attention on her. He valued order, efficiency, and the predictable rhythm of a soccer game. Gretchen was the antithesis of everything he valued. Her presence and chaotic behavior were actively fueling his exasperation.

The rhythmic crunch of their feet on the fallen leaves was punctuated by Gretchen's incessant chattering, a relentless assault on Travis's ears. Did he feel a prickle of annoyance and a stab of something darker: resentment? No, he wouldn't let himself go there. He wouldn't let her have that much power.

Davis, however, seemed to revel in the attention. His presumptuous smile widened with each of her childish outbursts. The contrast between their reactions was like a chessboard. Davis scanned the path ahead despite knowing the woods like an old friend. He could smell the sharp trace of pine and the earthy musk of the gorge. The unspoken communication between Davis and Travis was as familiar as the beat of their own hearts. Davis knew that Travis was reaching his limit; he was a master at reading his friend's subtle cues. He held back a teasing jibe, enjoying the power play. Then, a sudden break in the trees to their left caught his attention. Gretchen gasped at the sight. It was not a shriek this time, but something softer. She was awestruck.

Before them lay a canyon, a jagged scar in the earth, the steep borders dropped sharply, revealing a sheer, rust-streaked rock face plunging into its shadowy depths. The damp earth and sound of rushing water intensified the experience, filling the space with omnipotent threats.

Far below them, a river churned silver, cutting through the gorge. A rusty railing, mostly hidden by leaves, was all that separated them from the drop. Travis stared at the water in the chasm, feeling a sensation of smallness. He'd seen the gorge many times, but its size always impressed him. It was both amazing and terrifying. The meadow below was a mix of gold, russet, and orange, a beautiful contrast to the darkness of the shadowy canyon walls. A gust of wind, guided up by the cliff's rocky surface, stirred the leaves at their feet, forming tiny cyclones.

Davis lifted a hand. "Stop," he said, the gentleness in his voice surprised even Travis. "Gretchen, look." He carefully helped her dismount, his fingers brushing her arm. It was a simple gesture with profound meaning. Travis, despite his initial irritation, found himself mesmerized. The immenseness of the gorge was undeniable; a breathtaking natural masterpiece etched into the earth. It held dark, fearful energy, yet it was impossible for him to look away.

The river, a wild, untamed force carving through the gorge, was brilliant in its chaotic setting. He found himself momentarily captivated, forgetting the frustrations of the day. The silence, broken only by the ceaseless roar of the river, settled over them. Even Gretchen, usually a whirlwind of motion and sound, fell uncharacteristically quiet.

She stared downward with amazement; her attention-seeking behavior had been replaced by a quiet introspection. For a few precious moments, any tension between the three of them completely melted. The incredible power of nature held them captive. They shared in the experience silently.

Gretchen whispered cautiously, "They should have higher bumpers or something. If someone fell down there, they wouldn't have a chance."

Travis grasped the moment with long-awaited vigor, "No, definitely not. They would probably explode on impact." He paused and considered his next statement. He could not resist. He laughed incessantly, "Yeah, Gretch, they should totally have... higher bumpers." His laugh was an obvious ploy to elicit some ribbing from Davis. He did not take the bait. Instead, he was suddenly inspired to capture the moment on video. It became a social media moment, and he embraced it.

"You're ruining my shot!" Davis seethed before he began filming. His voice took on a practiced, theatrical tone as he positioned himself in the frame: "This is Davis Day. Live from the brink of eternity. Featuring the immensely stupid, Travis... the beautifully inspiring Gretchen... and yours truly, the only one here with any friggin' sense."

He aimed the phone at each of them, focusing on Gretchen's cartoonish pin-up expression before spinning the lens back at himself. "If anyone fell from here, scientists have confirmed that they would explode on impact and would..."

His words were cut short by a detonation. A primal, enraged sound ripped through the serious intensity of his live stream. Zack, a steely construction worker with dark hair and developed muscles, launched himself at Davis in a terrifying rush of brute force.

He grabbed Davis from behind, like a bear tackling its prey, sending him hurtling toward the edge of the gorge before yanking him backward with brutal force. Both guys tumbled to the ground in a crash of limbs and curses. Gretchen screamed a high-pitched, piercing sound. Travis, initially frozen by shock, reacted by sprinting away from the group, toward the safety of the trail. Turning around, the realization dawned on him; the ambush was a calculated act, a performance of friends.

Davis's face contorted with furious disbelief as he scrambled to his feet. Zack, laughing hysterically, stood slowly, revealing a muscular frame that exemplified unmitigated strength. He dusted off his palms by slapping them loudly onto his faded jeans. "I'm just fucking with you, Day," he guffawed, forming his full lips into a perfect, natural smirk. "Little dick." The anger flowing from Davis was undeniable. A purple flush rose from the center of him, staining the surface of his skin.

Davis's veins bulged in his neck as he roared, "ARGHHHHH! That wasn't funny; you could've killed me!" The heat of the afternoon was mirroring the fury in his eyes. The dirt plastered to his head settled into the sharp angles of his face. He postured as a boxer, ready to step into the ring.

Zack commanded the conversation with a condescending wave. "Nah, man. I had you." His sneer revealed a flash of perfect white teeth behind his calm tone. From the other side of the trail, a monstrous figure emerged. Cyrus rambled into the group, laughing on cue like a true simpleton. His obscenely muscular torso was clad only in a pair of poorly fitting briefs. His skin gleamed in the light refracted through the leaves overhead. He was a grotesque parody of fitness. His overdeveloped glutes strained against the fabric of his low-slung underwear. The sight was, somehow, uncomfortably comical.

Zack's eyes gleamed with malevolent amusement as he encouraged Cyrus, "Did you guys see the look on his face?" He gestured toward Davis with a casual flick of his wrist. He exuded an almost unbearable confidence, the type born of privilege. A healthy dose of sadistic enjoyment seasoned his taunting.

Davis, still simmering, snarled, "You're lucky I didn't lose my friggin' phone." His chest rose and fell in sharp, uneven bursts.

Cyrus, eager to stir the pot, mocked him, "Yeah, Zack, so lucky." He glanced at Zack with a look that defined unconditional loyalty, a slavish devotion that chilled Davis to the bone. Davis, understanding his position, forced a laugh in a desperate attempt to undermine the rage still coursing through him. It was a confrontation he knew was not wise to pursue.

"Screw you guys," he chuckled with forced levity. "Seriously, Cy, what the frig are you doing naked already? Did you guys not even wait for us?"

Ignoring Davis, Cyrus turned to Gretchen, "We got some killer weed," he announced, his voice was giddy in anticipation of her response.

Gretchen's eyes lit up, and a glint of experience replaced her earlier naivety. "I'm totally there." She turned to her cousin with genuine curiously. She stared at Zack. "How the hell did you guys even know we were here?" Zack mimicked Gretchen's shriek with an almost perfect imitation. He threw his head back and barked with laughter afterward. His attempt to degrade her was evident but ineffective. Over the years, she developed a tolerance to his brand of bullying. She was unfazed. His voice echoed through the canyon, adding to the surreal nature of the scene.

"I don't know, Gretch," he drawled, his voice dripping with false innocence. "Psychic powers, I guess?"

His eyes stayed on her. It was a protective confidence that made her feel at home. Zack, with an air of entitlement, turned and led the group away. They strolled past a rocky outcrop. A few feet past two large boulders, an immense clearing opened to reveal the rest of their waiting friends. The overwhelming scent of marijuana polluted the air.

Chapter 17: Kid Games

The granite boulders loomed, their rough surfaces slick from recent rain. Beyond them, the clearing opened. A ring of firelight illuminated the afternoon, highlighting a scene of casual chaos. Zack, his dark cowboy mullet shining in the firelight, swaggered back to his spot with a superior smile plastered onto his face.

"I'm just fucking with you," he drawled at Davis from across the lawn. His voice showed the confidence of inherited money and unabashed pride in his ten-inch appendage, which he constantly referred to. He'd already shown it off a few times that day, which the others found grudgingly amusing. Cyrus lumbered back after him, his underwear his only nod to modesty after a dare that went well. The cheers for his return were less about his bravery and more about his showmanship. His eyes, though, showed a desperate need for Zack's approval. The crowd didn't move him.

Davis plopped into his reserved space, his dark eyes scanning the scene with resignation. His confidence was shaken by Zack's ambush. Travis sat beside him with a measured calm, absorbing it all. He was the anchor, the quiet counterpoint to Davis's emotional volatility. He was also a primary reason the group hadn't completely imploded from the magnitude of Zack's imperial personality.

Gretchen stood at the edge of the circle, not knowing where she belonged. This was the first time she had been invited, despite having known most of the people there for years. The firelight reflected the uncertainty in her expression. Davis's call resolved her confusion. "Here," he said, his voice a gruff whirr, sliding over to make room. She was relieved to settle next to him. Her hand rested lightly on his thigh. It spoke volumes, a calculated move in a game far more complex than truth or dare. The circle pulsed with laughter and anticipation as the challenges and questions intensified. The smell of cannabis was undeniable, mingling with the pheromone of sweat and teenage hormones.

Each person was a character, playing their part in a drama as certain as Davis's unpredictable temper and as large as Zack's obscene wealth and physique.

Zack stated calmly and slowly in a matter-of-fact tone, "Anybody fucks with my cousin, and I will fucking kill them. Girls included." The nervous laughter that followed from the group was a thin veneer over simmering anxiety. He grinned a flash of sharp teeth in the dimming light. His smile didn't appear genuine. His eyes projected a chilling glint of instinct as he spoke. Everyone noticed the disparity, but no one pointed it out.

Cher, perched on a weathered log, slowly lifted her head. Her stare, clear as crystal, fixed on Zack. "I see you found our murder victim." She joked, her words full of dark, intoxicating sweetness only a goth chick could convey. Gretchen squirmed, accompanied by a pronounced sneer. Cher tossed her head without concern, a strand of silky black, obviously dyed, hair catching the light from the campfire.

"I see you. Don't be such an uptight bitch, Gretchen. You were screaming like a stuck pig. I was just joking.... Trying to be cool with you... We're cool, right?... Loosen up." She produced a joint and lit it, the pungent aroma of the smoke assaulting everything in its path. "Medical grade. No judgment... yet." The joint circled, a taboo invitation to group indoctrination.

Davis, his denouncement evident in the bold look of disgust on his face, watched its approach with detachment. His deep brown eyes followed the relay. He was not fond of drugs but tolerated being around them to be included. He wouldn't touch that thing. Not a chance. He smelled the desperation clinging to it like skin. Gretchen snatched it, her fingers surprisingly steady, and inhaled deeply, the smoke curling around her like a vengeful spirit.

Her breath became unsteady. "You can judge me all you want, Cher. I've known these guys my whole life. Zack's my cousin. The rest? I've known since I was five. You're the new one, the outsider. The one who doesn't know the rules yet." She coughed, a harsh, rattling sound that quickly dissolved into nervous giggles. She worried that the peace built on her kinship with Zack could shatter at any moment if she didn't play her cards right. This was his domain, and he had no tolerance for disruption... from anyone. Zack, his eyes moving to Davis, chuckled. "I was seriously just fucking with you," he muttered, a hint of menace supporting his words.

The game quickly resumed. Bare skin gleamed under the harsh floodlights. Sexuality, sweat and nerves fueled the adolescent machine. The bonfire cracked, sending sparks that matched the tense energy among the eight of them. Truth or Dare wasn't just a game; it was a weekly expectation, a descent into a darkness fueled by alcohol, drugs, and the need to test loyalty.

Davis eventually left the group and leaned back against a weathered oak tree. He was often voted out early because he refused to participate in riskier activities involving swearing, nudity, or drug use. The group tolerated his strictness for a while but eventually got tired of his constant prudishness. He scanned the scene from the sidelines, without taking issue. Being a spectator didn't bother him. He was already tired of the game, anyway.

Travis, who was also losing early, moved to stand beside Davis like a silent guardian. He was far bolder, in terms of willingness, than Davis, but also had ethical lines he would not cross. He appreciated the heat of the game, the reckless abandon, and the self-awareness it offered. His loyalty to Davis kept him from ever going too far.

Gretchen, sixteen but wielding the power of a seasoned temptress, watched Davis from the circle with interest. Her blonde hair cascaded down her back, framing a face that embodied ruthlessness behind innocent blue eyes. Each carefully chosen truth, never a dare, was a strategic play.

The game took a turn when Madison, a curvy girl whose apparent affability masked a sharp tongue, dared Cyrus. The ranch hand, obscenely muscular and impossibly stupid, was a willing and enthusiastic participant with no apparent limitations. Madison's challenge was predictable and commonplace: a full-body striptease in front of the rumbling bonfire. Cyrus, eyes glazed with bold excitement, instantly obeyed after receiving a nod of approval from Zack.

His movements were clumsy but eager. His awkward dance elicited a mixture of groans and cheers. It seemingly never got old.

Doug, Zack's quiet follower, his blond hair, a dandelion field standing atop his head, was next. Britney, a bundle of nervous energy, dared him to drink a spill of tequila from Madison's cleavage. His timid cheeks flushed a flustered pink. He hesitated for only a heartbeat before noticing Zack's stern nod before complying, the awkward silence broken only by slurping sounds and a few stifled giggles.

Britney was suddenly, and unusually, quiet. It was Matt who dared her to flash the crowd, an unexpected twist, given his secret infatuation with her. Her Boyfriend, Cyrus, looked on with amusement as she exposed her breasts. They both understood it was only a game. No harm, no foul.

The activity was a paradox of misplaced intimacy. It was guaranteed to escalate to something brutal and ugly. It always did. The jarring ring of Travis's phone changed his trajectory. His expression didn't indicate disappointment. He quickly moved to leave.

"I've gotta go," he announced. The response from his dedicated collection of friends and acquaintances was a chorus of jeers, slick with brutal hazing.

Davis worked to convince him, "Don't be a downer, Trav." His voice was like distant thunder. He was obviously frustrated. He didn't want to be abandoned. The other guys echoed the sentiment with cruel, directed attacks. Travis assessed the field of eyes aimed at him. He didn't try to conceal the insincerity of the feigned regret written on his face.

"Whatever, guys. My mom needs the car. And besides," he added, his green eyes flashing, "you're all just jealous because she's cool." His genuine confidence was a shield against the desperate guilt trip he felt washing over him from his best friend.

Davis stepped closer to him, whispering a plea in his ear. "Come on, man. Don't leave me hanging here. You know how this is." His words spilled rapidly with need. Travis, sensing the storm coming, suffered the icy chill of dread climbing up the hairs on the back of his neck. He had to go home if he didn't want any trouble later. Compromise was not an option.

"Not this time, Day," Travis said, his voice resolute. He wasn't falling for the usual routine. This standard manipulation attempt, containing whispers of camaraderie and duty, often turned into a list of unrealistic and selfish expectations. Davis began an argumentative, guilt-ridden, assault about his ride home. It devolved into an unending cycle of asks and denials.

Suddenly, a lifeboat emerged. Cher's voice ascended over the bargaining from the back of the clearing. "I'll take him home." Her voice held an authority and strength that silenced the others. Travis nodded quickly and grasped the opportunity, moving out of the group, with a panther's finesse, between the jagged boulders. He disappeared into the shadowy embrace of the woods as dusk continued its approach. The dying rays of the autumn sun chased him from the area until his presence was but a mere history.

The bonfire crackled, dying down and spitting sparks into the darkening air. Moods grew tense as the game ended, and smaller groups broke off. Davis dreaded the post-game conversations the most. Without Travis as a dependable buffer, he knew he'd be on the defensive.

On one side, huddled close, a pack of girls whispered secrets. Gretchen leaned closer to her best friend, Britney. A vacant cheerleader smile, and perfectly applied lip gloss defined her. She nodded dumbly. Her superficial expression was focused on the bonfire's other side, where her boyfriend, Cyrus... too adult to be her boyfriend but too malleable not to be, stood with the easy arrogance of a teenager, despite being twenty.

Davis sat quietly in his group, occasionally looking to Gretchen from his place across the fire with an irrefutable longing for not wanting to be there without Travis. He sat in silence, his presence radiating an energy that influenced everything around him. The girls were a flock of birds, drawn to his dangerous temperament. He'd heard some of their whispers, snippets about his relationship with Gretchen. She managed her contributions with a poisonous blend of possessiveness and control. He smiled at their jealousy, the thought being an experiment in tolerance. From where he sat, the girl's group was likely much more preferable to him, than his annoying group filled with testosterone and competing aggression.

Zack was sixteen but built like a man twice his age. His entire face curled into a sneer as he punctuated another boast about his "porn-star dick," as he held court. His anatomy was a weekly topic he rarely allowed to go unaddressed. It was an inarguable fact, widely and enthusiastically known, and all too frequently and explicitly backed up by him. His topical fixation was an indicator of his age and a declaration of what he considered to be dominance.

Cyrus always nodded vigorously when Zack spoke. He rarely made a sound unless it was to reinforce Zack's pronouncements. His own personality stayed hidden beneath his master's overwhelming presence. He was understood to be the ranch hand who clearly idolized the rich kid. The young men teased him about having a crush on Zack. It was a joke that was infrequent and unappreciated. Zack ensured that such teasing never went unpunished.

Brittle laughter from the girls felt like a taunt, a discordant melody against bravado brewing on the other side of the fire. This wasn't a casual gathering. On the contrary, it was a battleground of hormones, power, and boldly expressed criticisms.

"Women are fucking bitches! All of them," Zack snarled, his mullet swaying like a black flag. His tone was a roar that vibrated in him, and was validated by the aimless, but gleeful agreement of Cyrus, practically fluttering with validation.

"Except Gretchen," Cyrus added quickly, his eyes darting nervously to Zack. Davis felt the sensation of Zack's eyes on him. Zack's presumed hatred for him tapped Davis on the shoulder and slapped his ego.

"I'd hope not," Davis stated sarcastically. The cadence of his response was clipped and staccato. Zack exploded. He shoved himself to his feet. His posture took on a peeled, animalistic stance.

"Hope?... You fucking think Gretchen and I are into incest? You think we lived in some goddamn attic?" He managed the anger in his voice enough to display his willingness for conflict to the other young men in the huddle. The collection of them seemed to thrive on opposition. Zack clenched his fists. The tendons visibly tightened under the skin of his arms.

Davis withdrew, not from fear, but from the sheer overwhelming force of Zack's presence. It wasn't worth it. He watched the blood drain from the boy's face as he ranted. Zack produced a cruel, brittle laugh that precluded his return to his seated position at the head of the group. "I'm just fucking with you, kickball!" he sneered. "You take everything so seriously! Life's short. What's up with you anyway?" Everyone else sat quietly. Davis, acutely aware of the others' eyes on him, felt the familiar poke of intimidation. He'd learned to anticipate Zack's cruelty, the cold, deliberate slicing of his words. He prepared an answer and swallowed hard. The lump in his throat felt as immense as the boulders surrounding the clearing.

"What's up with me?" he repeated after clearing his throat loudly. The intensity of Zack's stare was a challenge, but he would not allow anyone to see him flinch. Zack's carved smile was devoid of humor. He leaned in close to Davis, his breath hot on his face.

"No car, no job. You're a fucking leech. No offense, man, but I'm looking out for Gretchen," he spat, the words guided by disdain. He grinned at Cyrus before returning his attention to kickball.

Davis looked at him without backing down. "Oh, I'm not offended. What you said was just...messed up and rude." He felt anger simmering but refused to let it show. He provided a relaxed counter to Zack's bluster. He knew better than to do anything else.

Zack paused with a look similar to respect, or perhaps grudging admiration, crossing his features. "You're... cool, man. You won't even smoke with us but still... You've got... good..." he searched for the word.

Matt supplied it, a thin, almost imperceptible voice cutting through the tension: "Morals?"

Zack nodded with superiority. "Yeah, morals. You're hard to read. You won't cuss or get your dick out at the games, like the rest of us. What's wrong with you? You think you're better than us or something? No... you're not that stupid. Maybe you're just ashamed of what you are packing... or maybe you just like to look at us." The others murmured their agreement in a chorus of subdued assent.

Davis seized the moment without taking the presented bait. He launched his counterattack with words as sharp and absolute as a surgeon's scalpel. "Oh, I have a job, Zack. I'm an athlete. I start with the Minotaurs next season. It's a professional soccer team." The quiet pride in his voice was a direct insult, a subtle but potent jab at Zack's privilege. A ripple of laughter broke the tension. The rare sight of Zack being outmaneuvered was a delicious treat. Zack's face flushed the color of hell.

He growled, the guarantee of consequence vibrating through his words, "I'm just saying...if you hurt her..." He paused; the implied threat hit home. The perception of his anger was as strong as the whiskey he'd been nursing all night. It permeated the group of young men. "...I will kill you." His eyes bored through Davis's body. The intensity of his stare burned with an organic fire.

Gretchen watched from several feet away. Her expression was unreadable. She knew the power she held in the group because of her cousin. There was a delicate balance she had to maintain to keep it. She thrived on the opportunity.

While her attention was split between distractions, her body reacted from Cher's sudden touch. It was a firm tap on her shoulder from behind. Gretchen jolted with surprise. Cher's purpose was quickly revealed. She wanted to close the unfinished business from a conversation Gretchen abruptly excused herself from earlier so she could police her cousin's conversation with Davis.

"You said you saw Davis and Travis following those girls earlier," Cher, offering genuine concern, reached out to Gretchen with support and friendship. Her carefree, hippie energy had transformed into something much more serious. Her gothic black hairstyle framed a face painted dark with worry.

Cher's emerald eyes blazed with an off-putting intensity. Her interest was deeper than childish gossip-seeking. "And you asked them to stop? That's not just creepy, Gretchen. It's fucking horrible. Those two… they're predators, and you're playing with fire."

The light from the dying campfire licked at Gretchen's face, highlighting the soft contours of her bone structure. She'd tossed her earlier statement about L.A. Brit-nay like a cigarette butt while she watched her boyfriend and cousin battle beyond the flames.

"Oh, yeah… just social media," she clarified absently, her voice a sugary coating over a core of disinterest. "They were following some influencer… Britney or something. I told him it was cheating. He whined about it, but he totally understands, now. It's no big deal. It's not like all that." Her soft glance moved back to Cher with a wide-eyed smile, seeking the approval that was her lifeblood.

Cher's face crumpled like a discarded bag. The impact of her expression hit Gretchen as a physical assault; the sheer weight of Cher's disgust settled on her like a shroud. "Cheating?" She fired the word as she would an arrow. The fire crackled in unison with her outward vocal display of disbelief in the new truth she had come to understand.

Gretchen tried a different approach. Her red nails dug into her palms from insecure irritation. "Well… it's cheating in your heart," she offered as a meek clarification. Her marked affect switch from friendly causality to dismissive instruction made everything worse.

Cher's eyes became hot pokers, readied and aimed to impale her. A cascade of stones emanated from her center before she exploded; the force of her building damnation shook Gretchen to her core.

"Holy shit," Cher breathed, her words were barely audible yet somehow deafening. She took a moment to process the information before continuing flatly, "Are you kidding me right now?" She flung her arms out, causing her expensive silk shirt with black sequins to sparkle in the firelight. It was a silent scream in its own right. "'Cheating in his fucking heart'? You definitely are kidding me!... Aren't YOU all over social media like paint?" The barbed accusation swung at Gretchen.

Gretchen, her innocence cracking open, matched Cher's attack with poised intention. "Yeah," she hissed tightly. "But it's different for girls. You know that. It is totally different." She created a barrier between them with folded arms.

Cher stormed out of Gretchen's sightline, "I'd have fucked you off right then," she snarled over her shoulder, her tone a hideous, mocking derailment. "That's the rankest, most controlling, codependent bullshit I've ever heard!" She paused, relishing the stunned silence before turning to confront her again at a distance to unleash a torrent of more public defamation. "People are allowed to have friends! If you don't trust him, fuck... him... off. Game over!" She returned to sit on the oversized log, which had come to be known as her seat. "Who's got the weed? I need a fucking ton after this. She's the reason ninety-two percent of women aren't believed," she muttered, her voice trailing off into a poorly done imitation of Gretchen's earlier words, "they were following girls, and I asked them to stop... What the fuck ever!"

Madison, grim-faced, handed Cher a joint. Britney raced to comfort Gretchen, offering a hug that felt more like a cover. Gretchen was beyond comfort. She tried to rally the other girls with her tears. Her eyes pleaded for support, but the young women only stared back at her with confusion and pity. Even Britney's hug felt cold, overweight with critical insincerity.

Cher took a long drag, her eyes softening slightly while closing the conversation. "Don't worry, babe," she said nonchalantly with the satisfaction of a supported purpose engraved on her face. Her voice quickly returned to a hazy, careless whisper through the smoke. "It's just my opinion. Everyone has one." She shrugged, marking the finality of her position. Her narrative, however, towered over them all like pyramids, standing in an immense desert of absolute truths.

Zack was noticeably pissed after helplessly witnessing the scene. He cut through the inebriated haze of the party with the cold authority of a dictator. He unapologetically barked, "Party Over!" His voice, armed with unrestricted rage, silenced the cacophony instantly. He pointed a thick finger at Gretchen. Her hair was disheveled. Strands were adhering to her tear-dampened face. She had lost her cool and embarrassed him. "Gretchen, Davis, get in the truck. Now."

He didn't ask them; he ordered them, suggesting an unavoidable threat of violence for non-compliance. He didn't bother to conceal his embarrassment beneath a suave attitude.

Davis's refusal to move met Zack's authority with obstinate defiance. He hated being in Zack's truck. His posture was taut with unsuppressed angst. Everyone knew Zack hated conflict unless, of course, he was the one orchestrating it.

He glanced at Cher with hope for rescue. Her earlier offer of a ride now was obviously as hazy and unreal as a forgotten dream. Her emotionless wave of surrender only solidified his mounting frustration.

Zack barked, "Cyrus, get these fuckers to clean up this mess and make sure that goddamn fire is out. Now." Cyrus reacted with superhuman speed, as expected. With the mindless obedience of a trained dog, he was already barking orders at the others with the fervor of a religious zealot. Zack, the ruthless leader of his motley crew, didn't need to say anything more. The silent weight of his presence, the pared power radiating from him, pushed them ahead like machines.

Davis felt the heat of Zack's stare burning into his back, and his frustration grew with each passing moment. He forced himself to stay calm. Gretchen ran to him, grabbed his hand, and forcefully pulled him toward her cousin. The three of them moved through the thinning crowd, a silent procession into the shadows of the woods. The cool, damp night offered a break from the remnants of what was, moments ago, a party.

There was no way around it. This was Zack's playground, and all of them were his toys. Davis now understood this more than ever. He wondered how Gretchen couldn't see it?

"I'm just fucking with you," Zack muttered under a smirk as the three of them walked through the trees. The words were a pointed jab at Davis, which only he truly understood.

Chapter 18: We Smell Like Weed

Zack's luxury truck boomed, a low growl swallowed by the vast Midwestern sky. Small particles of dirt danced in the bright blue beam of the headlights. The tense silence between the occupants made the trip miserable.

Davis sat rigidly beside Gretchen. His dark eyes stared, unfocused, out the passenger side window. He was intentionally speechless. His bare chest tensed against the constricting seatbelt with every bump. Gretchen played with her hands, clasped tightly in her lap, avoiding her cousin's attention. The truck's interior, smelling faintly of something musky, felt like a prison. Zack glanced at Gretchen intermittently, with silent judgment, as he drove. He noticed her discomfort with a smile.

The fifteen-minute drive seemed like an eternity. The cold of unhappiness radiating from Davis's thigh seeped into his girlfriend as a chilling reminder of his foul mood. The cab held the residual stink of weed. This compounded Davis's feelings of isolation and anger.

The dread of discussing the events of the evening with Davis once they were alone gnawed at Gretchen. It was barely buffered by the pathetic veil of avoidance she wore for Zack. Tears of regret stung behind her eyelids. She refused to release them. The heavy reality of her choices pressed on her. She was acutely aware of both Davis's stance on drugs and Zack's stance on public embarrassment. Her awareness of things, however, did not always foster an understanding.

Sleepover with Britney. Confirmed with mom and dad. Davis's parents are coming back tomorrow afternoon. She repeated the prepared facts in her mind, in hopes of speeding up time. It wasn't working. The chaos was too overwhelming. Harsh criticism sat on both sides of her.

Zack's silence was anything but reassuring; it was the calm before a storm. His piercing looks conveyed that he knew something. She felt someone must have told him about her plans for the evening. She refused to believe it was Britney. It didn't matter, though. Despite his feelings about Davis, Zack would never tell her parents. There would be a price for his silence, but he would never state it so soon.

Finally, the truck turned onto Davis's street, and his house came into view, gradually growing larger as they approached. The mundane yellow glow of a solitary streetlight blanketed the idling truck and glinted off the cellophane wings of insects that swarmed and danced in the humid air. Davis jumped out of the cab and slammed the door shut before Gretchen could move. In the dimness of the cab, Gretchen's delicate features twisted strangely into a shrug as she offered a guarded, appreciative, "Thanks for the ride, Zack."

Her gratitude was strained. Zack winked at her, a quick smile and wave as she opened the door and slinked onto the street where Davis waited impatiently. As soon as the passenger door clicked shut, Zack gunned the engine and peeled away without a word. Three quick bursts of his horn interrupted the evening quiet.

Gretchen watched him turn the corner before shifting her full attention to Davis. He was already turning away and heading towards his driveway with a brisk stride. It was still clear to her that he had not calmed down at all. Davis was not a master of concealing his emotions. She caught up to him and reached for his waist before reconsidering. Frustration sat solidly in her mind, replacing her previous hope for the romantic rendezvous, which had been planned for weeks.

Davis stopped when he reached the sidewalk. A muscle twitched in his jaw before he exhaled a long, drawn breath and then reached for her. His hand rested possessively on her lower back, a touch that felt like a claim. She loved it. The way his dark hair fell across his forehead and how the light glinted off his sculpted biceps could never go unnoticed. A blinking thought of quick resolution crossed her mind. The peaceful drone of crickets helped to create an oddly romantic potential. Maybe the evening wasn't lost after all.

The stale taste of weed burned in Davis's throat. He snarled, the words spat from his mouth like tobacco, "That friggin' weed stink! In the truck? He knows I can't stand it! It makes me want to…" He paused to think, offering an accusing frown to Gretchen as he processed. The look drilled through her. It hurt, but she accepted it without argument.

She reached out, her fingers traced the line of his hardened abs, a touch that was naughty and apologetic. "Relax, muscle-head," she encouraged. She could tell her sweetness was unappreciated.

"What, are you gonna cry?" she teased and softly moved to grasp his hand, hoping to conjure a smile.

She waited before pulling him in the direction of the front door. Her long nails lightly scratched his skin as he resisted. "It's better than your invisible truck," she teased again with a frisky pinch to his side. "And honestly, walking home would have been a real bitch." The playful giggle that accompanied her statement did not lighten his mood, as she intended.

Davis could feel the ire rising in waves to the surface of his skin. The muscles in his arms and shoulders tightened until they felt explosive. He inhaled deeply. The aroma of weed emanating from their clothes amplified his sour mood. Anger simmered and fueled a potent cocktail of helplessness and absolute disgust. "Don't," he ground out. "Don't defend him and don't you dare insult me. I don't need it. The stuff is dangerous."

Gretchen's smile didn't shrink. "Oh, god," she said. Her voice was soft and contained a superior understanding, which Davis needed. "Zack's a big boy. He'll be fine… Besides," she added with a wink, "I think he's practically immune to the stuff. Probably has a higher tolerance than a damn rhino." She leaned closer to him, passing a soft breath over his ear.

He wasn't talking about Zack's safety, and she knew it. The image of her cousin flashed through his mind, instigated by her reference. Zack, the spoiled rancher brat with his ten-inch weapon, who obnoxiously boasted about it and showed it to anyone within ear or eye shot. "I've got a dick like a porn star!" His voice echoed in Davis's head like an obsession. "Don't argue with me, little-dick." Davis couldn't help but feel fresh cuts from an evening he had barely started to put behind him.

"But now," Davis complained, underlined by a sneer and the harsh temperature of his stare, "We smell like friggin' weed... Strong." The hatred beneath his dialogue, projected onto the drugs but really aimed at something far deeper, was genuine. "I hate this," he grunted. "I hate everything about this. We should have ridden with Cher. That was our mistake." He pivoted to move in another direction, pulling at Gretchen's hand more forcefully than she had tugged at his moments before. His grip seemed inescapable. "It doesn't matter now. Let's go this way."

Gretchen aggressively slapped his arm and ripped her hand free from his. She stood firmly in place as he turned to look at her. The moonlight glinted off of her, revealing the strength she kept hidden beneath her seemingly fragile exterior. Her dissatisfaction, combined with controlled insolence, cut through the night. "I want to go inside. What the hell are you doing? It's dark, and I'm fucking tired."

He continued his growl, "ARGGGGH! We have to go in through the garage... especially since I don't even smoke the crap."

Gretchen was ready and willing to argue, to stand her ground. She had sustained enough judgment for one night. "I am absolutely not having sex with you in the garage, Day!" Her hair whooshed around her shoulders as she swung her head to keep from looking at him, daring him to confront her.

Day's laugh was a brittle, chilling sound. "You're right," he slowly articulated, as his voice morphed into the sarcastic sharpness of someone accustomed to getting his way. "Gretch! We are also not going into my parents' house smelling like freakin' weed."

She turned her back to him and folded her arms, refusing to bother looking at him. Her voice was flat as week-old roadkill, a blaring attempt to control his mood. "Oh, my god. What is your problem?"

She didn't address the words to him but to the empty expanse of driveway beyond. Then, she had a moment of brilliance. It almost slapped her. Arguing with him was getting her nowhere.

In an act of compromise, she turned to him and offered an olive branch. She approached him. Her fingers trailed lightly down his back, a touch that intensified the flirtatious glint in her eyes. She arranged her mouth into a pout, a look she'd rehearsed, specifically for moments like this.

"Don't be so paranoid," she purred, her voice became a honeyed caress that scraped against the brittle edge of his indifference. Her doe-eyes, now fixed on his, held a dangerous sweetness. "There's no one here to smell it, remember? They're gone." She leaned closer, even though she knew he could smell her.

His expression remained unchanged as he fumbled with the garage keypad. "Besides," she breathed, her voice barely audible, "it really isn't that bad. I can barely smell it. A light... a very light smell, if even that."

He stepped from her and began to open the garage door. His fingers fumbled clumsily against the rubber buttons of the electronic keypad. The motor groaned, vibrating the white concrete beneath their feet.

The door shuddered upwards, revealing a cavernous, meticulously ordered space. Neatly stacked boxes, a wheeled trash can, a shelf holding paint cans, cleaning supplies, and trash bags welcomed them.

His voice wound around the rustling noise of the door. "Of course, YOU can't smell it. It's because you've been SMOKING all friggin' day. It reeks. My mom could smell it from the interstate."

He didn't wait for a reply. Once the door was fully open, he jerked her inside with a strength that matched his words. His force, though firm, held a tenderness. He guided her past the door to the left into a shadowy space that was somehow both cluttered and orderly. "It'll be in the house for days," he complained. His exasperation reverberated off the cinderblock walls of the building. He stood and waited until the massive door gently thumped closed.

Davis rummaged through boxes overflowing with cleaning supplies. Without acknowledging her, he moved with a sharp efficiency that indicated his urgency. Gretchen tickled his back with a touch that felt like a caress.

She whispered, cutting through the silence. "It won't linger like that, but I get it." He ignored her, his hands searched in containers over his head until he located his target: two crisp white kitchen trash bags.

Gretchen's flirtation thickened. "Don't be so grumpy, babe," she coerced him. Her hand found and gently stroked his backside for a moment too long. "We had an awesome time tonight."

Silence. Her smile faltered. She elected a shift in diffusion tactics. "That Cher girl was cool. I didn't like her at first, did you?" The question was barbed. She found Cher to be a threat.

Davis didn't look at her. Instead, he abruptly shoved a bag into her hands. His action was fluid and final. "Here... Yeah," he stated with no inflection, devoid of warmth. "She's a little hard, but she was cool." As he spoke, he tossed the shirt he'd worn around his neck all night into the bag in his hand. He stared at her, his expectation brooding and apparent. "Well, go on," he demanded, gesturing to the bag.

Her eyes darkened, opposition replacing her earlier charm. She encircled his waist with her arms. Her fingers dug into his warm flesh. "Are you trying to get me naked, Mr. Day?" she asked in a baby doll falsetto, batting her eyelashes in a display of stereotyped femininity.

He continued stripping, quickly placing his clothes into the bag with brisk efficiency. His frustration was finally beginning to boil over. "No! I'm definitely not! I told you. We're not stinking up the house. Put your clothes in there. Now. We need to wash them.

The washing machine's right on the other side of the door. Keep your friggin' underwear on. Come on, let's go."

Despite their disagreement, Gretchen's eyes met his near-nakedness eagerly, the chiseled lines of his soccer-honed legs and the prominent bulge beneath his spandex boxer briefs filled her with an undeniable adoration.

Still, she stood with rigid refusal, like a marble statue. Her fists clenched. Her breath became forced. The delicate curve of her breasts rose and fell beneath the thin cotton of her tank top. Until now, she'd tried reason, attempted to flirt, anything to make the night better. She had tried her hardest to abate her feelings of frustration. Now, the dam burst. Her limbs, a blur of motion, reacted in edgy protest. A high-pitched shriek marked her dissent.

"You are being an asshole!" The trash bag, a crumpled insult, floated to the floor, landing like a feather at her feet. "This is perverse!"

The stomp that followed it bounced off the walls; a tremor of the rage which flowed around her. Davis stood there staring with disappointment. He was a study in lean muscle and smoldering inflexibility. His bare torso caught the dim light as he looked at her expressionlessly. Without a word, He slipped through the door into the house, like a ghost through a wall. The click of the inside lock was a gunshot in the aggressive quiet.

His calm voice eventually filtered through the wood. "Do it or not. Your choice. You can spend the night out there with the spiders and ants if you want. It's up to you. You're not coming in."

The squeaky hinge of the washing machine opening and the almost imperceptible rustle of plastic grabbed at her. She heard him humming over the soft thud of garments falling into the metal drum. It pushed her past her limits.

A growl poured from her mouth. "You are a complete fucking asshole," she vocalized through tears she could no longer contain.

Her words were flat but composed of the poison only defeat could brew. "And you know it." Her shoulders slumped. The fight had been slowly drained from her, leaving behind only powerless obedience. Slowly, defeatedly, she reached for her discarded bag. Davis had won. This game, as all games, belonged to him.

Chapter 19: A Love-Hate Relationship

The morning sunlight painted stripes of light across Gretchen's tanned skin. Her long leg lay heavy and warm across Davis's waist. Her arm was a protective barrier spanning his chest. She felt the calm drumming of his heart. A single stray hair tickled his jaw. The scent of her shampoo drew a subconscious smile from him, despite his being on his back in deep sleep. A restless energy coursed through him. He shifted and moved his hand along her side, gingerly tracing the curve of her hip. A contented warmth ran through her, producing a gentle sigh.

She moved in closer to him to rest her head on his collarbone, her breath warming his skin. He mumbled something in his sleep, creating a soft rumble in his chest. Gretchen's other hand rested on his, their fingers laced together. The anger and harsh words from last night were already fading, washed away by the morning sun and his comforting weight. The moment was constructed from a silent understanding. She had never woken up next to him before, and she liked the protection she felt there.

A tremor in Davis's body startled her. She gently pulled away, being careful not to disturb him. The crisp white sheet glided over his skin as it clung to her thigh, leaving him exposed to the cool morning. There was something about seeing him at rest that resonated with her. She couldn't recall ever seeing him this untroubled.

"God, he's perfect," she breathed aloud, her whisper stealing quiet. Her stare devoured him. The hairlessness of his body was no longer strange to her. It had become an alluring contrast to the dark, thick thatch on his head. The care he took to maintain himself fascinated her. The smooth expanse of his tight skin felt like art; a canvas stretched taut over the intricate network of muscles she knew so intimately. The smell of him, a unique blend of sweat and something purely Davis, filled her nostrils. His aroma was intoxicating. Then, her eyes dropped, and the sight hit her with the force of a train: the pillar of his erection rising from the otherwise barren landscape of his smooth, flat frame.

Her mind drifted. Why do guys get turned on when they sleep? she pondered. The question amused her as she secretly stared while he was unaware. The phenomenon was a puzzle as complex and combustible as the man himself. She knew his brash swagger, his volatile temper, and the dangerous undercurrent of childish inexperience that lived inside his charm. Even after months, Davis remained a landscape she was only beginning to explore, but it was hers. The unlimited energy she gained from owning him both confused and excited her. The merged emotions were a powerful combination, pulling her inexorably closer to him.

Her arm telescoped from her delicate torso, fingers closing around the cool glass of her phone on the nightstand. She wasn't as covert as she had hoped to be. Her movement awakened him. His eyes shot open to the morning and the sight of his own nakedness. No shame colored his eyes as he met hers. He merely chuckled and stretched.

"What time is it?" he mumbled, his voice the rough croak of a sleepy child.

Gretchen didn't answer aloud. Instead, her eyes widened and filled with frantic energy. They were glued to the phone's screen. Then, she launched herself out of bed explosively. The blur of her flesh contrasted with the faded blue comforter.

"Get up! Crap! Get up!" The words were intense bullets of panic racing through the morning peace. Her urgency consumed everything around her. Davis crossed his arms over his chest. He knew this Gretchen. Her drama was typical. He sat up slowly, pulling the sheet, a flimsy mask, across his waist. It was an instinctive gesture of modesty as pointless in theory as it was in practice.

"What's wrong?" His voice was calm. He attempted to anchor her with composure. It was not his best skill, but it felt right.

"I told my mom I was at Britney's," she panted, feverishly dialing the phone. The words, "I was at Britney's," hadn't left her mouth before a crazy, anxious shake seized her hand. She gripped the phone and shouted into it.

Without provocation, she jabbed a finger at Davis; the silent "shhh" was a warning. He giggled in disbelief. The phone, salvation in her hand, was pressed to her ear as she glared at him, paced, and gathered her belongings. Her bra and panties flew from the floor and onto her body, like prayers. He watched her, mesmerized. The irrationality of her movements was somehow beautiful.

He heard fragmented bits of her conversation. High-pitched torrents were interrupted by gasps and frantic assurances. "...Oh, thank God!... Brit? I know, I know. She did...?" She darted out of the room. The hallway swallowed her, leaving only the muffled echo of her voice.

Davis stood up, retrieved his rumpled boxers from the floor and pulled them on. The snap of the waistband disturbed the sudden silence of her exit.

She returned as quickly as she left. Her management of the situation was followed with relief. She shook her head with a sigh that indicated a solution to her problem. She slipped her dress over her head, revealing the delicate curve of her spine as it flowed around her hips before she plopped onto the bed to sit and gather her thoughts.

"Gotta pee," Davis announced, a grin tugging at his lips. He pointed at the insistent bulge straining against his spandex briefs with a raised eyebrow. "Gotta get rid of this. Watching you definitely isn't helping."

Gretchen's laughter resembled the chime of tiny, whimsical bells. She struck a pose, arching her back seductively, embodying both innocence and utter... sexiness. He left the room to resolve his identified problem. Gretchen looked out the window and assessed the upcoming day, optimistically. Outside, the sun beat down on the lawn. She was relieved that Britney was on her way.

The shrill ping of her phone sliced through the bedroom. She quickly lunged, fearing it might be her mother. She looked at it apprehensively. It wasn't hers. Another ping.

Davis?

Carrying the boldness of teenaged curiosity, she strolled to his dresser and picked up his life. A tap brought the screen to life and her breath stopped. Horror bloomed across her face, reddening it like strawberries unfurling across her alabaster skin. The discovery transformed her from tranquil to a storm about to break.

A single word hissed through gritted teeth, "Motherfucker."

Davis sauntered in, whistling while pulling his jeans from the floor. He slid them carelessly over his hips.

"Brit on her way, babe?" He noticed her expression and became concerned. "What's wrong?" The worry in his voice was genuine and childlike. Gretchen didn't answer. Instead, she repeatedly tapped his phone screen.

"L.A. Brit-nay... just... accepted... your... friend... request." The words fell with discord. "You couldn't last a day, you fucker?" Davis, his confident swagger replaced by a stammer, waved a hand defensively.

"Wait," he sputtered, his voice now a plea. "That was from yesterday! I told Travis to ask her... she must've just... now... I swear!" His eyes darted to his phone as another notification announced itself. Gretchen peered at it, her fingers flying over the screen. She slammed the phone into his face, the image of L.A. Brit-nay's now-active follower profile became an unadulterated accusation.

"She's following you now? You were trying to hook up with whores while I was asleep!" Gretchen's voice became a shrill siren.

Davis's denials were lost in her screams. He took a step toward her, but she stepped away. She raised her hands in front of her. She glared at him with accusation, daring him to move.

"BULLSHIT!" Gretchen shrieked, the sound shattered the sanctity of his bedroom and rattled the soccer trophies with the power of a vengeful god. Her voice vibrated through him. "You LIAR! She was already following you. You told me that. Then, you blocked her! Now you're saying she conveniently wasn't actually following you after I caught you trying to cheat. You unblocked her last night! You asked her again!" Her stare, eyes blazing with a hatred that chilled him to the bone, pinned him in place.

A single tear, a fat drop of pure sadness, escaped the corner of his eye. It was unfamiliar because it was not formed from anger, like the tears he'd grown a tolerance to. He felt a sickening twist of helplessness in his guts. He collapsed onto the bed with his hands cupping his face. Gretchen was unmoved. She stood over him with her hands perched on her hips, demonstrating her disgust.

"How is it even cheating?" he choked out, genuine tears now streaming down his face and wetting the desert of his abdomen, his voice cracking. "No, I didn't block her yet! We were all hanging out, we came here... laundry and everything! I just... forgot!" The words were desperate, pathetic. A compromise fought its way out of his soul. "Give me my phone. I'll block her right now. You can watch me. I swear!" A jarring car horn intruded on the moment.

Gretchen's voice was ice.

"I'm not going to do this. You were lying then, or you're lying now. Either way, you're a liar.... I don't have time for liars. I don't trust you. I'm officially fucking you off." The statement was a dart, hitting its target with the accuracy of a sniper's aim. She gently placed his phone on the bed beside him. She stroked it like a consolable child.

The soccer star looked utterly broken. Leaning close, her breath was warm against his ear. She whispered words dripping with painful sweetness, "Keep your whores." Then, with a ballerina twirl, she was gone, a funeral march out of the room. Her shadow faded into the hallway behind her. Davis was shattered. He scrambled to his feet, pursuing her through the house.

"Listen! Please, please, please listen! I'm telling you the truth. I love you!" He said it. His heart syncopated a frantic rhythm from within. It begged a pulsing need for understanding, for mercy, for sanity. Affected, she stopped at the door and turned to him with empty eyes. Another impatient blare of a car horn, this one longer, discounted her acknowledgment of his emotion. A single tear emerged and danced from her eye to her chin on a twisted path.

"Britney's here. You fucked me, then you tried to talk to whores while I was sleeping. " Her voice cracked, her wall finally crumbled. "Fuck you, Davis. You're a piece of shit. I told you. Leave me alone. Don't call. Don't text. Don't even think about me." The door creaked open, and she stepped through. The violent slam behind her ended the conversation.

Britney sat outside, waiting in her car. Her impatient stare fixed on the scene of her best friend stumbling from the house to greet her. Gretchen, her face a death mask, slammed the car door, and the girls drove away. Davis stood alone. The only sound was his Heartbreak, ticking the moments between his betrayal and the harsh experience of angering her.

He stared through the picture window, watching Brit's car creep down the driveway until it vanished. He wandered to his bedroom; a slow crawl wrought with self-loathing. He threw himself onto the bed, hitting the mattress with a heavy thud. He was imploding with the newfound and unexpected weight of his unpredictable world.

"She's fine," he reassured himself, the words unconvincing. "Just give her a minute, buddy." He started rocking to soothe himself. The action did nothing to lessen the burning in his chest. Finally, losing his composure, desperation escaped from his guarded core. Molten lava teardrops burned a path through the layers of his managed persona.

Gretchen had vanished. His parents, those obscure figures who'd always felt more like observers than caregivers, were miles away and unreachable. Travis... even Travis, his rock, his grounding force, was absent. He was isolated and drowning in foreign emotions. Pressure built in his chest. It hurt like a demon clawing its way to the surface.

The feeling of self-hate was not enough. He added a raging inferno of contempt, a hellish tide pulling him under. He clenched his fists with force, bone cracking against bone, a prelude to the brutality he was about unleash. The punch landed with a sickening thwack; the blood inside his cheeks perversely soothed him. He screamed a howl that destroyed the quiet. It was a mad plea for relief he learned in his childhood to manage intense internal pain.

"What… is… WRONG… with… YOU?!" He roared at himself, punctuating the words with repeated thuds of his knuckles pounding against the solid bones of his jaw until he could taste the iron in his blood. His eyes blazed with a ferocity that revealed his nature. The building pressure of his swelling face pleased him.

He knew her, her seductive power, the way she could twist him around her finger with a single glance or an aimed word. She'd simply walked out on him without reason. She left him to wrestle with the wreckage she'd created.

He found himself wishing for Travis to be there; his level-headed nature and rational opinion always calmed him. He wondered if even his best friend could save him from himself. The emptiness surrounding him was asphyxiating. Davis, in all his swollen-headed, volatile, undeniable rage, felt irreparably destroyed.

The god had fallen in a cataclysmic crash to Earth.

Chapter 20: The World Tilted

The late afternoon sun, a molten orange, dipped behind the bleachers, turning the soccer field's vibrant green to a muddy brown. Davis moved in a haze against the fading light, amateurly lunging for the ball.

Unable to maintain focus, his muscles responded with consistent painful tension. His feet were repeatedly tangled. The usual confidence of his stride vanished, replaced by frantic flailing that showed how off-balance he was. The field felt wrong. The turf slipped under him, like it was actively resisting. He struggled to control the ball. It avoided him; every play he attempted was met with failure.

Each time he tried to catch it, it slipped just out of reach. His legs moved too fast, too slow, out of sync with the speed of his thoughts. His body didn't respond the way he directed it to. His chest tightened. He missed another pass. His cleats, kicking at nothing, caught the earth and scattered it in front of him. The game was slipping from his grasp.

Frustration built in his chest as he worked. Nothing came easily. His movements were frantic and uncoordinated. Even the simplest actions felt foreign. Soccer appeared to be abandoning him, too.

The encouragement of his team and the shouts from his coach faded into a hum. It was all diminished by the pounding in his ears. He noticed Travis was watching him with concern from the sidelines.

Davis instantly pivoted to avoid witnessing his friend's disappointment. The self-conscious turn cost him another interception. The ball shot past him unnoticed. He groaned in frustration before throwing himself to his knees, punching the ground with force. The coach's whistle pierced the air. "Davis! Focus! You're better than this!"

The words landed like a bomb. The shout, meant to snap him back, only deepened the unbearable self-deprecation. He saw his own reflection in every mistake, a reminder of how far off he'd drifted.

The coordination he once relied on had vanished. His body moved like an anchor now, dragging behind his thoughts. Sluggish and disconnected, he pushed through the remainder of the practice as if the effort might tear him apart. Another stumble pulled him off balance. The field no longer made sense, and neither did his place in it. Nothing aligned. Even his feet moved apart from him as if someone else were pulling the strings.

Once his domain, this was no longer a place where he felt in control. The ball rolled past him, and he didn't bother to chase it.

There was no point. It was like his body didn't know how to act anymore. His muscles didn't react the way they used to. He did not know how to fix it, how to get it back. He looked for Travis, but he had turned away.

After his exhausting failure, the locker room felt empty as he walked in. It used to be full of energy. The sounds of laughter, the slap of towels, and the rush of the game fed him. Now, it was just a room full of ghosts. Teammates moved past him without a word, without a glance. No one reached out to him. The bench caught him. He sank into it and stared at the floor. The weight of the past several weeks was closing in around him.

Travis finally arrived, clapping him on the shoulder as he passed. "Don't let this be the day you give up," he said. His tone was reliably calm. Davis didn't look at him or respond. He didn't have the energy. Travis departed through the maze of lockers, toward the rushing sound of the tepid showers.

The room pressed in until there was nowhere else to go. Davis's body felt present, but he couldn't tell if he was still inside it. It was as if the world had slowed down, and the prodigy had run away.

The memory of Gretchen's gentle smile, her innocent eyes, her quirky gifts, "just because" rode on a carousel of memories. He never intended to hurt her; to inflict the same pain she'd given him. He had never experienced such a deep and unreachable ache. It was an agonizing sting, providing no promise of relief. He raised his head to study the shattered image in the mirror on the wall across from him. He stared at himself blankly, and a stranger stared back.

Chapter 21: An Invitation

Only weeks earlier, the locker room still buzzed with hushed whispers that clung to the walls. Davis heard them all: every whispered jab, every shift in conversation when he walked in. He'd once been the standard. Now, he felt like a benchmark for failure. He didn't defend himself. Staring at his hands, he curled his fingers, clenching them into a hard fist.

Travis sat hunched on the bench between two locker rows. His elbows rested on his knees with his jacket oddly zipped all the way up to his throat. Beside him, Davis leaned back. His head pressed against the cold locker door. One leg stretched out in front of him, while the other tapped an aggressive rhythm on the scuffed tile with his foot.

Davis flexed his hand, admiring the strength of his forearm. It reminded him that he hadn't disappeared. His skill hadn't gone anywhere. His strength was still his. He had begun to believe the hope was gone. He knew, deep down, that his current circumstances had nothing to do with his ambition.

"Remember what I told you, Trav?" he said. His voice was low and gravelly with a roguish edge. "I ain't finished yet."

Travis nodded with small, almost imperceptible, movement. Davis always had an addictive need to prove everyone wrong. He was reclaiming the confidence he had misplaced. He appreciated this about his friend. Davis always bounced back.

"Nope, not finished," Travis replied with a supportive smile. "Not by a long shot." Davis's Minotaur contract was looming on the horizon. The frigid autumn afternoon brought with it a renewed promise of a stunning career.

"Glad you're snapping out of it," Travis said. His words were accented with an involuntary twitch in his jaw. The encouragement left a trail of satisfaction that traveled across his face. He jabbed Davis hard in the ribs; the force of it was surprising, even to himself.

Ignoring the friendly assault, Davis pressed his thumb hard against his phone screen and answered without looking up. "It's been two weeks." He swallowed hard. "She won't even answer a text or anything. And for what? It's insane."

Travis, ever the pragmatist, tried a different tack. He was more than tired of hearing about what Gretchen wasn't doing. "You think this is going to win her back? Hell, no. She wants a battle, Davis. A chase. She wants to see you fight for her. Show her you're sorry. Show her you care."

Davis scrolled through unanswered text messages on his phone. The muted glow lit his face, accentuating the grim set of his chin.

He turned the screen toward Travis, a gesture both hopeful and defeated. "Called her. Texted her. A million times. Nothing. See? Even blocked the girls. Every single one. Most of my followers." The defeat in his voice was almost unbearable.

Travis stared at it. The phone's cold light reflected in his own tense eyes. He swallowed his Adam's apple, bobbing. "L.A. Brit-nay?" he asked flatly.

"Especially L.A. Brit-nay! This is all her fault!" Davis's voice was sharp, a staccato drum.

Travis shook his head. The movement was pointedly sharp and exasperated. He spoke slowly, with control. "No, Davis. No, it's not. You've got a crazy girlfriend, just like the rest of mankind. L.A. Brit-nay's not the problem." He paused for a moment and allowed the silence to build and the tension to thicken for dramatic effect. "And let's be clear: she's probably never gonna add you back." His tone was devoid of sympathy. The truth of it settled firmly between them.

Travis leaned in, his green eyes thick with intensity. His stoic expression morphed into an impish grin. "Davis, man, you have to come to Zack's ranch party. Gretchen'll be there. This is your chance."

Davis nervously ran a hand through his hair without commitment. His eyes flickered with doubt. He could practically feel Gretchen's rejection already. A chill ran through him that had nothing to do with the excitement of the soccer field. Zack's party was the event of the year, but he knew he wasn't meant to be there. Every part of him understood he wasn't part of that world anymore. After a moment, he shook his head slowly in disagreement.

Travis pressed on; his plea evolved into a full-on beg. "Macy's going to be there. Please, dude!" he whined, his voice low and urgent.

Her name was a potent lure, a glittering hook. Davis knew how interested in her Travis was. He felt the thrum of desperation from his friend. The temptation of being a good wingman pressed down on him. Travis had faithfully been a consistent rock of steadfast support. He needed the soccer star to help him gain a girl's favor. The tension in his jaw tightened. He vividly imagined his likely humiliation and the sting of Gretchen's public rejection. The thought of facing her made him sick to his stomach. At the same time, obligation was tugging at him.

"No," Davis finally stated. His single-word response was a determination. It was laden with unspoken fear and a painful dose of self-preservation. "It's just not a good idea. She told me to stay away from her. Besides, she probably won't even go. I really would look like a loser in front of everyone if that happened."

Travis let out a bark of laughter. It was exaggerated like a cartoon. "Outer space, man! Outer space!" He caught Davis staring forward. There was still a chance. "When have you ever known her not to go to that party? Every FUCKING year. Everyone goes. You already know, man."

Travis's tone was a challenge. "Unlike someone else I know, Gretchen Stiles is not gonna be dragging her ass around like someone died." He extended a hand, looking for a high-five. "If it works, it works. If it doesn't, it doesn't. What's the difference? Huh? At least you'll know where you stand."

The warmth of his best friend's enthusiasm was irresistible. Davis's expression altered, indicating he may be wavering. "C'mon, man. Do your boy a solid. Please?" He paused, then nodded slowly. The corners of his mouth barely moved. "I'm right, and you know it." His hand stayed, steady between them, waiting for contact.

Davis returned a hesitant, almost sheepish smile. He raised his hand and slapped Travis's with a single powerful rep. Travis's smile widened. "Thought so," he sang with a brimming affection. "I'll drag you there if I have to. I'm more tired of this break-up than you are."

Davis moved his eyes back to the tiled floor, watching the shadows from his legs shift behind his shoe. He pressed a toe forward, then drew it back again. The point of his movement didn't matter. It simply filled the space between his thoughts. Travis stood beside the bench. Nothing about him pushed or pulled. He just stayed.

Davis traced a narrow line on the dirty floor with his foot. He followed it with his eyes, then drew another, slower this time. His focus was beginning to return, shaped by his introspection.

A faint whistle carried through the hallway beyond. It was the notification that the custodian was locking up for the night. Before long, he would be strolling through to kick them out.

Davis wasn't fazed. He continued to track the lines he formed on the floor. Then he reached forward, just once, and tapped the back of Travis's hand. The gesture didn't mean anything special. It simply acknowledged the fact that he was listening.

"Okay... I'll do it. Let's get out of here." he mumbled with tired resignation. His shoulders dropped. The fight left him. Travis was probably right. He usually was.

Chapter 22: Favor for a Friend

The mirror in his bedroom interrogated Davis as he prepared for his grand entrance. His eyes, fixed in a scrutiny bordering on self-loathing, scanned his reflection. Three crumpled shirts lay discarded on the bed, casualties of his hour-long war with his pursuit of perfection. Each rejected garment felt like a lost opportunity. Every choice he made was a shred of confidence sacrificed on an altar built of low esteem. Travis slapped his hand on the dresser in playful frustration. "Enough! You've had three days to figure this shit out. It doesn't matter what you wear. You'll look like a fucking god in any of it. Let's... GO! At this rate, everyone will be gone by the time we get there. And, just a warning, if I have to see you in your drawers one more time, I'm gonna punch you in the face!"

Davis, usually quick with a retort, remained quiet and stared at himself. He had wrestled with his decision to go for days. The gnawing hope for a potential reconciliation with Gretchen and the fierce loyalty he felt for Travis stood on one side. The other option dangled a fear of rejection and humiliation over him.

Davis finally snatched up a worn, red-and-brown Minotaurs practice jersey. He wore it frequently, even though he hadn't officially started practice. Before he could pull it over his head, Travis's hand clamped down on his arm, a firm grip that pulled him from his reflection.

He dragged him from the room impatiently. Using more force than necessary. He jerked Davis forward, groaning as he followed. He managed to pull his arms through the jersey along the way and haphazardly tuck it into his too-tight blue jeans.

They thundered through the house, waving at Max and Ellen as they walked by. The sound of Ellen's encouragement was muffled only by the urgent race of Travis's brisk lead. The front door called back as they made their way to the soccer-mom chariot in the driveway.

Travis grinned. A flash of white teeth brightened his tanned skin. "Showtime," he said. His tone revealed a hopeful excitement. Davis swallowed hard. A lump in his throat, the size of a baseball, was forming. As the passenger-side door slammed closed, the situation became real for him. He was definitely going now. Did he make the right choice? The sickening certainty of his doubt settled in. He knew he wanted to see Gretchen but did not know if he had the courage to face her or try to convince her to give him another chance.

Manicured lawns, each a perfect emerald square, blurred past Davis's window. He pressed his forehead against the cool glass; the chill was a different experience from the burn in his throat. There was no conversation between them as Travis navigated the side streets and merged into the interstate traffic. The rhythmic hustle of the freeway matched the frantic drumbeat in Davis's chest. He watched mile markers flash by like taunting scoreboards. He tensed with every bump in the road; each jostle started an independent engine inside him.

Travis, hands firm on the wheel, glanced at him. "You okay, man?" he asked, almost too casually disrupting the silence.

Davis remained tense and refused to look at him. He looked at the van door, instead. "This was a bad idea," he mumbled to the window. His response was lost in the sound of the engine. He cleared his throat and spoke more distinctly, "A really bad idea." He felt the churning of adrenaline racing through him. Waves of angst were starting deep in his stomach and rising to choke him.

"Relax," Travis said. His voice was a solid reassurance. His hand momentarily left the wheel just long enough to slap Davis's knee before returning to position. "She'll come around. You know how they are."

Davis shook his head, the movement jerky, uncontrolled. "No, I don't. That's the problem." He felt the tremor in his hands. His own heartbeat echoed in his ears. "I shouldn't have listened to you. I should just... leave her alone until she's ready." The van continued, hurtling down the freeway, carrying them towards a dream or a nightmare. It was too late for either to matter.

Memories of past parties danced in Davis's mind as the sounds of livestock, and the smell of manure replaced the oil and electricity of the suburbs. They were entering a world of green, untamed wealth. Houses, spaced like constellations, grew grander with each passing mile. The price tags were implied invisibly by the pretentious landscapes.

"Randall Street," Davis muttered. He leaned forward, returning his forehead to rest against the glass. A street named after Zack's family was the last place that he wanted to be. The music on the radio, unnoticed until now, pulled Davis from his assaultive thoughts. He subconsciously held his breath as they passed under a sprawling sign spanning the gated entry: RANDALL CATTLE RANCH.

The twisting concrete driveway swallowed the surrounding nature, leading them to a mansion that dwarfed everything around it. The spacious clearing beside the estate looked like a used car lot, each gleaming vehicle a harbinger of the party beyond.

"Maybe I'll just blend in," Davis thought. Something didn't feel right. He gripped the worn leather under the passenger seat and braced himself. The van lurched as Travis expertly navigated the throng of vehicles and found a place to park in front of a barn. The steel structure loomed above them.

"Damn, look at this," Travis said with awe, taking in the space as if he had never been there before. His bright green eyes were nervously scanning the cars around them. He pointed a finger toward a purple sports car. "That's Macy's ride, alright." He rubbed his hands together. A greedy excitement replaced his nervous demeanor. "Odds are good, brother. Odds...are...good."

Travis's optimistic tone didn't soothe Davis. He saw the reflection of his own tight face in the window, the sharp angles of his jaw, the dark circles under his deep brown eyes, and felt more insecure. Travis, noticing the sheen of welling tears, asked with irritation, "Dude, What's wrong now?"

Davis sat up slowly, rubbing at the faint lines of worry etched across his forehead. His voice was a defeated breath. "Nothing. Just...nervous, I guess."

Travis turned the key and the engine stopped, a final sputter of sound was swallowed by the night. The parking area, bathed in the sickly yellow glow of security lights, felt miles from anywhere.

"Lucky spot, huh?" Travis's grin was tight with amusement. He leaned back against the worn leather of the car seat. The scent of the cheap air-freshener hanging from the rearview mirror suddenly became noticeable in the small space of the cab. Pine.

His tone shifted; the teasing edge was gone. "Listen," he said with firm, clipped intensity, "I'm hitting it with Macy... I hope. You're fixing things with Gretchen. And, Davis," he paused and fixed on his buddy with an imposing stare, "It's not gonna happen for either of us if you go in there like a bitch... so fucking chill. It'll be fine."

Davis noticed Travis's tension in the artificial light. The seriousness of Travis's next words paralyzed him for a moment: "Don't fuck this up for me, Davis." He swung the van door open and energetically hopped out. The click of it closing behind him announced the start of the evening. Travis's unyielding, but supportive, criticism met Davis as he wrestled with his willingness from his seat.

"Let's go," he whined, stepping out of the van and onto the ground. They walked toward the massive house. It was a fortress of darkened windows and ominous shadows. The sight of it promised an night weighted with expectation and fraught with either thrilling celebration or devastating failure.

A deep, resonant "MOOOOOOOO" erupted from Travis as they strolled by the pasture. Travis grinned, his short brown hair catching the light.

"This is gonna be awesome! Do it, Day! Remember? Tradition!" Travis chirped. Davis barely glanced at him.

His own "MOOOOO," a robust and playful outburst, drew a chorus of bovine response from the herd. He grinned widely. He remembered he had that effect on animals, and people, too, when he wanted. Davis's mood lightened and he began to call upon the confidence he knew he had. A positive energy pushed its way through his anxiety as his characteristic confidence stepped into him.

Davis strode forward and spoke with practiced ease, "We'll walk in like we own the place." He adjusted his stance. The muscles in his broad shoulders shifted beneath his boastful jersey.

The house became much larger with their approach. It was a monstrosity of dark wood and ornate stone. The double doors shone with a hard, dark polish. The place reeked of a life Davis had only ever dreamed of. He had to hold it together. Control was everything. He would not show even a touch of weakness. He put on a slow, cocky grin. It almost erased him. The swagger was a character of its own.

"Ready? Three… two… one… and go!" he announced. His jaw tightened to accentuate the angles of his face. His breath stalled in preparation for his entrance, then flowed freely as he squared his shoulders and moved into action.

With a powerful shove, he threw both doors open at once. The dramatic entrance he executed was enhanced by the cavernous interior. He stepped inside, radiating relaxed assurance and complete command. Beneath his social media-inspired persona, a silent scream was trapped inside his bravado. He glanced at his feet. The polished floor reflected the smugness painted on his face. He noticed it and approved.

Chapter 23: The Outcast

A tidal wave of sound and movement engulfed the two newcomers as they entered. Warmth slammed into them, followed by timed waves of bass from a local rock band that vibrated through the tile floor, resonating deep in their guts.

The Randall's house wasn't ostentatious, but it brimmed with wealth. Richly stained wood paneling covered the walls. A crystal chandelier, the size of a small car, pulsed with the rhythm of the loud music, showering the room with a dizzying kaleidoscope of light. Davis grinned with confidence, his deep brown eyes scanning the scene.

Travis stood beside him. He was a calm center to Davis's storm. He took it all in with a calm acceptance. The room was full of energy. Teenagers, a mash of jeans and cocktail dresses, swirled in a dizzying dance. Some chatted in hushed groups. Others were on a mission to stand out individually through bold demonstration. The collective voice was a wild chorus against the music. A girl in a shimmering gold dress brushed past them. Her perfume was a heady mix of sugar and flowers that lingered for several moments after her departure.

"Look at this," Davis murmured with a chuckle reverberating behind his rib cage. He casually gestured to a trio huddled near an improvised bar. Their faces were illuminated by the flickering candlelight. "High school's version of a Wall Street power lunch."

Travis raised an eyebrow. "More like a popularity contest fueled by daddy's money," he countered. His judgmental tone matched his friend's. "Still an impressive turnout, though." A group of girls giggled as their eyes darted toward Davis. He caught their glances. His hotshot smirk instinctively widened. This party was a happening event! It was lit. Everyone was there, as advertised. The music swelled, pulling them further into the vortex. It was a mind-blowing experiment in fleeting affluence, a shimmering, temporary kingdom built on borrowed privilege.

Travis's eyes snagged on Macy across the haze-filled room. She was an ebony goddess in floral-patterned silk. The loudness of her dress was a splash of vivid color among the muted tones of the room. She waved at him shyly. Her happiness to see him was a perfectly applied cherry on top of a flawless confection. He managed a whisper, "She's there...right there."

Davis noticed his friend's posture stiffen. Travis straightened his shoulders like he'd swallowed a lightning rod. A grin stretched across Davis's face. "Dudes got it bad," he thought, then clapped Travis on the back. "Go get her, man."

Davis watched him go and then launched into action with a burst of restless energy. He strutted deeper into the room! Crowds were his element. He maneuvered through it. The disgusting reeking smells of beer and a trace of funk... definitely marijuana, defined the ambiance.

He found his way into a semi-cleared space, allowing a testosterone-fueled bellow to rip through the chatter, "I'M HERE! Now, this thing can really start!" His levity was known for its contagion, but this time his viral attraction died in his throat. Smiles didn't reciprocate; only annoyed glances and disregard were returned. The room, holding his hope moments before, felt cold and exclusionary. People reacted as though he was not even there. He shrugged, his natural charm faltering only slightly. He had faced tougher audiences, though he couldn't quite recall when.

"Anyone know where the drinks are?" he called out, a little louder this time. He desperately tried to capture the supportive energy he was accustomed to. A nondescript kid, with barely a glance exchanged, shoved a bottle of soda into his hand and vanished. It was cool against Davis's throat. It was welcomed in a place that smelled like it had nothing useful to offer him.

The bass from the band vibrated Davis's body. It was accompanied by the shimmering heat radiating off the scores of teenagers packed into the room. He slipped through them, brushing against friends and past acquaintances until he found a better vantage point to observe his mission.

In the far corner, he noticed a baby grand piano serving as an impromptu table. It sat bathed in the glow of dim lights, away from the other guests. Around it, a familiar cluster materialized:

Britney sat in the center wearing a strapless dress covered in loud, hot-pink sequins with a clueless smile painted on her face. Next to her, Cher's stoic expression was lost in the haze of smoke rising from her mouth and nostrils. It reminded him of what a dragon might look like after a kill. Then he saw her. Hope and insecurity consumed him in tandem.

A white sundress clung to Gretchen's frame. Its fabric caught the light, sparking in tiny bursts. Her champaign-colored hair was styled in an elegant up-do. It was a deviation from what he was used to, but she was still beautiful.

He noticed a muscular arm draped possessively around her waist. The arm belonged to a man built like a Titan. He was all blond bulk and undeniable physical power. A wrestler, Davis thought. The idea brought the burning sensation of vomit from his stomach to the base of his throat.

Gretchen threw her head back and laughed with her companions, oblivious to Davis's presence. He remembered the sound of it, like tiny bells. It felt good to see her happy, although he was too far away to hear her. Her eyes were soft, alight with a joy that felt agonizing to him in its context.

She comfortably leaned against the wrestler with her head pressed into his shoulder. She appeared to be utterly lost in him. Britney shrieked with laughter, piercing through the music. Cher echoed the laugh with a throaty gurgle, followed closely by a fit of coughing. Their reactions were identical to the ones Davis remembered.

The same attention they'd always given him was being offered to someone else. He felt a cold knot forming in his gut. Was something off? Or was it just him? The music swelled, drowning out any other sound, any other thought. His questions remained unanswered.

He felt the presence of the crowd, a rolling sea of faces, and a barrage of shouts and laughter that beat over him. His vision was clouded with a strange confusion. Why did he agree to come here? Unshed tears he refused to let fall pricked at the corners of his eyes, dulling the bright lights reflecting from the slick tile floor.

Then, a shift in the current. The host, sharply etched against the swirl, moved through the throng. Zack swaggered ahead of a small group of boys like a dictator. His black hair was slicked back, framing a face that was both pretty and brutal. His full lips formed a perfect, satisfied smile. Trailing behind him were Cyrus and Matt. Two other young men, strangers, followed the others like trained hounds. The hierarchy was clearly illustrated.

The crowd parted like the Red Sea before Moses so they could pass without obstruction. Murmuring compliments and accolades from friends were drowned out by the roar of the entertainment. Zack shifted his direction from Davis's path and the others followed like segments of a centipede. It was an intentional shift in trajectory. Davis felt the weight of many eyes on him throughout the room. He offered a shaky wave toward Matt. A meek smile was offered, quickly evaporating as the five moved forward, slicing through the crowd and out of the room to the freedom of the porch. None of them bothered to acknowledge him.

Davis was stymied; the echoing music became a grounded reminder of his confusion. He was acutely aware of how easily he could be swept away again, lost in the tide of this densely populated but desolate place. His question was answered. Something was definitely off.

Feeling as though he was the object of attention... negative attention, he tried to pull himself together. Rejection is what he had feared above all else. This is why he didn't want to come. Cortisol coursed through him as he scanned the room before returning to his purpose... Gretchen. Eighteen years hadn't prepared him for this feeling of invisibility. His dark hair felt plastered to his scalp. Each strand was a tiny antenna perceiving a silent hostility.

He shifted. Banishment. The concept unsettled him more than he had anticipated. He'd known coming to the party was risky. A sudden feeling of fear hit him like an earthquake under his skin. He continued to look for an opportunity. The prismatic rainbows from the chandelier were almost degrading him. Each glittering refraction seemed to exacerbate his apprehension. He forced himself to focus. He took a deep breath and tried to anchor himself.

Gretchen.

The name was a lifeline, the one, single thread binding him to his purpose. He moved, cutting through the room's oppression. His steps were strong and resolute. He could feel eyes following his progress. Each glance became a tiny dart thrown in his direction.

Noticing his approach, an annoyance overtook the revelry in Gretchen's face. A flash of angst, forming a white-hot spark, ignited in her eyes. She motioned to Cher. Then to Britney. An urgent exchange passed between them: a snap of a wrist, a returned nod. Three shadows retreated through a nearby door, leaving behind only the mystery of their departure. Gretchen's companion remained; his stare fixed hard on Davis's approach.

Davis continued toward the menacing figure without pause. He navigated through the group until he stood before him. Justin, his face sneering, was a beacon of danger, making a promise of violence.

His voice ascended over the music, adding a formidable baritone dissonance. "Dude! What are you doing here?"

Davis squared his shoulders and stood the ground he had claimed. He casually placed his soda on the piano, noticing the condensation sticking to the bottle like tiny beads of sweat.

His voice was calm, controlled, arrogant, and respectful. He had an image to maintain. Trashy was not an option. "Nothing, man. I need to talk to Gretchen, that's all."

Justin's reaction was sharp enough to cut steel. He positioned himself as a rampart between Davis and the exit. It was a physical dare for him to test his fortitude with a challenge. "I think it's pretty clear she doesn't want to talk to you." He moved closer, fearlessly. The stench of beer on his breath was appalling. "Haven't you done enough... man?" A dismissive chuckle escaped him. He leaned over Davis, their noses almost touching. "I'll give you this, Kickball. You've got some serious brass balls showing up here. Nobody wants you here. In case you haven't noticed." The threat festered heavier than the smoke curling from the corners of the room.

Davis paused for a moment and noticed the room's attention before mentally accepting the challenge. Anger twisted his face into something ugly. His jaw tightened. His knuckles ached. His hands clenched into fists. He braced himself for a fight. But Justin merely stared at him with amusement, unshaken. He had anticipated the response.

Before Davis could move, a firm grip was clamped around his neck, yanking him off of the floor. Breath whooshed from his lungs as Justin's face, just inches away from his, returned to a formidable snarl.

The music filling the house with a vibrant rhythm, died abruptly. It was replaced by the hushed amazement of the guests. Their faces were a sea of judgmental stares, amusement, confusion, and awe.

"You aren't her boyfriend, prick," Justin yelled, slicing through the silence. He shook Davis like a rag. "Who does it look like she's with, huh? You're making everyone uncomfortable, dickhead." Davis's eyes darted around the room, catching glimpses of everyone he had ever known looking on in disbelief. Justin, enjoying the spotlight, leaned in closer, his voice dripping with menace. "Who invited you? Don't make me kill you in front of everyone."

The scene was already a social murder with evidence permanently drawn onto the stunned faces of the witnessing guests.

Davis couldn't register a response before he was airborne, crashing with force onto floor and sliding across it. The impact of the cold tiles jarred him to his core. His embarrassment burned hotter than his anger. He scrambled to his feet, sinew screaming in protest. His eyes locked onto Justin as he slowly began to exit the room to rejoin his party.

Davis's urge to chase him, to retaliate, was immense, but the impulse quickly died. A second defeat would be catastrophic. Instead, he stood frozen, watching with derision.

Justin paused at the door. His voice echoed across the room, ushering a scathing finality to the night. "I suggest you get the fuck out of here," he spat. It was another promise. "I dare you to talk to her again. Quit stalking her. She showed me your texts, psycho. Get lost!" A scoff, the slam of the door, and then nothing. The deafened room became full of empty. Davis was alone in public. The weight of this realization was heavier than the humiliation he had experienced.

"Where's Travis?" he called his voice a crack against the conversations rebuilding around him. He felt discord hardening in his jaw, like a dam against his rising panic. You will not cry, he repeated silently, the words a mantra against the encroaching fear of further emasculation.

As if nothing had occurred, the music swelled again. A youthful wave of sound enveloped him. The crowd, a jumble of adolescent indifference, resumed its activity without exception.

His eyes searched the room. No Travis. No Macy. A cold sweat slicked his palms. He pushed through the group, cutting a swathe through the careless partygoers. "Have you seen Travis?" he asked different attendees repeatedly as he moved. The hopelessness in his voice was barely heard against the throbbing music. He was met with shrugs, averted gazes, and polite dismissals. The room became a pool of vile dread.

He reached the double doors and called Travis's name twice. It was a pointless challenge against the music. Everyone around him remained absorbed in their own worlds; their faces offered no solace.

Defeat finally settled on him. The feeling was unfamiliar and frightening. The front door creaked open, guided by his shaking hands. No one noticed him leaving. The cool night infiltrated the warmth of the room. Davis stepped onto the porch and gently closed the door with a deafening click of the latch. Now bathed in cool moonlit air, he realized his world had been shattered. His unshed tears, a reservoir of suppressed frustration, finally broke free.

Rivers traced paths across his tanned skin. His controlled emotions collapsed into the harsh representation of a heartbroken boy. Travis's absence taunted him in a quiet reproach to his own helplessness. He was mortified. "I should never have come," he whispered to no one.

Davis dragged his feet, each step a slow, stubborn intrusion on the packed earth between himself and Travis's van. The moos of the cows, a comforting tradition only an hour ago, felt meaningless. The sounds were dissonant notes in the vacuum that existed between him and his destination. He called out, a low call from the pit of his stomach, "Travis?" The name remained suspended, frozen by the vastness of the field. He called again, the second attempt lacking even a pretense of optimism.

He already knew. He knew. The van, parked sadly by the barn, seemed to be miles from the house. Davis felt relieved to reach a sanctuary. He enthusiastically pulled at the door. The handle was cold and unyielding... and... locked. He slammed his fist against the van's roof. The dull thud echoed in emptiness. A resentful laugh moved through him. It was cut short by the undulating wrecking ball in his chest. "Of course it is!" he muttered, his words lost in a sigh. His head slumped as he sank to the ground. The hard earth provided a cold comfort for his body. He simply sat on the ground and stared at his hands, preferring to simply watch his fingers bend. He needed a break from trying to figure out what had just happened.

He thought about Travis, who was likely having the time of his life with Macy. Scenarios circled like wolves in his mind's eye. It was a grim realization of his solitude. The overarching feeling of abandonment in this desolate place suddenly became real.

Chapter 24: An Unlikely Savior

The humiliation of the evening seared. Davis leaned against the cool metal of Travis's van, the music from the mansion now a dull throb behind him. The echo of Justin's words still rang in his ears. The night air offered no relief for the churn in his stomach. Questions looped rapidly through his mind, each one a fresh stab. He indulged in his contemplation until a sound interrupted his thoughts.

A latch clinked from a short distance beside him. The suspended barn door groaned on its wheels like a wounded beast. Davis's head lolled upwards. He wasn't asleep, not really. He was trapped in a murky, half-conscious swamp of thought.

"Day? That you?" Zack's voice, rough as bark, broke through his lucid dream. Davis squinted, his dark hair falling across his forehead. Zack, a weirdly welcome presence against the barn's steel wall, grinned with his grubby hand outstretched. He smelled of sweat, hay, and something pungent: weed, probably. The gesture felt both patronizing and condescending, precisely the kind of thing Davis typically loathed about Zack. Zack's mullet, black and greasy under the barn light, seemed to vibrate with smugness. Davis felt a surge of irritation, but it quickly dissolved.

"Yeah," Davis rasped, his voice flat, his eyes fixed on his hands and then on Zack's unusually kind gesture. "Seen Travis?"

Zack's smile tightened. He stepped back, arms crossing his broad chest, his posture radiated aggressive nonchalance. "Nah." Davis's eyes, usually so sharp and confident, were dulled with exhaustion.

He mumbled, "I just wanna go home," into his lap. Zack's personality shifted. An expression of genuine concern momentarily eclipsed his arrogance. He dropped to the dusty ground beside Davis, his leg bumping the other teen's thigh.

"But you just fucking got here, man," Zack resolved, his voice softer now, almost compassionate. "Come on, hang with us. It got kind of lame in there, huh? The guys are just smoking weed and chilling." He clapped a hand on Davis's shoulder; the pressure felt oddly heavy, almost convincing.

Davis shook his head in a sharp, definitive motion. Zack leaned back, the movement revealing a glimpse of taut skin behind a faded band t-shirt. The slight tightening in his neck suggested increasing impatience. "What's wrong? You sick or something?" His eyes narrowed. He clearly did not like being refused.

Davis remained silent for a moment, staring at the dirt and gravel under him. His demeanor was completely absent in the moment. "Nah, man.", he sighed. "You know I don't smoke. I just need to wait for Travis. I wanna get outta here." He paused, "Crappy night. It's not your fault. I'm just... not feeling it."

Zack, a silhouette of broad shoulders and coiled rancher's strength, remained impassive, yet every line of his body provided a silent threat. Behind him, the barn loomed, a metal behemoth eclipsing the last light in the bruised purple of the night sky.

Zack rose to his feet and stood utterly still. His eyes scanned Davis like a predator for what seemed an eternity. Finally, he spoke. His words were delivered without emotion. His statement was a sheepish admission that seemed to originate from the very stillness of the night:

"Alright, I saw Travis... a couple of seconds ago. In there."

Davis began to protest suspiciously as Zack reluctantly pointed at the barn behind him. His eyes were narrowed with doubt.

Zack cut him off. A warm smile split his face. "He was hitting a blunt," Zack said with a coy chuckle. "I didn't want to break the news; you get all uptight about fucking pot." Zack turned and his voice rebounded off the corrugated metal: "Hey, Cy! Travis still in there? Travis, you around?" There was no response. He shrugged his shoulders and stared forward. "Sorry, Davis, we're high as fuck, that's all."

Cyrus eventually called back. His hesitant call from the barn's shadowed interior cut through the darkness: "Um... yeah. Travis... um... he's here. He was, uh... hitting the blunt right before I got up." Zack spread his arms wide, mimicking a bird taking flight, the gesture somehow conveying supreme confidence seasoned with amusement. He again offered his hand to Davis, "C'mon, don't bring the whole party down," he sang with the tone of a guilting mother.

Davis accepted Zack's hand and pulled himself to his feet, contrary to his better judgement. He peered into the barn's dim interior, then, in a gesture of booming authority, cupped his hands around his mouth. "Hey, Trav!" he bellowed.

Zack's laugh exploded before he swatted the makeshift megaphone from Davis's hands. "SHHHH!" he demanded. A controlled giggle shook his shoulders. "We ain't trying to move the party out here. Just... get in there." His eyes released the hint of entitled amusement he always carried. The faint smell of marijuana wafting through the open doors helped to support his story.

Davis watched Zack disappear through the opening and followed him in with hope. He stood in the doorway for a moment while his eyes adjusted. Davis recognized Matt and the two strangers from earlier, Corey and Thomas, sitting on a low stack of hay fashioned into a large square bench at the rear of the structure.

"Where's Travis?" Davis stage-whispered to the guys, not intending to stay any longer than necessary. A small butane fire pit cast a strange orange glow on their blank faces. Davis's eyes, deep brown and sharp in the gloom, landed on them. He leaned in with impatient resolve. "Where's Travis?" he repeated more firmly.

A flash of pale skin caught his peripheral vision. Peeking from behind a slatted wall, Cyrus emerged, completely naked again. The sight was so commonplace it barely registered surprise. Davis's head returned to Zack, who leaned against a tool rack, motioning him inside with a beckoning hand.

"Shut the door," Zack implored, his brown eyes glinting. "Were you born in a barn or something?" His calm voice, balanced with a casual sharpness, was as familiar as the smell of hay and manure.

Cyrus answered Davis with an annoyed whine, "He just went to take a piss." He stepped fully into the light, putting himself shamelessly on display. His eyes fixated on Zack for permission before he spoke. "Trav… Hurry up, man… pinch it off!" he barked over his shoulder. The command seemed oddly deferential.

The heavy barn doors slammed shut as Davis yanked them, metal teeth clicking with finality. He rolled his eyes.

He turned around. Then, a fist. A blurry streak of skin smashed into his jaw. The world exploded in a burst of pain, shortly followed by the sickening thud of his body hitting the packed earth floor. Two figures, Corey and Thomas, emerged from the shadows, leaping over him as though it was a choreographed dance. Their sprints were as swift and precise as bullets, landing like cats in front of the exit. The strangers became a barrier to escape.

"What are you doing?" Davis groaned in blind confusion. Zack's hair framed a face that burned with anger. He crouched, his slit eyes pinned Davis to the ground.

"Shut the fuck up, rapist," Zack demanded. His composure was chillingly calm. "You picked the wrong family to fuck with."

Davis tried to speak the word "What?" but a strangled grasp stole the question from him. Another blow landed: a brutal kick to the face. Stars exploded behind his eyes as his neck snapped back. The pain shouldn't have been this numbing or cavernous.

Zack, now a dark mass looming above, seemed to have the strength of a god. Davis saw the fire blazing in him and felt true fear clawing at his throat. The word rapist circled in his head. It became a twister intensifying the confusion behind his attack.

Chapter 25: Prologue to a Nightmare

Hay pricked Davis's cheek. It was sharp against his skin. Blurred shapes swam in his vision. The dusty brown of the dirt flecked with needle shards of hay, and the faded blue of Zack's jeans clouded his sight. The menacing gleam of a boot sole imprinted on his jaw felt almost visible. The disco beat of blood-filled bruises, discoloring his young skin, pulsed. Each movement of his swelling face was a dull thunder in his ears, distorting the muffled sound of Zack's voice.

Davis mumbled, "I didn't…" The whisper felt lost. It was masked by the ringing in his head. Doubt moved in his gut. Had he even spoken? Was this a hallucination from the undefined edges of grief?

The hay smelled faintly of sunbaked earth and sweat. Zack's face slowly came into focus. It wasn't the misty, spectral menace of a moment ago. Instead, it was a sharp, cruel caricature. The sixteen-year-old's face reflected danger. Black hair cascaded over his brow, making him look feral.

The imposing figure paced erratically. His muscles were convulsing under his shirt. Davis tried to speak again. This time, the words were clearer. A risky plea originated from his very essence. "I didn't..." Zack's reaction was empty. He stepped closer without speaking. The smell of leather and something vaguely animalistic clung to him.

"I'm just fucking with you," he sneered, his voice seething with disrespect. His hand brushed against the handle of the hunting knife fastened to his belt. The habitual gesture spoke volumes. His words were constructed of the cruelty of someone who'd never faced real consequences. His tone was condemning. Zack paused. "Or maybe not," he added. A sinister smile directed his intention. He then crouched until his breath was hot on Davis's face. The smell of cannabis clashed sharply with the scent of iron and dirt.

Zack maintained a chilling monotone. His expression was a grimace that underscored blank eyes, the color of mud. "You did it, Davis. You fucking did it." Each word was a pronounced sentence. He firmly pressed his index finger against Davis's bleeding mouth. The pressure was excruciating. "I dropped you off at your... shitty house. And you raped her. You used me to get her there."

Davis's breath stopped. Panic dug its way outward from his center. An atrocious, silent scream was trapped in his mouth behind Zack's touch. He tried to speak, to deny it, but only a strained gurgle materialized. His deep brown eyes stared widely. Zack swayed casually as he leaned even closer. His dense breath filled Davis's ear.

"Shh... Tonight, it's an eye for an eye. Me and the boys... we're gonna take your ass, man... rape you like you did my cousin." Zack laughed menacingly as he stood up. The firelight glinted off the steel in his gaze. He was a sixteen-year-old rich kid with a rancher's build, but he held the composure of something far older... and far more dangerous.

"Now," Zack said before pausing. He gestured toward the dark, shadowy mass of hay bales in the corner. "You can man up and walk over there... or we can do this another way. Makes no difference to me." He waited; an ugly patience had settled on his face. His attention poured on Davis's darting eyes, then dropped to the young man's trembling hands.

It was a direct threat, a challenge Davis had no option but to take. He contemplated his options from the dirt floor. His silence was punctuated only by the rhythmic drip of his own blood falling from his mouth to the surface below him. Zack slowly stood back and motioned a path toward the hay bales with an outstretched arm and waited patiently for a decision.

Davis saw it all in a horrifying flash: Cyrus's blatant nakedness; Zack's unsettlingly calm demeanor; and the bold-faced lie about Travis. It was all a perfectly rigged trap. His heart hammered a wild, turbulent tempo. His eyes flew across the room. Focus landed on a rack of tools: shovel, pickaxe, pitchfork. He slowly rose to his feet but didn't accept Zack's invitation.

Instead, he leapt across the room to save himself. His trembling fist closed around a long pitchfork's rough-hewn handle. The tines scraped against the packed dirt floor, producing a sound reminiscent of nails ripping through canvas.

A guttural roar erupted from his throat. He swung the pitchfork with the force of a broadsword, skillfully aiming for Zack's throat. Zack barely moved. He gingerly stepped aside with the grace of a seasoned fighter. The weapon missed its mark and barely grazed his side, tearing a shallow gash. Red blooms blossomed on Zack's shirt. Tiny, angry polka dots appeared on the torn fabric.

Davis froze, doubled over with frenzied breaths. He was a gladiator awaiting his execution. Zack, unfazed, examined his wound with a bored glance.

"You're gonna have to do better than that, boy," he said flatly. The words dropped slowly like cotton. He laughed toward the others with a low, menacing sound that echoed in the barn's confines. "Looks like we got ourselves a fighter… good."

Corey and Thomas advanced toward him. Davis lunged and swung. The pitchfork whistled but didn't make contact. A crushing blow pulverized his head from behind. Strong arms clamped around his neck. He couldn't breathe.

The pitchfork was ripped from his hands. Another blow, this time to the stomach, returned him to the dusty floor, knocking the wind out of him. The boys' steel fists and hard boots pummeled him like hail. Through the pain, Davis heard Zack's voice, crisp and authoritative: "Kick his ass!"

He tried to scream, to protest, to explain. "Just let me go! I didn't do it! It's a lie! I only… I only had girls on my phone…" his effort was lost in gasps between waves of abuse. Darkness threatened the edges of his vision. He felt the crushing weight of their violence, the searing hurt, and the certainty that this night would be his last.

Travis was nowhere to be seen. The satisfied face of Zack, illuminated by dim light, remained central. Davis curled into a protective ball and screamed as he weathered one assault after another until he was bereft of sound.

Zack's sudden blast, a powerful "Stop!" seemed to disrupt time. The world compressed. The thumping and thudding sounds ceased. Davis was left abandoned with his racing heart. Swollen eyes, blurred with tears and the physical reminder of his beating, registered the approach of heavy boots on the packed dirt floor.

Zack hovered for a moment before squatting, a hulking shadow in the gloom of the barn. His fists roughly tugged Davis's blood-soaked hair, forcing his head up. Oil-slick black eyes bored into his. A disappointed stare consumed Zack's face, revealing teeth just a little too sharp. "Had enough, bitch?"

Davis spat. A discolored spray of saliva arced high and landed squarely in the center of Zack's oppressive sneer. "FUCK YOU! I didn't do it! I swear I didn't!" Denial clawed its way out followed by an irrational emotion of guilt for the forbidden word he used. Hot tears streamed down his face. They were a mixture of humiliation, fear, and a gut-wrenching desperation that stole the oxygen from his lungs.

Zack wiped the blood from his face with the back of his hand. His movement was a jerky, almost manic swipe. His body trembled. A growl slowly built from within him. "You need to cry, bitch. You spat in my fucking face!" He shook Davis's head violently; his grip was like a vise. The words were a battle cry assaulting the corrugated steel walls until they rumbled. The shock on the faces of his friends momentarily abated the brewing storm.

Suddenly, he remembered his audience and composed himself. He spoke behind a cruel, childish laugh. "He spat in my face? This is a badass bitch here. Isn't it?" His attention returned to Davis. His eyes narrowed, and a satisfied glow appeared. "You think you're a badass, bitch?" The world tilted with the question. The floor unexpectedly began to move under Davis as Zack dragged him backward by his hair, a slick rope in Zack's grasp.

The floor was cold and hard under his body as he was moved through the barn. His scalp burned hotter with every step, but he could do nothing. A chilling calmness had settled over Zack: an icy nothingness that was far more terrifying than the animated rage he stifled. Davis's screams, ragged and broken, bounced off the metal walls, each syllable an indication of his helplessness.

The soccer star's athletic frame was a broken vessel, completely overwhelmed by the young rancher's brutal strength. The rich kid's sneer was a testament to the ferocity of his determination.

Zack towed his dead weight to the towering bales in the back of the barn. Davis's struggles, frantic thrashings of limbs, only slowed the procession and increased his pain.

With perspiration beaded on Zack's brow, He turned and dropped his prisoner. His gaze fixed on the others, "What the fuck are you jokers doing? Get him up there! On his feet! MOVE!"

Matt, his face pale beneath his dark hair, swallowed hard. Unanticipated fear vibrated in his voice. "Zack, this is fucked up. I think…"

Zack cut him off with a scoff. "Do you think I give a shit what you think? Get him over there!" Matt and Corey obediently pulled him from the floor and held the boy upright. Davis, eyes swollen half-closed, fought back weakly. It was useless. His constitution had been decimated.

Zack's fist, a blur of motion, struck Davis's diaphragm with another sickening thud. He went down hard, face-planting onto the hay platform, his legs dangling precariously over the edge, and his toes barely scraping the floor. He attempted to scramble up, a feeble effort against the intensity of the blow, before slumping back into a broken heap of flesh.

Matt's voice, a choked whisper, cut through the abstruse silence. "Zack, man, you said we were just gonna scare him, maybe rough him up a little."

Zack chuckled, a sound absent of humor. "He's scared, alright. Trust me, he is scared. Just do what you're told. You're in this now."

He barked at Cyrus. The hulking figure emerged from the shadows of the barn. His obscenely muscular body was formidable.

Zack commanded, "Cy, hold him down!"

Davis could do nothing but wait. His vision continued to blur as Cyrus pinned him down, blocking out the light, and settling onto his back hard. The weight was crushing. The hay flattened under them, pushing sharp stalks deeper into Davis's skin. His breath became more labored. The suffocating feeling was lessened by the intense heat from Cyrus's nude body pressing against his battered trunk.

Davis's arms flailed helplessly underneath the immovable force. Cyrus crushed him harder until he lay still and his eyes stared blankly at Zack between the blades of hay under him.

He was kneeling, again. His face inches from Davis's. He contemptuously disregarded him. This time, there were no games. The victor postured with a sadistic display of triumph.

Matt whispered. A terrified expression dominated his face. "Is he dead?"

Chapter 26: Dead, Not Dead, Dead

"No, Nimrod," Zack drawled. His voice was a low, flat whisper devoid of any warmth: "He's not dead." He nodded curtly to Cyrus with a silent command. Cyrus grinned, revealing a flash of bright teeth. He then yanked Davis's hair in obedience. A groan ripped from Davis's swollen lips like that of a tortured animal. Zack's assessing stare pinned Davis. "Are you, rapist?" Tears, hot and fast, streamed down Davis's cheeks, carving clean paths through the grime on his skin.

"I didn't do anything! You know me! I swear!" His voice cracked. Desperation defined each disregarded plea. "Please believe me!"

Zack shook his head slowly; disappointment etched into his sharp features. "But you did, rapist. She wouldn't lie about that. You raped her. You know you did. You did it." He paused. A cruel smirk played on his lips. "She has no reason to lie, but you do. Don't you? You do because you're fucked…" A controlled giggle emerged before he continued, "Well, almost fucked, anyway." A long silence stretched, broken only by the rustling of hay.

Then, Zack's voice changed. A sugary sweetness coated his words as he offered an option. "Tell you what," he said casually with a glint of something hopeful in his brown eyes,

"Admit it, and we might go easy on you." Davis stared at him with disbelief. Zack leaned closer. His voice was gentle and influential. "Go on. Say it." Cyrus released Davis's hair, letting his head fall back onto the hay with a thud.

Davis lay still, his breath ragged. The seconds stretched into an eternity. Then, a sudden surge of energy engulfed him. He bucked and twisted to free himself from Cyrus's iron grip. He wrestled and fought, but it was pointless. He knew it but didn't care. He was overpowered. Cyrus and Zack erupted in laughter while the others looked on nervously. The sounds of the boys' sadism were echoing through the barn, cruelly and triumphantly. Davis's endurance eventually weakened, and his strength drained away.

Cyrus's body slid across Davis's sweat and blood-slicked jersey. The hay was mercilessly scratching at his broken body through the fabric, producing involuntary groans of pain with the slightest shift. The whimpers pouring from him were crude and muddled.

"I... I didn't... Please, believe me..." His voice cracked, choked by a sob that tore through all of his defenses. Terror, clear and genuine, owned him. Zack's temporary satisfaction evaporated. In its place was a pointed fury that emitted fire.

His eyes locked onto Davis as he interrogated him more, "Is that what Gretchen said? 'Please don't...'"

The words were delivered in staccato bursts. Each syllable dripped with unalterable judgment. He savored the tremor in Davis's eyes, relishing how his prisoner's glances darted away and back again. The sweat beading on his forehead felt like vindication. A cruel rage enveloped Zack's expression, revealing the spoiled, entitled monster beneath the surface. Zack stepped away and began to pace. The rhythmic thud of his boots echoed the frantic rush of Davis's blood. The other boys watched in silence. Their eyes shifted with fearful uncertainty.

"Well?" Zack demanded, his voice a growl. Only restrained gasps answered him. He glared through Davis. "That's fine, then." He paused, letting the anticipatory silence build with asphyxiating dread.

"Matt?" The called name was a whiplash, causing Davis to flinch violently with repeated shudders convulsing his body. Zack's finger, thick and strong, jabbed forward, a steel rod pointing directly at his target. "Get his fucking pants down!"

A scream ripped from Davis's throat. The sound echoed off of the metal of the barn's walls. He thrashed. A renewed burst of adrenaline momentarily overrode his exhaustion.

Cyrus erupted into another fit of laughter, mimicking the bucking of a mechanical bull on Davis's back. He refused to be unseated. He made exaggerated rodeo sounds in a grotesque mockery of the terror unfolding beneath him. Cyrus was enjoying this. Zack had his own agenda.

Matt stood frozen, paralyzed by fear. Zack's patience snapped. "MATT!" he shouted again, the sound a thunderclap that shattered the twisted display. He approached the boy and slammed into him with a firm shoulder, sending him sprawling to the barn floor.

"I SAID, GET... HIS... FUCKING... PANTS... DOWN!" His voice carried an authoritative urgency. Every word was a divine command. Matt struggled to his feet with fear and indecision painted across his face. Zack's eyes continued to blaze with violent energy. The sight of Matt's hesitation ignited a dangerous spark. "Fuck it," Zack snarled, "Fuck it, I'll do it myself." "Get out of the way," he barked as he shoved him aside.

Zack was an unhinged force in the barn. His words were built upon a foundation of chaotic intensity. Davis's screams for help went unanswered as Zack reached for his waist, deftly avoiding the powerful kicks from Davis's legs. With a swift movement, Zack unfastened the boy's jeans, along with his underwear, and aggressively rasped them down the thickness of his soccer-trained thighs until both were tightly pooled around his ankles. The fabric was then crushed under Zack's foot, pinning his victim's feet to the floor in a direct and physical display of total dominance.

Davis's vulnerability lay hopelessly exposed. Zack wasted no time, administering a series of sharp slaps that cracked through the space. Cyrus whooped with delight. His laughter filled the air as Davis screamed and fought the stinging whacks that left red, then purple, handprints on his skin. Zack showed no sign of stopping. His taunts were relentless. Each strike was designed to humiliate and break Davis's spirit. The lashing beat at Davis's already battered psyche.

The barn fell silent, with the exception of Davis's labored shrieks and Cyrus's occasional snicker. Zack stood tall, his eyes cold and unblinking, surveying his abuse with sinister satisfaction. Davis, once proud and strong, now lay defeated. His body heaved with the effort of his futile struggle.

The quiet in the barn was broken only by Davis's agony. Zack's mood continued to darken. He stepped closer. His eyes were firmly fixed on Davis's exposed form. With a swift motion, he gripped the flesh of Davis's backside, spreading the muscles until chills of panic raced over his captive's body. A powerful groan built in Davis's throat, but it was swiftly silenced by Cyrus, who forced something into his open mouth. A sock? He pressed it firmly against the cut flesh of his lips. The room became a tomb as Zack waited patiently for the noise to subside. His eyes never diverted from Davis, who had fallen silent. With a nod from his leader, Cyrus removed the gag, and Zack's breath washed over Davis's skin, an unwelcome caress.

"Well, well, well," Zack purred. His eyes gleamed with malicious enjoyment. "What do we have here?" His eyes roamed over Davis's body, taking in every detail with a sense of ownership. "Lookie here, boys. Looks like we got ourselves a virgin." Davis felt the sting of every eye examining his shame. "Look at the tight little pussy."

He paused, his eyes narrowing. "Shaved, Even?... Nice!" His voice turned accusatory as if Davis's personal grooming choices were further evidence of his guilt.

"You a virgin, bitch?" he demanded, his voice became harsh and emasculating. Davis, paralyzed by fear and shame, could only focus on the hay beneath him, praying for this nightmare to end. Another sharp slap to his bruised flesh shattered all hope.

The pained cry that escaped him was met with another beating, this time from Cyrus, who joined in with glee. "He's talking to you!" Cyrus chided, his eyes alight with cruel authority, "Answer him!"

Zack's voice was a menacing growl. Davis knew that any resistance or denial would only prolong his torment. Sobs of dread and fear wracked his body. A quaking tremor began in his feet and raced to his skull, ravaging him. Tears blurred the harsh lines of his sight.

"No... yes," he choked out, the words swallowed by fresh bursts of grief. "I... I mean..." His presence, usually radiating a potent, almost unstoppable magnetism, was crumpled and broken. "Please... don't... rape... me." His response was a strangled gasp, punctuated by the shuddering collapse of his composure. Then, from the shadows behind him, came a voice with a chilling casualness. Zack's. The entire world was weighted with his looming presence. He cleared his throat and spat a slow, thick stream of saliva. It stretched from his lips and landed with a sickening splat on Davis's back. The hot liquid seemed to burn his flesh.

"Good," Zack continued. His voice dripped with a seductive sweetness. "They say you always remember your first time the most." The coldness of the liquid seeping between Davis's spread legs intensified the fire of humiliation that engulfed him. It triggered a wave of primal fear as he felt it was running closer and closer to its goal. This wasn't a joke. This wasn't Zack's usual bravado and posturing.

This was real. The terror ignited a surge of energy. The cocky swagger, the volatile edge, the inherent self-belief; all roared back, fueled purely by a need for survival.

Davis lashed out, his muscular body exploded with a furious energy that defied his earlier helplessness. He fought with the desperation of a cornered animal. The strength from finally realizing the seriousness of the game he'd found himself playing emerged.

Zack just smirked, with a hint of something akin to respect showing briefly in his eyes. He was enjoying the fight. The power. The control.

This wasn't about sex at all. It was payback. He had an obligation to his cousin to destroy her rapist's image and break him down. There was also a need to demonstrate the reach of the Randall family's power. The only path for both was this brutal confrontation. The resolution laid before him was far more significant than simple dominance.

Davis's eyes, wide with a terror, rasped, "Wait... stop... Wait... please." His voice became a choked whisper and cracked like chalk. He provided a boy's Hail Mary to save himself from the losing game. He needed to strategize.

He would bargain. Davis's plea was a grave croak, "Okay... okay. I'll suck you. All of you. I'll swallow... everything." His tears indemnified his sincerity. His offer was met not with action but with the chilling weight of appraisal. Doubt tightened its grip on the faces of the young men surrounding him. His body trembled with a vulnerability that revealed his deepest fear. He scanned their faces, searching for a sliver of mercy before he collapsed into a broken wail of inconsolable sobs, "Please... please... don't... don't rape me, man."

A meek voice sliced through the tension. Matt, his face pale as bone china, spoke with a trembling breath. "This... this isn't what we... we agreed to." He paused and glanced at Davis with pity in his eyes before appealing to the others. He searched for an ally, a lifeline. Instead, he only found indifference in their stares. He bolted like a gust through the space, toward the freedom of the field beyond. The barn doors slammed open before him. He passed through without any intention to look back.

Zack screamed after him, "Matt! You fucking say anything, and I swear to God, I'll kill you. I'll fucking kill you. You're on my fucking list!" His voice was rife with power and unadulterated conviction. He stood frozen with contempt. He became a barely controlled animal poised to strike. He clenched his fists, and his dark eyes burned.

Within moments, the sound of a vehicle door slamming, followed by the sudden screech of tires, was heard. The bluster of a truck accelerating away cut through the expectancy. A slow, toothy smile spread across Zack's face. He crossed the barn and confidently closed the doors. They groaned with surrender under his powerful hands. He stared at Davis with intent before turning to his accomplices. All but Cyrus were aghast with shock. Zack casually leaned against the door.

"See?" he said with conviction. His voice was dangerously smooth. "Bye-bye, Matt. We're good." He adjusted his jeans with a subtle, almost unconscious gesture, hinting at the monstrous reality of his penis. He absorbed confidence and exuded threat by nature. His dominance in every situation enabled him to thrive. To Davis, fright was the only emotion he could identify. Bravado did not exist.

Chapter 27: Rebirth

Davis watched Zack's casual return with gut-churning dread. Cyrus, a hulking behemoth of a man, pressed obediently onto his back, a silently bound proof of Zack's absolute power and influence. Davis's own failure to escape was a weight pressing down on his pride, an onerous cover woven from threads of fear and humiliation.

A pathetically weak hope had ignited when Matt, the bookish misfit, had seemed to offer a lifeboat. That hope, now extinguished, left behind only victimhood. He was trapped, utterly at the mercy of a boy who reveled in his suffering. Zack was a boy who wouldn't even hear his screams, a boy who'd never known the true experience of anything close to the agonizing helplessness that now consumed Davis.

A foreshadowing clang sliced through the silence as Zack rummaged through a crate near the butane fire, its orange glow painting the barn in flickering shadows. "Aha," he breathed. The object he pulled out, a cattle brand, sent a wave of nausea crashing over Davis. The world became smaller. The barn dissolved into a blurry haze as Zack casually placed the brand into the fire, the metal screaming under the heat. Davis's eyes were fixed on the encircled "R" at the brand's head, a searing symbol of Zack's callous dominance. The metal shifted in slow motion from dull grey to searing orange, then a blinding white.

Suddenly, Zack's face appeared inches from Davis's, blocking out everything else. He was kneeling before him, pointing at the fire. The intensity of his hatred could burn holes through stone. "See that? Hot... isn't it?" Zack's voice, a flat monotone, complemented the chilling silence. He didn't wait for a response; his words were defined by a tone of certainty. "You're done screaming. I'm serious. Do you understand me, boy?" The threat stuck to Davis's soul. Zack's glare locked onto Davis's surrender, leaving him no room for escape, no hope for rescue. This was a declaration of a war Zack had already won. Davis nodded his head with resigned affirmation. Hay continued to puncture his skin, rough against his exposed body. There was no fight left in him.

"Please, don't hurt me," Davis begged with a reverent whisper, the words a rasp of desperation against the overwhelming dread of what he knew was coming to him. His voice was dead, brittle, and pathetic.

Zack mirrored Davis's flat tone. "Admit it," he demanded, the words smooth as polished stone. His voice, even at his young age, carried heavy influence. "What you did."

"Zack, I swear, I didn't rape her. You know me," Davis choked out his defense between shallow breaths. Each inhalation was a struggle against the significant weight on his back and the growing knot in his throat. He fought the ripples of terror churning within him as he hoped for mercy, understanding, or both.

Zack's response was a slow, exasperated drawl. He held a demeanor as cold and cruel as a judge delivering a death sentence. "That was your last chance." He stood. His movements were languid yet charged with menace. The denim of his jeans labored against his powerful thighs as he peeled them down, revealing the monstrous length of his flaccid penis. A sadistic grunt emanated from his lungs, a predatory sound that sent icy tendrils down Davis's spine.

He'd seen Zack's gift many times before, the infamous porn star dick, but always in the spirit of a game to feed his ego. Never like this. Never as a chilling, deliberate threat.

Zack gripped his mammoth appendage, its veins protruding as he handled it. With cruel pleasure, he waved and slapped it repeatedly against Davis's face. Its thick shaft assaulted his cheek with more and more force as it became more engorged. The degradation continued, punctuated by his aggressor's menacing laughter. Zack then slowly guided the bulbous head to Davis's trembling mouth, gently tracing the outline of his lower lip. The glide of smooth skin sent a shiver of disgust and fear through Davis.

He smelled the musk of Zack's sweat, the cloying sweetness of his cologne, a sickening exclamation point to the unseasoned terror seizing him. Zack's laughter created a chilling sound that redefined the confined space.

"You said you wanted this instead?" he teased, almost singing while the others watched. Davis buried his face in the coarse hay; the scratchy texture was a small comfort compared to the horror unfolding.

He could feel Zack's hot breath on his neck above him. The words, "Come on, buddy. Open up and say ahhh…" were a grotesque misrepresentation of childhood coercion. Zack's voice, usually aggressive, was dangerously soft. "You need to wake him up," Zack continued, a manic glint in his eye, "He's sleeping. Be careful, though! He gets really angry when you wake him the wrong way."

Davis remained still. This isn't real was a frantic mantra cycling through his mind. The phrase was a feeble attempt to cling to some assemblance of reality amidst the encroaching nightmare. His limbs flexed and contorted rapidly. The disobedience he displayed was a dangerous cocktail that threatened to destroy him.

Zack snarled at Cyrus. "Hold his fucking head up, asshole!"

Cyrus, whose boyish giggle contradicted his brute strength, obeyed with a booming laugh. "This is fucked up, dude," he wheezed with a hint of something more than amusement coloring his voice.

Davis stared blankly ahead with a mixture of terror and something analogous to… forfeiture. Zack's burgeoning erection stood before him in the dim light. Just do it, Davis convinced himself. A single, almost inaudible "Ahh" escaped Davis's barely parted lips, choked back by a sob.

Zack, grinning from the dopamine-high of absolute power, grasped Davis's chin to pull his mouth open wider before offering a demonstration. It was a dramatic and sick impersonation of a motivational speaker. His tongue, thick and pink, slithered out, covered with saliva. "AAAAAH! Come on, bitch. Open up real wide! You gotta try harder. You gotta make some room. This motherfucker's big," he roared. His loud voice vibrated the hay bales beneath Davis's pinned body. Zack's fingers caressed the boy's cheek, sending chills down his spine. "C'mon, boy. Get that tongue out. AHHHHHHH!"

Davis produced a fibrous, primal "AHHHHH" from his throat as he obeyed. Three dirty fingers, powerful and invasive, plunged into his gaping mouth and slowly turned like a key to extend his jaw fully. Zack's voice was constructed of hyperbolic condescension.

"Now that's more like it... nice and wide... Tell us all how bad you want to suck this big dick and swallow my big load." The pressure intensified with the rough texture of Zack's fingers tickling Davis's tongue. It was an agonizing catalyst for the acid in the back of his throat. His tongue, straining to its limits, tasted of his own blood. He pushed himself harder, driven by a perversion of fear and a need to... to what? Serve his unjust sentence? He didn't know. "AHHHH," he repeated with his tongue pushing beneath the intrusive hand blocking his mouth.

"That's right... good boy! Do you want it, bitch?" Zack's voice was a nail driven into Davis's fragile composure, ending his thoughts.

Davis's head shook violently, a silent battle raging in his eyes. "No! No! No, I don't! You know I don't! Just get it over with!" He snorted before defiantly meeting Zack's eyes. His look was direct and absolute. One final, agonizing "AHHHHH" forced from deep in his lungs. His body trembled with exertion. The idea of his own fear clung to him, mingling with the musty aroma of the barn. Even Cyrus, usually so eager to please Zack, looked away; his face became a mask of uneasy curiosity.

The breath paused in Davis's throat, a strangled gasp as he witnessed Zack's massive shadow slowly retreating without delivering on his threat. He waited for Zack to say, I'm just fucking with you, but it never came. Nothing was making sense.

The sight of Zack pulling on his jeans, concealing the throbbing phallus that had moments before dominated Davis's vision, sent a fresh wave of ice-cold terror through him. Oh God, I messed up, he thought, the words tormenting him.

Zack's voice, complete with bored disdain, sliced at him. The dismissive wave accompanying them only served to amplify the degradation. He gave an order. "Corey, fill his tank."

Corey, his face a flurry of bewildered confusion, hesitated. Then, Zack's outcry shattered the silence with a command that vibrated through Davis's very bones. It rattled the steel barn walls like a struck gong. "DO IT! FUCK HIM! NOW!"

Corey's eyes, wide and terrified, mirrored Davis's own growing panic. His hands, trembling, fumbled with his belt, his pants collapsing in a heap at his feet.

The searing touch of Corey's calloused fingers on his skin ignited a primal scream of defiance in Davis. He writhed, he thrashed, screaming in protest as he fought with a ferociousness that surprised even himself.

His voice, full of consternation, humiliated him as he begged. "Yes! Yes! I want it! I want it so bad!" Tears returned to his cheeks, blurring his vision as he gasped. The choked confession ripped from his soul, "I swear... I want... to suck all your big dicks..." He opened his mouth repeatedly and extended his tongue, "AAAAAH!"

The sting of Zack's slap to the face sent fiery stars behind Davis's eyes. He then moved with animalistic intent toward the fire. The iron, glowing an infernal orange, became an extension of his cruel purpose. Davis's heart battered him, a frantic drumbeat against the unnerving muteness that descended when Zack disappeared from view. The only sounds were the crackling fire and the frantic pounding of his own pulse. His universe became the dancing flames in the butane pit.

Zack's voice, low and chillingly calm, broke the silence. "I said you were done being loud." His tone, shifting seamlessly from enraged violence to bored, clinical detachment, was an alarming transition. "Problem is," he mouthed, the words barely a whisper, "if you're asking for it, it ain't rape, is it, faggot?" Before Davis could even process the logic, the white-hot iron seared into the flesh of his buttock, the burning agony eclipsing every other sensation. A shriek tore from Davis's throat, a primal scream that defined both terror and pain.

The smell of burning flesh filled the barn. Zack's laughter, a cruel, triumphant howl, began as a solitary subjugation. It soon mingled with the others, who followed his lead obediently.

Cyrus released him, leaving him crumpled. He collapsed from the dais onto the dirt floor. Pain and humiliation drove him to want to soak completely into it. The laughter surrounding him, a morbid symphony of his utter defeat, was haunting. This assault had left the eighteen-year-old shattered, both physically and emotionally. The star athlete was bested by the arrogant, entitled power of a sixteen-year-old.

A scarlet, bleeding bloom on Davis's raw ass pulsed with each ragged breath as he hauled himself upright. He winced as he forced his jeans over his swollen wounds. His body, usually taut with seamless excellence, was a disaster of bruises and blood. Each crippled step was a searing agony, carrying him toward the door; the sounds from his attackers followed him like a death knell.

"Davis? You in there?" Travis's voice, a light in the blinding darkness, cut through the cacophony. Travis's call held a grim urgency. He had always been the structure to Davis's volatile chaos. Even Travis's unflappable demeanor was frayed.

Escape and a very real need to survive fueled Davis's violent rush. He fumbled with the door latch, the cold metal bit into his trembling fingers. It wrenched open, and he threw himself through the doorway, landing face-first in the dirt. He crawled past Travis and made his way to the van. He held firmly to the door handle with a scream tearing from his throat. "Help me!

They're going to kill me!" A cry from his tormented soul echoed in the starry, silent night.

Travis didn't hesitate. Guilt, a cold fist clenching his heart, fought with the ingrained loyalty that bound him to his friend. The burning stench that followed Davis out didn't matter. He didn't question it. He quickly opened the door and shoved Davis into the seat. The impact of his force elicited another agonizing sound from Davis's ravaged lungs.

From the doorway, Zack watched, unmoved, with chilling amusement. "We were never gonna rape you, rapist!" he called after them, his voice a gravel-laced taunt. "You're marked, motherfucker! Marked with an R! I want you to say something... I really do. I want a reason to finish the job, bitch. Run, rapist, run!"

The image of Zack's enormous penis flashed before Davis's eyes as he listened to his threats. As the van lurched away, the scene shrank in the rearview mirror. Travis was overwhelmed by waves of guilt. *He told me no. I made him come here.*

He watched Davis, broken. A sobbing mess on the floorboard next to him. The compulsion to know, to understand the unspeakable horrors that had just transpired, was a screaming riddle in his mind. He didn't ask. He didn't need to. Instead, he placed a gentle hand on Davis's head. His own tears blurred his vision as they drove away.

Chapter 28: The Morning After

The kitchen timer ticked, each second a rifle shot against Ellen's skull. Thirty-seven years old, but fine lines around her sapphire eyes spoke of a life far older, one lived in the shadow of her son's destruction. Her dark brown hair was unruly, mirroring the chaos inside her. Davis, her Davis, lay sprawled on the couch like a discarded rag doll. He was a crude representation of the boy she'd known only yesterday. His stillness was more frightening than any temper tantrum he'd ever thrown; he was catatonic.

The word tore at her soul. It defined the helplessness she'd felt since Travis brought him home. She hadn't slept. Sleep was a luxury she couldn't afford. She couldn't justify rest at all, while her son was slowly dissolving before her eyes. Every maternal impulse screamed at her to cradle him or to offer reassurances. Her efforts were met with dismissal and were devoid of emotion. He refused to tell her anything. The fear of her own inadequacy paralyzed her and rendered her helpless.

She had always been the fixer, the one who smoothed over the rough patches of his life. She had made it her mission to rescue him from the consequences of his choices. A crippling fear of failure had fueled her compassionate habit. Now, she was drowning in the wreckage of her good intentions. He was hurting, and he wouldn't let her in. She wrestled with the question of whether it had been for her son or herself.

He was unrecognizable; the vibrant spark in his eyes had been extinguished. It was replaced by a horrifying emptiness that exemplified the cavernous hollowness, also consuming her. The urgency in the room was a toxin, slowly poisoning everything around her. She pretended to do housework to stay close to him. The feather duster became a pathetic weapon against the invisible enemy that had claimed her son. The television sat in darkness. Its black reflection was a physical representation of her life.

Any minor change in position produced a suppressed groan from her son. Even then, he wouldn't look at her. The sound sent jolts of agonizing need through her. Ellen, with a perception only a mother can possess, acutely felt the pain radiating from her son into her own body. A sour, burning acid was blistering her flesh.

The urge to rush to him, to pull him into her arms and somehow erase the brutal damage inflicted upon him, remained strong. She knew better than to act on it again. It was the deep yearning that tore at her. It hurt her that he wanted none of her compassion. What if he did, she thought. Would she fix this, too? Would he ever tell her what this is? Would she again engage in the behavior that was systematically destroying him? Why was he alienating her? The questions continued. None were answered. Waves of self-deprecation coursed through her veins.

The floorboards groaned beneath her weight, a mournful surrogate for her despair. The only thing she was certain of was the throbbing, pulsing helplessness inside her. She reminded herself that everything was going to be fine in an effort not to burst into tears again. Was it, though? Was anything going to be alright?

The scratch in her throat felt like sandpaper. "Davis?" she whispered. His previous reactions to her made saying his name feel like a felony. He didn't answer. He didn't even acknowledge that she had spoken. He just sat there, a broken statue, picturesque even in his ruin.

His tall frame slumped over the arm of the sofa. His athletic grace was all but gone. It was replaced by a desolate nothingness that chilled her to the bone.

"Please," she choked out, the plea catching in her raw throat, "Tell me what happened. Tell your mama." She reached for him instinctively. It was an overpowering maternal need to touch him, yearning to feel the warmth of his skin. She hoped that if he allowed her gesture of compassion, it might somehow break through the wall he had built around himself.

He did not. Instead, he flinched away from her with a violent recoil that sent a fresh wave of agony over her. The rejection slammed her growing insecurity against the brutal reality that he had shut her out. She begged, "Please, Davis, I've called everyone," she etched through tears she could no longer contain, "Travis, even. No one knows anything." Hope fluttered within her when he finally turned his head so his eyes met hers. Just as quickly, they made their way back to his lap. He faded back into the abyss of vacancy.

Panic overwhelmed her rationality. She grasped at straws. "Is it drugs? Did you do something… illegal?" His eyes rolled with a sign of disdain in their depths. Normally, she would have scolded him, but now, the subtle shift in his expression was a lifeline. She, at least, had evidence of a connection. Something. Anything. She resisted reaching for him. Her hands were trembling as she prayed for guidance.

"We can help you, Davis," she said sincerely. He stared at her for a moment with a long, soul-crushing glare, nested in lifeless apathy. The indifferent bleakness in his eyes was killing her. This was behavior she had never seen.

"No one can help me," he whispered behind a forced breath. There was no movement until his father's shadow fell across the room. A quiet, somber presence followed it in. Max's return only deepened the anguish. Ellen stood motionless as Max settled beside their son. The horrific replay of the last sixteen hours, the gut-wrenching silence, the chilling emptiness of Davis's lethargy was evident to both of them as they sat helplessly and watched him… and waited.

Ellen felt as though she was hosting a stranger in her home. Her eyes, usually bright with a fierce love for her son, were clouded with gloom so profound it threatened to end her. She felt the accusations of her own failures rising in protest against her. She questioned whether she was somehow stealing her son's pain and somehow twisting it to become her own cross to bear. She contemplated whether her concern was about him or about seeking her own validation. The creak of the front door cut her introspection short.

"Did we figure anything out?" Max's voice was roughened with the harshness of the restless night. He had just returned from speaking with the police. Nothing. Ellen simply shook her head. Her hands fluttered before her. She wrung them in an uncontrollable gesture of defeat. She glanced at Davis to draw her husband's attention. Her towering athlete sat slumped to one side in a heap. His confident energy was muted. She had gotten nowhere with him while Max had been gone.

"He won't tell me anything," she whispered. She felt choked by a mixture of exhaustion and a love that felt blinding. Max offered his hand, calloused from years of hard work. She took it eagerly. His touch was gentle yet urgent. She needed him.

"Just… come clean, kid." He addressed Davis with understanding and frustration. "Whatever it is, we can handle it." The dismissive wave of his hand, an attempt at confidence, felt pathetically inadequate against the intensity of his fear. His son did not reply. The silence stretched taut. The only sound was the low hum of the refrigerator, a mechanical heartbeat in the tense quiet. "Do you understand, buddy?" Max's voice cracked. "We're on your side. No matter what." But even as he spoke, doubt was consuming him. Could they really handle whatever storm his son was hiding? His charismatic, damaged boy seemed determined to drown them all in this colossal shipwreck.

Davis's attention, dark and shadowed, finally fell on them. Ellen felt another flicker of hope. These moments had briefly blazed in arcs throughout the night, only to be resolved by emptiness.

His words, tight and brittle, scraped against the silence. "I said it was nothing. A stupid fight. Over nothing. I am sick and tired of talking about it."

Ellen pressed on. "Nothing? Travis dropped you off, beaten to a pulp. Is that a friend? How can you be so... tired of it when you haven't said a thing about it? We need answers, Davis. We can see the blood, the bruises..."

Davis's jaw tightened. The muscles in his face spasmed with deep-seated anger. "I told Travis to leave it alone!" he ground out, the words tight as a tourniquet. "He wasn't even there. He just drove me home." Davis played with his fingers, the purple bloom of bruises blossoming across his knuckles, mirroring the darkening storm in his eyes. "Why are you calling my friends, anyway? Stirring up crap? I want to forget about it, okay?" The "Okay?" was a choked whisper that shattered into a carnivorous yell. The carefully built dam of his control burst.

Ellen watched helplessly as he fought himself from the sofa and to his feet. A groan of pain rushed from his lips. The sharp crack of his back rumbled like an earthquake as he laboriously stood. The sound represented the shattering of his mother's composure. He stumbled toward his room without looking back.

Ellen looked to Max for help. She saw a reflection of her own fear on his face. He simply looked back at her with distant eyes. The inability to reach Davis was clearly a shared failure. She watched as Davis slowly navigated the hall. His limp produced a sickening sway in his gait. It was disturbing. His strong stature was marred, ravaged by a fight... or something else.

Max intervened with worry drawn deeply in the lines of his handsome, squared jaw. He called after Davis without approaching him. "You sure you're okay? Something may be broken. Come here and let me see your leg."

Davis's angry snarl instantly sliced back at him. "Forget it," he fertilized the poisoned words with contempt. His voice was hoarse and fortified with pain. "I'm friggin' eighteen. I think I would know if something was broken. In case you didn't notice, I took an ass-whooping last night. Do you think I might be embarrassed? Leave me alone!" His bedroom door slammed behind him. The force of it shook the foundation of the house. The muffled moans of pain that followed tore at Ellen's heart. She saw the tremor in his powerful shoulders. Her perfect, damaged boy was breaking.

A repressed, agonizing cry forced its way through her. It wasn't only his pain; it was hers as well. She had always been his balm, patching him up, preventing him from experiencing the lessons of failure. This time, however, the crushing realization that she had failed him blocked her view of her boy. Tears stung Ellen's eyes, blurring the already indistinct lines of the hallway. She felt the familiar tightening in her shoulders, the brutal grip of regret closing in. Max's hand gripped hers more tightly than before. A weak smile of appreciation formed on her lips as she looked at him.

His touch was both reassuring and strangely inadequate. "I don't know what to do," she whispered. "I'm not letting him leave this house until he tells me what's going on." Max's dark eyes held hers captive. Understanding and weariness battled inside him. He pulled her close in a tight embrace. His arms were strong and warm. She felt safe, yet his protection failed to reach her. His reassuring hold was somehow not comforting. It felt like nothing more than a diversion. His arms were a paper shield against an unknown storm. Max knew, as she did, that the pain in the back bedroom was far more profound than a fractured bone.

Chapter 29: The Hollow Boy

Davis glared at his bedroom's pine door. The tension built within him made it appear to vibrate the longer he focused on it. Relief washed over him when the drone of his parents' questions ceased. He slumped onto his bed with an accompanying groan. The antiseptic-soaked gauze rubbed against his raw left hip. Fire shot up his spine. It was a searing pain that jolted to the top of his skull before racing back down his left leg. Even the slightest movement ignited fresh agony in every inch of his skin. He flopped onto the bed, landing on his stomach. The simple act of moving was a torturous exercise of endurance. He clamped down on the tears that threatened to spill with every passing second.

He had endured many injuries in his lifetime. This wound was a different category of hurt. He surveyed the space of his room. It had always been an inspiring haven of posters and trophies which celebrated his achievements. It suddenly felt meaningless, almost hostile. He didn't feel like the space was his. The jarring smell of antiseptic canceled the comforting familiarity of his environment. He closed his eyes and prayed for sleep to dull his pain. He longed for a temporary escape through dreams. The constant burning sensation drove all hope of respite away.

Zack's face swam into his mind continuously. His dark demeanor, his lifeless brown eyes, and the sadistic, arrogant smirk took turns pursuing him. The memory of Zack's words spat out with casual cruelty also refused to leave his mind. He heard them behind every thought, "I'm just fucking with you," he'd sneer. He seemed to be next to him. Davis knew better, but knowledge did not lessen his suffering. A cold dread engulfed him. True fear returned with the repetition of every threat. Had Zack really meant it? Would he finish the job if Davis told anyone? He was not going to risk it.

The thought of Zack's retaliation and his ridiculously oversized… Davis cut himself off. He had to find a way to stop thinking about it. The ruminated taunts about his "little dick," the boasts about Zack's "porn star" cock; claims confirmed in a vivid living nightmare weren't harmless humor anymore. They were intrusive traumas which only served to rekindle the flames of fear that were ignited.

He would no longer think about Zack's swagger, his smirk, or the way his gang of rancher buddies bent to his will. It was all a darker motivation for control, kept strong with the understanding that he and his family owned the town. In the events of one night, Davis realized that no one disputed the notion and that none of it ever was a game.

Davis's soccer career overshadowed everything. Ten days until practice. Ten days until his dream of being somebody was scheduled to arrive. He would leave this small pond. The entire town could evaporate afterward, for all he cared. Last night felt like the ending of any remaining ties. He had to focus on healing and moving on.

The agonizing pain and betrayal fueled by the mere thought of Zack having the power to permanently derail his future, chased the physical pain away for a moment. Davis clenched his fist. The sharp stab in his back from the tension diminished the pressure in his mind. A knock on his door interrupted him. The sound of knuckles against wood were feather-light, yet they sparked an inferno in him.

His voice pushed out of him, demonstrating his simmering rage. "I said, leave me alone!" A hesitant response cut through the silence of the room. It wasn't his parents.

"Day? It's me. Can I come in?" The door opened slightly without waiting for a response. Travis's silhouette framed the entry. His friend's bright green eyes met his, followed by an uncomfortable, sympathetic smile.

Davis conceded with a curt, "Yeah, fine." His veiled agreement produced a physical tremor, barely perceivable. Travis approached with quiet confidence. He gingerly settled onto the edge of the bed beside his buddy. The consideration he demonstrated with each action spoke volumes. "You doing okay? You alright?" His voice was soft and was a reassuring anchor in the stormy ocean swirling around them.

Davis's laughter was brittle. "Yeah. Great. Look at me. Can't you tell? I'm peachy." Insincere levity coated each word that fell from his mouth.

Travis's compassion held a reassuring intensity that challenged his guilt. He studied Davis, searching, weighing, considering whether to broach the subject of the previous night. Davis knew this look, and concern washed over him. Travis's grief, a laser beam honed by seventeen years of soccer fields and hard-won victories, pinned Davis to the bed.

He stared at his best friend stoically before speaking, "People are saying some bad shit about you, man," Travis said. His tone was nothing less than a threatening whisper. The word "rapist" was unspoken but implied. Davis saw the contemplation reflected in Travis's features and appreciated the thoughtful, but obvious, omission.

Davis's pulse increased to a hurried rhythm. His blood boiled in his veins. "It's not true," he insisted, his voice a pathetic whisper. The topic brought back the memory of the preceding night.

Travis leaned closer, "I know it's not true, but she's saying it is, man. You gotta talk to her. Make her understand." The earnestness in Travis's voice was a hard shove. The honesty battered at Davis's protective walls.

Davis scoffed, a bitter laugh escaping his lips. "Screw it. It'll blow over. She's... she's with someone else now. Besides, I can't... I can't even talk to her, anyway."

The words twisted like a serrated hunting knife into his every muscle. The gossip enraged him. He loved her with a fierce, possessive grip, which controlled him. He could never believe that this started with her. Earning back Gretchen's acceptance was a constant throb beneath the charade of indifference he showed to everyone else.

Travis's hand rose to his chin. "Dude, you don't get it. This isn't going to go away by itself. She isn't playing around. This is your life. You need to fix this shit now." Davis flinched at the memory of Travis's last attempt at "help." His friend's insistence on attending the party in the first place was a well-intended but disastrous intervention.

The thought was a fresh wound he didn't want to open but had to. "Yeah, well, your advice worked out great last time, didn't it? Look at me? Just… drop it, okay?" His voice was stifled by a despair that was as much more self-directed as it was aimed at his friend. The words were bullets. The young men stared at each other. An awkwardness developed, each of them grappling with the strained search for a smooth escape from their guilt.

The sudden ringing of Davis's phone ended the churns. Travis grabbed it from the nightstand. His eyes instantly narrowed. "Speak of the devil," he murmured.

Davis snatched the phone like a need. He pressed it to his ear, his long fingers trembling slightly. Gretchen's voice, a honeyed sound, filled his head. "Hey… look… I can't talk long. I'm just… worried you might want to do something stupid. You aren't going to put Zack in jail, are you?"

Davis stared forward in disbelief. There was no sympathy for him, no "Are you okay", no "I'm so sorry". Travis eavesdropped with an unabashed transparency; disbelief also carving into him. He could actually feel the tension radiating from Davis. His friend's life-force was laid bare.

Davis's voice cracked slightly. "No. Never. Only Travis knows. Can we talk? Meet... somewhere? I miss you so much." He was despondent, pleading for anything she might offer.

Travis whispered with condemnation, "Davis... are you crazy?"

A sigh, dense with relief for her cousin, reached Davis through the phone. "Maybe later. This... the phone is best right now." The short coldness in her voice was a numbing slap. Davis's forced calm disintegrated into a pile of ash.

The question flowed naturally from him, unversed and impulsive, "Why did you tell people that?"

Gretchen's tone became a confrontation. "What did I supposedly tell people, Day? That you raped me? I said it because it's the truth." Her statements stung like wasp attacks.

Davis's body tensed; the color drained from his face. His heart was a drumroll. Travis's hand closed on his shoulder. He gave a silent instruction to end the conversation. Davis could only sit frozen, stunned.

Gretchen's voice, edged with annoyance, cut through his grief. "Are you there? Is that Travis? Look, Day, if you're too busy to talk to me, I can hang up." The phone felt like a weapon in his hand. It was a conduit for a statement that was both devastating and utterly untrue. Davis's torso pressed into his mattress, guided by the weight of the experience. He simply stared at the phone clutched in his trembling hand.

Travis, a muffled thunder from the other end, fought for dominance against her disgusting sound. He waved his arms and mouthed instructions. He felt like a ghost. He appeared to not exist.

"When... when did this happen?" Davis's voice cracked. Travis's agitated pleas for him to hang up were increasing beside him, demanding to be noticed.

Gretchen's offended laughter, sharp and brittle as shattered glass, continued. "Which time, you mean?" Her speech was a brutal condemnation. "I Should have seen this coming, you know?" she sneered, her innocent facade crumbling. "Just... go away." Davis's jaw clenched. He ran his fingers across the bed in front of him. His nervous gesture was an indication of the turmoil within.

"What do you want me to say? It's not true. You know it's not true!" His voice rose... fearfully.

Gretchen's response was a slow, deliberate exhale. A cruel testament played in her voice. "No remorse, Day? Shocking." She paused, the silence, punctuated only by Travis's frustrated mutterings in the background. Finally, cold as winter ice, she pierced the silence. "Got nothing else to say?"

Davis's eyes darted to Travis for help. He sputtered, the words choked with disbelief, "What?... Are you asking me to apologize or something?" The question, rhetorical, slid from him.

Gretchen became gentler. Compassion leaked through her harsh expectations. "It would be a start," she pouted, a caress against the raw nerve she hit in him earlier. "A start to fixing this... getting back to normal. I do love you, Day. But this... this is tearing me apart.".

Davis leaned into his bed, the fabric of his comforter cool against his skin, "How does apologizing for something I didn't do magically fix things?" he asked incredulously. His words were, unexpectedly, sharp as razors. Anger burned in his every nerve and he took control. "I didn't rape you. Never. Once."

Travis flinched. He'd seen Davis unravel before, but this was different, unsettling, dangerous. He intervened so she could hear him. He needed to save his friend from a danger he saw coming. "She's definitely Crazy, Davis. Hang up. Just hang up. That's a crazy bitch"

Gretchen's sweetness shattered. A guttural thunder encroached on the exchange. "Tell Travis I'll show him crazy," she snarled. Her voice, previously melodic, was now a weapon. "Tell him to say that to my face. I heard him, you lying sack of shit. You don't get to decide if I was raped, Day. The victim gets to say. I was the one who was raped. I know. Fuck you! And fuck you both! I'm done. Don't. Ever. Call me again!" The line went dead. She was gone. Davis stared blankly at his phone, his face the color of bone. Gretchen had eaten through him, leaving only a notched carcass.

"She hung up," he said to Travis with bewilderment. A grimace pulled at his split lips, stretching across his face, encouraging a fresh shine of blood to emerge. "She gets to decide? After everything? I was there, Travis! I was there!" He started typing, fingers blurring across the screen, each tap was a punch of redemption. A calculated text, unripe and incandescent, blazed across the screen.

He read it aloud with an invigorated energy, wrapped in a blanket of terrifying calm: "Okay, Gretch, I'm sorry I 'raped' you. Does that make you happy? Does that make it all better?"

Travis lurched and complained outwardly as he unsuccessfully grappled for the phone. "Stop, Day. Just Stop." Davis defended the interception. Travis's face displayed absolute fear. "Did you... actually just say that?" he stuttered, his voice full of disbelief that vibrated in Davis's ears. The question lingered like smoke.

Davis laughed inappropriately, a harsh, brittle sound. "'Raped,' Trav... In quotes. Sarcasm, man. I'm not putting up with her lies. Look at me, dude." Travis complied with silent reluctance as his friend clarified his purpose. "She caused it. This... this is insane."

It was of no solace. Travis felt a cold dread creep into his bones. He felt instant nausea, a churning wave of revulsion. "Day... I don't think you should have done that," he said, his voice strained. His good-natured support was barely hiding his panic.

A text alert, again, invaded the room. Davis commanded the phone with a vengeful gleam in his eyes. He read the message, his face twisting into a mask of sardonic triumph. "See? I got her hooked. She can't help herself."

He raced through the words, reading aloud Gretchen's reply in a piercing falsetto: "Of course I'm not happy. You think that makes it better? Never talk to me again. I hate you. I will never be better." His fingers elegantly danced a tango across the screen. His movement was oddly graceful, a macabre ballet of destruction. "Every boyfriend you've ever had can't rape you, babe! I hope that jerk you're with rapes you too. How many times has he raped you already, Gretch?" His responses were arrows poisoned with Davis's own truth. They were directed at her heart.

Another alert. Davis's breath wavered. His eyes were dark pools of rage. "I'm blocking you, never contact me again.", he read, Then, the dam broke. His face, an unstoppable fury, contorted. His ears burned hot. The veins in his neck pulsed like angry worms. Adrenaline, sharp and bitter, flooded his system. The disabling pain from his battered body, fueled his fire. Suddenly, he felt none of it.

He leaped to his feet, a roar ripping from his throat – a primal scream of death and heartbreak – "ARGGGGHHHHHHH!" He hurled the phone against the wall, shattering it into a thousand pieces. Plastic and glass rained in the bedroom. It was a brutal metaphor for the destruction within him. Travis dodged the flying debris with genuine fear. He saw, in the wreckage of the phone, the fractured representation of his friend's life.

"Davis! Chill out, man!" he shouted with unbridled concern. He knew, with a chilling certainty, that this was only the beginning. He knew the man in front of him. The striking, athletic, damaged Davis was unraveling.

Gretchen, with her innocent approach and calculating mind, had pulled the first thread. He had always sensed something about her that slowed his blood. Travis called to Davis with a repeated "Chill out man!" The door splintered inward, slamming into the wall of the chaotic bedroom behind the sheer force of Ellen and Max's combined passion.

Ellen screamed a high-pitched shriek that ricocheted through the core of the chaos unfolding in her home. "What in God's name is happening here?!"

Davis remained frozen, mesmerized by something wild and broken in his eyes. His tall frame slumped, radiating a fragility that somehow supported his inherent strength. Max, a force of nature in his own right, a carbon copy of his son, stepped forward.

His voice boomed a rumbling bass that shook the very foundation of the home. "Knock it off, Davis! Stop this now!" The unmistakable order reverberated. It was a verbal counter-assault that sent tremors through the already tense room.

Davis toppled, collapsing onto the bed in a heap, his body wracked with tremors. A sob stole from his throat. Adrenaline that had fueled his reckless abandon was finally spent, leaving him incapacitated. The harsh light of the room reflected the sheen of sweat on his skin, highlighting every sharp angle of his bone structure, every muscle. His body was tense with the aftermath of his ordeal.

Ellen advanced on Davis like prey. Her blue eyes were engulfed in untamable flames. "No one leaves this room," she roared at the very edge of her breaking point. Raw emotion and absolute exhaustion had finally broken her control. "Not until I understand exactly what the heck is going on. This... craziness... it's over! I've had enough of cleaning up your messes, Davis! Enough!" The finality simmering beneath her fury was undulating. It was a chilling emulsion of her unshakable love and utter fatigue.

Years of enabling his self-destructive tendencies had finally reached its omega. Her internal fear of failure, of losing him entirely, abandoned her. The exit of a lifetime of guilt was as powerful as the silence that followed her outburst. For the first time ever, she felt empowered by the energy of everyone's full attention.

Chapter 30: Metamorphosis

Gretchen re-read the text messages from Davis. An intense anger was burning in her stomach. How could he deny her experiences and cheapen her? He knew her history, the years of trauma reinforcing walls built around her fragile heart. He'd reached out with such understanding. He had been a bandage for her wounded soul.

The reflection staring back at her from the small desk mirror in front of her wasn't the naive face she presented to the world. It was a stranger, a calculating creature she barely recognized.

Travis's words echoed in her mind. Maybe she really was a crazy bitch. The thought dug deeply. It planted a seed of doubt in the fertile ground of her insecurity. Was it possible? Was she the architect of her own misery?

Ethan?... Davis? Were they merely reacting to some inherent flaw within her? The idea was repulsive to her. It was a betrayal of her self-worth, a surrender of an agency she refused to accept. At the same time, a chilling possibility gnawed at her, demanding anxious contemplation. She had manipulated situations before. She had used her appearance and charm to get what she wanted.

Had she pushed Davis too far? Had she inadvertently provoked his coercion? This question pounded at her, pitting her careful image of self against a terrifying suggestion. She clung to the truth of her experiences. It was her shield against the common social expectation of owning culpability for an unprovoked act of covert violence against her.

Internal conflict was mounting in her thoughts. It was lodging accusations against her she couldn't ignore. Davis, with his insecurity and damaged soul, shared many of her own vulnerabilities. Seeing him as her antagonist felt increasingly hollow. Perhaps their combined pain was inextricably linked, a disaster of their own making.

Then, Travis's face dominated her mind, sharp and clear. He was always a comforting presence, even though he was her polar opposite. She knew he would disapprove of her holding Davis accountable, of making him regret his callous words and actions. She also understood it had nothing to do with him.

It might seem manipulative and cruel to anyone else, but the need to control the situation was overwhelming. He had hurt her. Tricked her. Lied to her. He had taken advantage of her. He alone made his choices. She also made hers. She had come to regret her foolishness deeply.

Any regret she may have had felt like a price worth paying. It was a necessary alternative to the cost of staying silent. A growing voice whispered to her that perhaps, just perhaps, Travis was right. The possibility briefly caught her off guard and made her question herself.

No, she confirmed, Travis couldn't be right. She continued to assess herself through her reflection. The light from her vanity caught the devastation in her eyes. Returning to her phone, she paused once more to process Davis's apology. His passive dismissal of her assault was heart-wrenching.

The memory of the violations and their brutal, degrading aftermath devastated her. How could this happen to her again? Tears, mixed with mascara, stained her face. Davis basically called her a whore. How dare he?

An ember of retribution tugged at her. She should be angry. She was entitled to be, damn it! Davis was a bastard, a user, a rapist. He turned out to be a monster. But... a sliver of doubt softened the fury. Davis: attractive, athletic, impossibly tall... Davis, with his disarming smile and the way he could make her laugh until her sides ached... Davis, who was also insecure, damaged, fiercely needing validation. The image of him, vulnerable and weeping filled her with sadness.

Travis's words, his consistent support for his friend, wouldn't leave her. He had witnessed the same messages, the same apologies, the same sickening lies. She heard his reactions. He advocated for Davis. He announced openly that she was crazy. He obviously made a terrible mistake arising from his own deep-seated problems.

Travis was right about some things, at least. He knew the Davis, who was kind, funny, and fiercely loyal. He knew the Davis who was also intensely fragile, covering his own pain with bravado. The monster and the man, within the same body, he knew them both.

Her options pulled her in different directions. Should she report him to the authorities? Expose him?

The memory of Davis's tears, his broken apologies, and his pleas for forgiveness resonated with her own lifelong insecurity and strong need for connection. This knowledge weighed heavier than justice. For just a moment, she told herself to avoid facing the terrifying truth: She would be protecting a rapist if she remained silent. Protecting a man who had stolen a part of her, out of the fear of shame, placed every other woman in his path in a dangerous position. Deep down, she knew what she had to do. It cut her deeply. Her image taunted her with disgrace.

She sat there twice violated, twice... by boys lauded as pillars of the community, boys whose smiles had concealed an evil darkness. She discounted the notion that the physical assault was the most damaging. It wasn't. It was the insidious erosion of her self-worth, the whispering doubt that maybe, just maybe, she had somehow deserved to be the victim of the crimes that haunted her.

That thought slithered around her throat. Was it even about her, or was it about fearing the reactions of those around her? The attention made her feel dirty. She had always prided herself on her strength and integrity. Yet the insurmountable self-doubt gnawed at the foundations of those beliefs.

The thought of reporting him, of exposing his depravity, paralyzed her. What if they didn't believe her? What if she was proven to be a liar, a troublemaker? The fear of further humiliation from accusations surrounding revictimization was a cold hand gripping her heart.

She lost her composure, her strong wall of survival shattered. Her nails tore at her skin. She attempted to erase the marks, the memories, the shame. She was Helen of Troy, but instead of launching a thousand ships, she felt she was destined to be wrecked on the rocks of her own damage. The red trails on her face blurred into angry welts. Her melancholy sobs turned into angry wails. How could she exorcise the demons? What if the demons weren't inside her but were a twisted revelation of who she was?

The reality presented was cruel: report the man and risk everything, or bury the trauma and silently succumb to the self-hate that was beginning to consume her? There was no question. She knew, with a chilling certainty, that choosing silence would be a betrayal of the countless other women who had suffered in silence. Although the thought of this awful, destructive decision filled her with regret, the fear of doing nothing was stronger.

Until this moment, guilt gnawed at her. She hadn't asked Zack to retaliate against Davis. She would never have done that. She would never wish such pain on anyone… or so she'd believed. Zack, her fiercely loyal, terrifying cousin, had defended her. She was inextricably bound to protect him, even if it meant compromising her own morals. That's why she'd reached out to Davis: to ensure Zack wouldn't face the consequences of his actions, requested or not. She had no intention of bringing up the assault. Davis was the one who broached it.

After talking with him, her regret shattered. It splintered into a thousand jagged pieces scattered around her. Her current state was his fault. He forced her hand. His fate rested not only with his actions but also with his brazen disregard for accountability. A burning contempt for Davis was now real, undeniable, an alien force that consumed the passive innocence she once held. Davis deserved it. He deserved the humiliation, the public exposure. He deserved to feel the crushing weight of the betrayal, the abuse, the destruction he'd wrought.

Confiding in only Zack, of all people, had felt safe, like a no-lose gamble at first, but not now. She'd chosen him because he was the only one who seemed to even vaguely understand the bond that drew her to Davis, the effortlessly charming, golden boy who could crush her with a look, let alone a hand.

"Being a victim ends now," she announced to the empty room. She became a victorious warrior, a girl unmarked and untouchable. The antagonist wasn't some external force; it had been the chilling familiarity of her own past, whispering shameful doubts. This newfound strength, this energy, demanded a price. To truly escape the shadow of her victimhood, she had to confront the man who had inflicted it through his biggest passion, social judgment.

The purpose inside her screamed for retribution, a brutal, satisfying end to her quiet suffering. The hot pink welts bisecting her face throbbed a dull rhythm against the pulse in her temples.

Her hair, tangled like a battlefield, fell around her face. This wasn't merely the end of passive acceptance; it was the gut-wrenching, bone-jarring reclamation of a life violently stolen. The dignity she wore was now a superhuman shield, forged in the fires of her humiliations, each one a motivating rung on the ladder of self-respect.

Her fingers, trembling, tightened around the metal of her car keys, a solid link to the future she would seize. With a power that duplicated the storm brewing inside, she slammed her driver's side door shut. The sound of it echoed the war cry of a girl who had spent her life fighting for survival and who now, finally, was ready to unleash hell. This was about becoming an army instead of waiting for one.

The chipped paint hanging off the siding on Britney's porch swayed gently in the breeze. Gretchen, manic and swollen, stood on the step, her eyes fixed on the door. Britney flung it open before Gretchen even knocked. Her greeting was a gasp. Her hand flew to her mouth at the sight before her. The next moment, Gretchen was engulfed in her arms, sobbing.

"Oh my God, Gretchen," Britney whispered, her voice trembling, "Tell me everything." Gretchen, with her delicate features, told her story with controlled grief. It was a different tale from the one she had told at the party about a simple breakup.

The real story was revealed in a rush of painful words. Each moment that passed carried a shameful weight. Britney supported her with unconditional love. Fifteen minutes later, they were hurtling down the highway in Britney's cherry-red convertible, eventually screeching to a halt in front of Cher's sprawling Victorian house.

An ornately carved door opened a crack, revealing Cher's bored expression. Her lips were painted a garish shade of ruby red. But then she saw Gretchen. The goth chick's costumed apathy evaporated like morning mist. Her face softened, pulling the visitors inside with instinctual words of comfort.

From there, the three girls drove to Irene's office building, a sleek glass tower that gleamed under the afternoon sun. Inside, Irene, a vision of professionalism in a crisp white pantsuit, waited behind a minimalist desk. There was a sharp intake of breath upon their arrival. Her daughter sprinted to her and fell into her arms.

"Gretchen," Irene reassured, "We're going to handle this, honey. I'm so sorry this happened again." There was a sacred, but unspoken, understanding between the four women. A silent pact sealed the shared gravity which pulled differently within each of them.

Gretchen would not relive her experience again, not like she did with Ethan. This time, she had the support she needed. She was no longer afraid. A dark butterfly emerged.

Chapter 31: Full Circle

The worn sofa cushions sank under Davis's weight. He watched his mother from the corner of his eye. She had been pretending to clean the living room for the past hour. A sitcom blared; it was a discordant symphony of canned laughter that bounced off the cream-colored walls. Davis barely registered it. Instead, his attention was fixed on the phone clutched in one hand as he rapidly scrolled through social media posts with the other.

It had been four months since the attack that promised to shatter him. Four months of his mother's hovering before there was a shift.

He felt a phantom jolt of pain in his hip, a twitch under his jeans. It was a frequent, recurring memory of the autumn in the barn. He moved nervously; the sofa momentarily creaked a protest under him. Physical pain from his attack was all but an occasional dull ache now, a remote echo. The flashbacks, however, were excruciating. He sat silently and breathed until the moment passed.

The scar, a jagged R that created a depressed channel in his skin, was the only physical evidence of the worst night of his life. The problem was that it called to him daily. Sometimes, fear overtook him, and he was incapacitated. Other times, it was simply a passing fog, a sticky morning dew that evaporated with the rising sun. He was handsome, even if damaged. He had only recently begun to accept this fact again. A smile brightened his face as he glanced at his follower count: 536,018. It was a long way from his goal, but in his small town, it felt like he was scaling Everest.

He tapped at the screen. His insecure side battled with newfound confidence. Ellen glanced in her son's direction, wearing a faint smile. It was a combination of pride and support for the progress he'd made over the past few months.

"Everything alright, sweetie?" she asked. Her voice was soft. Davis shrugged. A tint of vulnerability marked his face before he masked it with a confident smirk.

"Yeah, Mom. Just… making some moves." He didn't need to explain. She wouldn't understand anyway.

He'd learned the hard way to trust the quiet strength hidden beneath his mother's surface. He recognized the strength that had enabled her to finally let him go… mostly. Her decision to allow him to stumble and possibly fall was encouraging him to grow. He was finally learning to believe he could make it on his own. Growing up didn't seem to be so scary for him anymore.

"You ready, buddy?" Max's voice felt like a skipping record. Davis nodded his head meekly, the gesture weak and unconvincing, even to himself. Cold, clammy fear gripped him. He knew exactly what his father was referring to. Every inference of the Minotaurs' tryout sent a fresh wave of disappointment through him.

This wasn't a sore subject in and of itself. It was a festering wound, a constant, throbbing reminder of his nightmarish humbling that threatened to destroy him. It was also the source of a deep-seeded resentment. He'd already passed through tryouts two years ago. He was good, maybe even great. He had gotten an offer. Then it happened. If not for Gretchen, he'd be playing right now.

Her jealousy, her demands, her false promises of a future together had all led to this. The brand on his flesh was a permanent reminder of a night that had destroyed his dreams and left him with a shame he couldn't outrun. His recovery was a sentence.

He needed this chance, this redemption. The Minotaurs were his only hope of escaping the shadow of his past, of proving to himself that a single, catastrophic event couldn't define him. But the brand, a permanent tattoo on his ass, felt like a mark on his soul. How could he explain it to his team? There was absolutely no way they wouldn't see it.

The lie he considered about a fraternity initiation felt unbelievable, even as the story formed in his mind. He also knew nothing about fraternities, and the thought of his teammates' skeptical stares made him even more uncomfortable.

Dishonesty felt wrong, a betrayal of the integrity he was trying to rebuild. But the truth? That felt like self-destruction. It was a choice between two equally devastating failures. He thought about his reflection in his grandmother's mirror. His body and talent felt like jokes, glittering prizes tainted by his bad choices. Then, Gretchen's image forced its way into his mind. Why did this happen?

She'd spun a web of deceit, so intricate and perfect that he'd walked right into it, blinded by desire. He had once experienced a pathetic need for her love. He hated how often the memories still tormented him. She was a constant, unwelcome guest in the chambers of his heart.

His entire family had vowed never to speak her name out loud again. It was forbidden, an imposed exile, yet it seemed to have the opposite effect. This practice of avoidance only served to amplify her presence in his thoughts.

She had become a dragon, stronger in her absence. He feared her. It was a fear that went beyond the simple understanding that she was manipulative. Cold chills shot down his spine as he refocused on his phone and tried to clear his mind.

Three sharp, bold blows, like wrought iron striking wood, shattered the quiet. The sound screamed through the old oak door. His mother's eyes clouded with a sudden, chilling premonition. Her years hadn't prepared her for this. Her dark brown hair seemed to darken further in the dim hallway light.

Max's posture stiffened. He glanced at the front door's frosted glass; the faint, ethereal glow of streetlights outlined two figures. They were unmistakably uniformed. Blue and red strobes pulsed brightly outside the house, a silent, ominous heartbeat.

Davis, his handsomeness marred by a nervous tremor, felt a cold dread blooming like spring crocuses. It was irrational. He knew he had nothing to fear. His family was safe, wasn't it? Perhaps there was a neighborhood disturbance, or a simple misunderstanding.

Max casually opened the door to greet the officers standing stoically on his porch. The easygoing smile that he naturally wore rapidly faltered. The atmosphere teemed with a sudden, critical tension.

"We're sorry to bother you this late, sir," one officer said, his voice flat, devoid of warmth. "We need to speak with Davis Day. Is he here?"

Davis's heart sank. He moved toward his father with a slow, reluctant shuffle. The sound of each step echoed in his mother's mind. The officer's words pierced the fog of her panic: "...accused of rape..." The distinct ratchet of handcuffs interrupted the peace that had existed within the family before their arrival. The cold steel bit into Davis's wrists. He looked to his stunned parents for rescue. Instead, they only watched him helplessly.

Cold sweat slicked Davis's skin as his body was turned away. He was being led off. The colored lights painted the night an eerie violet. In the windows of neighboring houses, curious faces appeared, blurred by the harsh glare; their expressions were odd combinations of pity and judgment. The prodigy's world tilted. This couldn't be real. His mother's face, frozen in fear and disbelief, swam in his vision as he was shoved into the back of the waiting police car. The slam of the door was final.

The ride to the station was a blur of red and blue. The shattering bangs on the door that had started it all reverberated and replayed in Davis's mind. The interminable crawl into the caged back seat played in slow motion. Each second stretched, a rubber band threatening to snap. He was a wreck. His confidence, a shimmering armor, was shattered again.

The experience was an explosion no one was prepared for; the fallout was raining down on him months after the childish bomb of that night had detonated. Over time, he had somehow managed to calm the tremors, but dread now consumed him again.

He hadn't raped anyone. He knew he hadn't. Knowledge, once a comfort, felt like a paper lantern. The detective's arrival was an anticlimax. A tired, cynical slob of a man who smelled of eggs and urine slumped into the metal chair across from him. The scrape of its legs rasped on the concrete floor of the cold interview room.

No water, no cigarettes; the predictable props of a thousand cop dramas were absent. This was an execution. No real questions were asked. Pronouncements dominated the interaction. Each was a mark on Davis's already fragile composure.

The false facts presented as irrefutable truths chipped away at his defenses. Impenetrable silence between words amplified Davis's loss of faith. He was in a vacuum. He was already caught in a series of lies, but they were not his. Anxiety clamped around his spine; each vertebra was a ladder rung as his honesties were dismissed with a casual wave of the detective's hand.

The final play, a thud of a manila file folder on the steel table, was deafening. The detective's finger stabbed at a text transcript, the words leaping from the page and compressing the boy's airway: "I'm sorry I raped you."

The blood drained from Davis's face, leaving him pale and weak. Travis, his unfailingly pragmatic best friend, had been right. Again. The following events were a blur of indignity and humiliation: the photographs, the fingerprints, the brutal violation of being stripped naked, and his body subjected to detailed examination.

A fat cop's verbal indignation, hit home from behind him as he faced a cinderblock wall. He snickered at Davis's exposed skin, the boy forced to stand before him, spread eagle: "Nice R, boy wonder! Let's see if we can find the O. Bend over and spread 'em wide, boy. I'm sure it's hiding around there somewhere." The words burned into Davis's shame as he complied without pause, relegating the worst day of his life to a joke. "Lookie here, boys, we got us a virgin", he recalled, feeling the cool air hit him.

After a full body assessment, which seemed intentionally slow, a filthy jumpsuit that smelled of someone else's armpits was casually tossed to him. He instinctively caught it and forced it onto his body before being herded into a room defined by the stench of mildew.

It was a concrete box filled with men. The memory of the barn, the claustrophobia, and inescapable fear returned. He was back in a cage. This time, he was surrounded by strangers. His trust was irrevocably broken, but he refused to show it.

He was alone again. The distant and surreal echoes of Travis's voice repeated in rounds, "I don't think you should have said that."

Chapter 32: The Lesser Evil

Every footfall on the cracked asphalt was a lead weight, dragging Davis toward his parents' car. Ten days he spent in a concrete coffin. The injustice still clung to him, despite his release. He glanced over his shoulder; the definition in his strong back seemed to shift with each jerky movement. The crispness of the Spring morning felt suspicious. His freedom felt fragile, ready to shatter. His face was pale, marked with the shadows of confinement. Insecurity owned him, a constant rattle beneath the surface. Had his release been a mistake? Were the uniforms lurking, ready to snatch him back into his cage?

The anger toward his parents, a resentment that had fueled him throughout his incarceration, faltered and died as he saw his mother's white sedan. The lie of "no bond available" still echoed in his mind. The truth of their helplessness felt like a backstab. He would never believe that his parents couldn't have helped him if they wanted to.

He slid into the backseat, the leather cold against his back, and respectfully closed the door. He expected a torrent of questions. Instead, he received only the awkward presence of his parents' concerned glances, clarified by an overarching sense of sadness. It felt like judgment; more absolute than the prison bars he just left behind.

Did they know something he didn't? Some hidden clause to his freedom, some ticking time bomb waiting to detonate? The questions he would never ask mounted. The engine's quiet turning vibrated through the floorboards. The city blurred past the windowpane as the car began to move. Color and motion through the window served as welcomed distractions. They couldn't erase the abandonment he felt. The lingering ache of his recent confinement and vulnerable insecurity surrounded him. With each receding block, the detention center shrank, but the scars it left behind felt permanent.

The asphalt reeled out under Ellen's tires, the bold yellow lines on the pavement echoing the grim set of her mouth as she steered into the lot. The building slumped low, a monotonous beige smear against the vibrant green park behind it. Nothing about it stood out, except for the hard gleam of gold lettering: Edward Gerald, Esq., on the heavy oak door.

Max held the door open. His expression was grim, mirroring the tension in his son's face. Davis concentrated on the brass numbers on the door, each a small, glittering challenge. His eyes held something fragile, like stone on the brink of fracturing.

Ellen's hand rested briefly on Davis's arm with concern. As the family walked into the building, a long hallway stretched before them, a yawning void of pale, institutional green. Glaring, overhead fluorescent lights emitted an annoying hum. Each step unnervingly heightened the silence that lay between the three of them.

"Hi! You must be the Days! Welcome!" A floral whirlwind, a young woman whose smile seemed ready to crack her rosy cheeks, practically launched herself before them. Her dress, a gaudy explosion of too-bright blooms, fit poorly against her curves. Her eyes entirely missed the icy daggers exchanged between Davis and his parents.

"Attorney Gerald has been looking forward to meeting you," the woman chirped. Her cheerful welcome was a sugary contrast to the moods around her. She practically skipped toward a corner office. Her movements were too brisk and too sharp for her to be taken seriously.

She motioned for them to follow, opening the door and ushering them inside.

Three mahogany chairs, polished to a deep, mirror-like sheen, stood rigidly aligned, facing a man who dominated the meager space. Attorney Gerald sat behind a massive desk. It was empty, except for a single sharpened pencil and a thick manila folder. The steel rims of his glasses reflected a sliver of light, catching the slightest twitch of a smile, a thin line that didn't move beyond the edge of his mouth.

Wooden joints creaked as the family took their places. Gerald remained impassive. The pencil, untouched, lay poised on the blotter like a loaded weapon.

Ellen barely breathed the words, breaking the uncomfortable stillness: "Attorney Gerald, thank you for seeing us." Her voice, a frayed thread, caught a twitch in her chin. "It is good of you to see where we are with this mess." Max copied her apprehension, his eyes locking with hers between the chairs. Then, Davis erupted. A volcano of discontentment was unleashed in the sterile space.

"Where I am at, you mean," he spat, "in crap and lies! Jail, lost friends, online trashing, wasted time… and getting jumped by my so-called friends. Branded like some… animal." His voice carried a wounded tone. He fidgeted. The fabric of his shirt clung to his shoulders.

He turned to his mother, his voice oddly composed. "Did you call a plastic surgeon… yet?" Ellen's silence was effortful, broken only by the rhythmic tick-tock of a grandfather clock and Gerald clearing his throat to speak. She motioned to Davis to pay attention. He dismissed Gerald with a curt flick of his wrist.

"What?" Davis sputtered, "It's okay, we're paying him. We're just gonna talk for a sec, then he'll prove I'm innocent." He paused for a moment before continuing, "In the meantime…" Gerald opened his mouth. Davis's finger instantly shot forward, silencing Gerald before he could form a word. The gesture was a punctuation mark. His voice, when it returned, was a resentful growl. "Meanwhile, I have a giant 'R' branded onto my ass that you don't seem to give a damn about."

His father's voice, a controlled tremor of authority, was condemning. "Davis, that's enough."

Davis was a wildfire, already beyond control. His eyes blazed. "No, it's not enough," he bellowed, his voice emphasizing a new, wounded desperation. The words slammed against the walls and bounced off the furniture. "I have an 'R' burned onto my ass because someone I've known my whole life went ballistic because someone I don't even know accepted a friend request! Then she accused me of things I never did!" He ran a hand through his thick, dark hair.

Gerald, seated behind the desk, had reached his limit. The quiet simmer of his patience finally erupted. A powerful interruption was slowly building, increasingly audible above the persistent drone of Davis's voice.

"Well," Gerald began, the words hard enough to dent metal, "it's not as simple as that. These cases... never are." His eyes closed to mere slits. They flicked to the ceiling as he let out a weary sigh.

Davis, oblivious, continued his tirade, his voice a high-pitched whine that grated on Gerald's nerves. "What do you mean, it isn't simple? Are you any good at your job? It's open and shut! Anyone can see—"

BANG! A loud thud cut Davis off, turning everyone's attention to its source.

The attorney's interruption was brutal. His hands slammed onto the desk, a sound like two rifle shots before the hush that followed. The wood vibrated with the impact. Davis flinched. The action, direct and calculating, silenced the boy.

"I need you to stop talking," Gerald's voice was controlled with a dangerous edge. "Listen. Look at me. And shut the hell up. Do you understand?" Davis could only nod, a tiny, jerky movement. The man resumed with his professional composure, settling back into place. "I've been practicing law for a long time, and I rarely come across someone as unconcerned as you, Davis. You waltz into my office, full of bluster and self-importance. Let me make one thing clear: this is my domain. My job is to help you, but I can't do that if you don't cooperate and recognize the severity of your situation. You're facing multiple charges of rape, son. Do you understand that?"

The lawyer's words reminded Davis of the gravity of the allegations against his client. Davis's mouth opened and closed, but no sound emerged. He seemed to be struggling to find the words; the assurance that had characterized his demeanor moments ago became noticeably absent. His parents remained silent, their eyes fixed on their son. The reality of the situation was setting in. The family was bracing itself for the challenges that loomed ahead.

Davis began to speak, his voice a deep roar. "But it's all lies. I thought your job—"

Gerald's finger, a rigid metronome ticking in time, silenced him. His eyes bored into the boy.

"Yes or no," he clipped, his tone a polished blade. "I don't need a dissertation on my profession. You focus on your responsibility... or rather, your lack thereof."

Max intervened, his voice a rumbling train. "Wait a minute! He's been through a lot. How is attacking him going to help?"

Gerald didn't falter. His stare, a glacial weight, settled on Max. Davis and Ellen remained still. Gerald's voice, though calm, carried the chill of the mountains. "Do you want to leave? I can probably keep your son out of prison. But good criminal defense lawyers in this backwater town are rare. I happen to be one. You can listen to me or thank me for my time and go. No offense, but this boy needs representation, or he'll be in prison. I have no doubt." He rose, his chair scraping harshly against the polished floor. "Do you want me to step out? Your call. No hard feelings either way."

Ellen, uncomfortable, her blue eyes wide with sunken regret, jumped in. "I'm so sorry. He's just stressed. We all are."

Davis, jaw clenched, glared at Gerald with a refusal to yield even under pressure. "I don't like you," he finally said firmly, "but we're staying."

A slow smile spread across Gerald's face. The sound of his laughter changed the temperature in the room. "Not sure I like you, either," he replied, his words short. He didn't elaborate. Davis shifted in his chair; a nervous twitch played in his face. "But I believe you," Gerald continued, his voice dropping to a conspiratorial whisper. "Those texts... they're a train wreck. The explanations you gave to the authorities are worthless. Forget intentions. Forget the past. Forget the fairy tale you're living in. None of it matters." Gerald punctuated each point with a sharp tap of his pencil on the table, and the sound disrupted the stillness. "Get it?"

Davis's shoulders slumped. His voice was a pathetic squeak compared to Gerald's booming tone. "I guess I do get it, but it's crap." He twisted a silver ring around his finger in an attempt to ground himself.

Gerald leaned forward, softening with a weary understanding. "Agreed," he stated, the word a final judgment. "And nobody gives a damn."

The silence returned, heavier now with the implication of future consequences. He leaned back, a slow grin cracking the granite of his face. The corners of his eyes crinkled kindly. His voice, initially tight with tension, eased. "I've got something," he said, the words carefully chosen. "If this were just, he-said-she-said, we'd have a fighting chance. But..." He paused, letting the suggested outcome air out before them.

Davis interjected. "...texts," he muttered, the word a deep regret. Gerald nodded in affirmation as he looked at Ellen. "Yes, his 'brilliant' text idea. From where I see it, we have two options: one is better, the other... a bit riskier. Neither is ideal, I'm afraid."

Ellen met his gaze. Her hand made a decisive gesture. "The better one."

Gerald shook his head, accompanied by a deep sigh. His breath spoke volumes. "Good choice. Which is precisely the problem, Davis," he said to his client with weary patience. "There's a pattern here... Impulsive decisions. Always." He rubbed a hand over his tired eyes. "At least he gets it, honestly. You haven't even heard the options yet." He paused, a thoughtful frown etching itself onto his face. "Let's start with the risky one. I have a feeling I know where this will go."

He cleared his throat, the sound sharp and brittle in the silence. "I've scoured this case for anything, anything we can use with a jury. And... there's the relationship with the young lady." His voice was flat and hopeless, yet he maintained a sliver of determination.

Davis's voice, unskilled and tight, wavered. "They... they burned me," he rasped. He pushed a hand to his side, a shudder wracking his body. "They held me down... burned me. That's... real. The rest... isn't." His focus dropped to the floor and quickly snapped back up, completely derailed. "I need surgery. That's proof."

Gerald's expression remained a consistent pose of practiced indifference. "We can show Pictures, vacations, love letters, the whole nine yards. We can even... display the damage to your person. Hell, we can have you drop your trousers right there in front of the jury. Show them the goods up close and personal." An uneasy pause broke his stride for a moment before he continued.

"...the texts. The apology. You admitted to writing them. You swore to it. We can spin it, sure, suggest a different context, but... a reasonable person... they'll see it. It's there in black and white. Your phone records will be right there in front of them." Gerald's overall vibe cooled dramatically. He let the silence speak volumes before adding, "Your bare ass might just look like justice to some of them. Like you got what you deserved."

Davis rebutted with incredulity. "If I raped her eight times, why would she keep coming back? It makes no sense! Wouldn't a reasonable person..." He trailed off, the question hanging.

Gerald leaned forward, the chair singing under his weight. His voice was as smooth as polished granite. "Let's say we can cast doubt. Nine times, by the way... not eight. Details, Davis, you should know the details of your own charges." He paused; his hard stare bored into him.

The silence stretched before Gerald let out a slow, theatrical sigh and settled back into his explanation.

"We're talking about a jury, son... people... Some with daughters. People who were not there with you. They'll hear your word, your friend's... and your texts.... Texts that scream, 'I raped you, and I hope you get raped again! Fuck off!'"

Davis winced, a visible shudder wracking his body. Gerald's voice took on a softer, almost paternal tone, yet it carried the weight of a sledgehammer. "That's not a strong case, Davis. They have to look at that young woman and tell her... we don't believe you. Even if we split the charges, four or five... each carries a maximum of twenty-five years. Hell, let's say we luck out and just eat one... Twenty-five years, Davis. That is longer than you've even been alive."

A single tear dropped, tracing a glistening path down Davis's cheek, then another, and another. His shoulders shook with the force of his sobs, as he fell into inconsolable despair.

"What's the other option?" Max asked in an effort to comfort his son.

Davis stared blankly ahead, "Yes, that's crap. Anything's better than that."

Gerald, a man whose tailored suit couldn't quite dilute his compassion, leaned forward and rubbed his hands together, his voice a low hum of practiced confidence. "I've spoken to the prosecutor. Multiple times this week. He's… optimistic." He paused, letting the significance of the word settle. "He thinks he can win this."

Ellen swallowed hard. "So, he thinks… he can win." Her addition was barely a whisper.

Counsel's posture shifted only slightly as he launched into the details of the other option. "We've discussed a plea deal. It hinges on the judge's approval, which is almost certain. If Davis pleads guilty to two counts… perhaps we can reduce it to one… of GSI."

Davis was taken aback with suspicion. He gasped with open-mouthed confusion, "GSI? What's that?"

Gerald's stoicism softened fractionally, but only for a second. "Gross Sexual Imposition. It is a much lesser felony and the definition's more pliable. For you, it means sexual contact with someone impaired by drugs or alcohol, incapable of consent. In this case, a minor." He said the last two words with careful precision.

Davis's head snapped up. His mouth pressed firmly closed. He squared his shoulders as though he was preparing for a championship bout. "So... it's basically admitting I raped her. You want me to say I raped her?" The question floated stagnant and accusatory.

Ellen finally moved. She pushed herself up, her chair scraping against the floor, an intrusive sound in the sudden silence. Her hands fumbled with her purse. The leather was squeaking under the tight pressure of her touch. Her movement was abrupt, standing out in the seriousness of the room. She looked at her son with sadness, her vision fixed sadly on his face for a moment before her hand, like a hesitant moth, touched his shoulder. It was a feather-light caress that traced the line of his spine before falling away in resignation. Tears were blurring the already indistinct lines of the people in the room.

"I'm sorry," she whispered, her voice choked with emotion. "I can't. I need to... I need some air."

She stumbled toward the door and turned the knob. The latch clicked open with the finality of a judge's gavel, leaving behind a dangerous silence. A single whispered, "I'm sorry," drifted behind her as she passed through.

The heavy door closed, leaving Davis and his father to stare at the lawyer in momentary disbelief.

Davis mindlessly ran a hand through his hair. His clouded eyes were painted with helpless disdain. He spoke with clarity. "All the options... they all suck! I will end up in prison for something I didn't do, either way!"

Gerald stroked his chin as he clarified the agreement. "No, Davis. The plea means a suspended sentence. No prison time unless... unless you violate probation, commit another offense, or fail to register..." His voice trailed into Max's explosive barrage, tearing through the office.

"Fail to register? As a SEX OFFENDER? My son? His name plastered on billboards, in the post office: a rapist, a child molester? That's your best offer for sixty-five thousand dollars?!"

Davis's body shuddered. Tears streamed down his face, and he buried his head in his hands. His body collapsed in on itself. "No! No way. It'll go online; everyone will see... it'll ruin me. We can beat this in court!"

Gerald's voice, though soft, held a steadfast steel. He remained steady. "Davis, you said she was high that last night at your house, right?" Davis nodded.

Gerald continued to press, "And you did have sex?"

Davis's protest was weak, lost in disbelief. "Yes, but hours later... it was her idea, though!"

Gerald crossed his arms, signaling he was out of options. "I'm not here to forge your path. It is important that you come to this decision yourself. I think we should stop and think on it. I want you to consider our discussion as a family. Call me in a couple of days. I don't need an answer now. I'll defend you either way, but a jury trial... It's not a good idea, in my opinion."

Davis's rage erupted, "This is BULLSHIT!"

Gerald looked at him with neutrality. "I agree."

Davis's whisper of resignation was barely audible: "And it doesn't matter."

His father's hand, strong and comforting, rested on his shoulder.

Gerald provided an affirmation. "Unfortunately, son… you're right." Moments stretched between them without interruption.

Finally, Max extended his hand to Gerald in an expression of genuine gratitude. The handshake was slow, a ritual exchange of understanding between men. "Thank you. We'll be in touch," Max said with emotion.

He then guided his son out of the office with his supportive hand still on his shoulder. He hoped to leave grieving and hopelessness behind them. They trudged back to the waiting car, where Ellen sat traumatized. Her silence showed the devastating burden of her newly revealed powerlessness.

Chapter 33: An Afternoon Jog

Travis and Davis stood at the mouth of the woods, taking in the late afternoon. They started on the same path where scraped knees and whispered secrets had once been their only worries. Today was different.

The boys fell into step together. Travis studied his friend as they walked. He moved like a wounded stag. His swagger was gone. It was overtaken by a formidable, melancholic gloom. Travis clapped Davis on the back. The summer's passing without contact between them had carved a gaping hole into their routine. The absence of Davis's company was a heavy weight.

"You've been awfully quiet, buddy. I'm doing all the talking here. I'm not used to it." Travis kept his tone light to mask his concern.

Davis's response was flat. "Yeah," his voice was a dry scratch against the distant roar of the river. He dragged his feet, each step a labored effort, kicking up small puffs of dust that swirled around his worn sneakers.

Travis watched with a tightening knot in his stomach. He noticed the subtle slump of Davis's shoulders and the way his jaw was clenched tight enough to make his temple throb. The aftermath of the hearing, and the passing threat of prison, stood between them for a while. Travis's quick, assessing glance was full of love, understanding, and frustration. He knew Davis was hurting. He opened his mouth to speak, then swallowed his words.

Sometimes, just the shared silence and the familiar path under their feet were enough. The twisted trail was a simple ribbon of black asphalt sitting atop brittle, ochre grass. Minutes blended tranquility into the early autumn sun until a crisp crackle of Davis's feet, leaving prints on the browning blades of grass beneath him, broke through.

He was a silhouette against the sunlight, tall and lean, with competitive agility still evident in the ease of his strides. He approached a gnarled oak and pressed his back against its strength. Its bark was a chaotic tapestry of grey and brown. The wood supported and comforted him as he leaned into it. The weight of the world seemed to seep from his shoulders.

Travis stood silently and observed the moment with reverence. Their presence was a striking contrast to the deepening shadows around them. A trailing Sadness ran along the contours of Davis's face. His natural beauty was marred by a haunting insecurity only noticeable by those who knew him well.

He spoke in a whisper, barely audible above the rustling leaves. "I come here... to think," he said, his voice husky. He paused and ran a hand over the rough bark. It was a gesture both tender and despairing. "Here... I'm not... a felon. Or a... a sex offender. This tree doesn't judge me." The distance in his eyes, the callow vulnerability in his stance, told much more than words ever could.

Travis's attention met Davis where he was. A lump formed in his throat. *What have you done, Gretchen?* His thoughts silently screamed.

"Man," Travis said, attempting to lift the atmosphere surrounding his buddy, "you know you aren't any of those things." He cast a meek smile. It was the kind that lifted his face, a genuine, abiding affirmation, and it felt safe. With a sure hand, he gave Davis's shoulder a firm, reassuring push. It was a declaration of their bond, forged amidst the sweat, competition, and years of shared experiences in their young lives. "C'mon, let's jog or something," he encouraged.

Davis stared forward vacantly, "I just feel empty. I am nothing. I am a complete loser."

"You are not nothing. You are not a loser. You are a great friend and probably one of the best soccer players I have ever seen. You are gifted," Travis said firmly, squeezing Davis's hand.

Davis, frustrated and laden with self-loathing, responded in a pitiful monotone, "After my attorney tricked me into a plea deal, all of that was gone. The Minotaurs dropped me in less than a week. They didn't even call me or whatever. They just sent a letter saying, don't bother."

Travis became insistent. The fire in his eyes burned with a fierce intensity. "None of that matters, Davis," he ground out. He saw the way Davis was clouded with a profound self-hatred. "There are other teams. Not just a couple of other teams, a legion of them. Hundreds and hundreds of professional players with rap sheets longer than the interstate. They've fallen; they've risen. They've won." Travis's voice dropped to a near whisper with an edgy softness.

Davis didn't flinch. "Name one," he challenged his friend. He knew the question would go unanswered.

Travis produced a heavy sigh. Disappointment, real and observable, was written on him. "Dude," he said, "There's college, trade school... hell, even the military. Do you think this is the end? You could see the world, Bro! Escape this. Start building something real." He shook Davis's shoulder; his fingers dug into his flesh with a downcast plea hidden beneath the forcefulness. He had to get through to him. He had to.

"I said, Name. One," Davis repeated, with a tone spiked with unshed tears. His voice was like brittle ice under the pressure of a thousand resentments. The shadowed emptiness beneath his eyes distorted the seemingly perfect symmetry of his face. "You can't," he said sadly and slowly. "That's the point. Every application, a rejection letter. They're all the same. Denied. Ineligible. Unacceptable."

"Campus life? A friggin' joke," he underlined his sentiment with his inflection. "The Air Force? The Army? More rejections. Security risk... Unfit." He laughed, hollow and resigned. "Even online school... even that last-ditch effort, they laughed in my face. Sex offender registry." His frame fell from its height. The athlete collapsed under the weight of his own despair.

"Davis," Travis started, each word illustrated an obvious challenge, "I'm not buying this self-pitying bullshit. Ethan, that skinny little kid, is younger than us, but he's managing college and life. You can do this. I know you can."

Davis held his breath and clenched his jaw, causing the bone to ache and pulse. Anger had become a familiar companion. Travis's easy confidence felt like a slap. He didn't understand. How could he?

"Then what, Travis? What the frig' am I supposed to do?" Davis's voice, rough and edged with contempt, shattered the mood. The rustle of leaves felt like rude whispers. "You think it's easy? My parents are broke because of me. Legit schools are a pipe dream. Girls? Forget it. The second they find out about me... poof! Gone. And probation? The weekly humiliation of pissing in a cup while some dude stares at my naked dick? A drug test for a guy who's never even touched drugs?" His voice became embittered with cynicism, collapsing into a raw, ugly cry of pain. "Oh. It gets even better... The rape classes, Travis? They are a friggin' blast! Three times a week, I get to sit there listening to these monsters. Then I have to find a job. A decent job doesn't exist for a felon. A job that any other teenager can do, I can't because they don't—"

"Don't hire felons." Travis finished his sentence. A touch of grim pity dulled his positive tone. The silence that followed was thick, disturbed only by the drumming of Davis's fingers against the tree trunk. The image of Ethan with his impossibly bright smile, his almost ethereal innocence, flashed in Travis's mind.

He agonized with Davis, slumped in defeat before him. The vibrant energy that used to surround him was extinguished, leaving only fragments revealed in memory.

"Look, man," Travis said with a steady cadence, "maybe you could... go stay with your grandma for a while?" Davis's eyes dropped to his scuffed sneakers; the worn leather mirrored the tattered state of his spirit. His absence of speech was accentuated by the rhythmic patter of wind hitting leaves for a moment.

Then, Davis's quiet retort invaded the stillness. "I thought about that, Trav. But I have to register everywhere I go. You know what that means: slashed tires, 'RAPIST' scrawled across my front door in flaming-red paint, broken windows, the constant fear of... of..." He choked back a sob, his voice cracking. "Screaming in the night... honking car horns... accusations... 'PEDOPHILE!'... 'PERVERT!'... My Grandma can't handle it." He trailed off, a torrent of tears flooded his cheeks and began to soak through the thin cotton of his shirt. The salty sting in his eyes was almost commonplace by now.

Davis looked up with a hopelessness that Travis could feel. "Where can I go, Trav? If I go out to the country; some lunatic could find me and... and murder me. No one would look for me for weeks. My address would be posted online, Trav. For everyone to see. To 'protect' the public."

The words stung Travis with injustice. He reached out; his strong hand gripped his best friend's shoulder. He provided another physical anchor. It was all he had to offer. The feeling of Davis's strength beneath his touch was a reminder of the boy he knew.

There was a young man, not a monster, hidden under layers of fear, confusion, and betrayal. Travis despised everything about this. He hated seeing the vibrancy of life draining from his friend. Regardless, he knew he would never abandon him. Never.

"That's fucked up, man," Travis encouraged. "But you can't let this... this shit... define you. It's going to take time, but people will forget. You gotta live your life. You owe it to yourself... to me."

He swallowed and continued, refusing to be shut down. "This isn't forever, Day," he whispered. His promise was a fragile thing. "It isn't." Travis forced a smile that didn't quite agree with his haunted eyes. "My mom always said God never gives you more than you can handle."

Travis sat next to him and offered what he could. Some of his support sounded stupid, even to his own ears, but he was happy he could provide it.

Davis's response was slow and melodramatic. He buried his face in his hands. Strong fingers clenched the hair at his temples. Travis's heart sank in the wake of Davis's inaction. What had he said? What had he done? Guilt hit him. He began to reach out again but reconsidered.

Slowly, Davis raised his head. His face slowly emerged from the shadow of his palms. It transformed to reveal a grin stretching across his cheeks. This appeared to be the brightest, most liberating expression Travis had ever seen.

"If this is God's plan, then He's pretty FUCKED UP," Davis said sarcastically before roaring with laughter. The sound echoed through the trees, conquering the oppression. He was on his feet in an instant. "Race you to the waterfall, loser!" He was already sprinting before he finished speaking. A flurry of long limbs driven by absolute power rushed past Travis.

Travis watched in shock, and thought out loud, "Like an athlete."

He took a relieved breath before allowing his face to lighten with hope. Accepting the challenge, he called after Davis, "If you get there first, it's because you cheated, Dickhead!" He pushed off the ground and launched himself after his friend until both figures were absorbed by the emerald-green hillside.

Chapter 34: Another Day at the Office

Davis stared at his reflection in the plate-glass panels; the wind whipped his dark hair across his face. The sight reminded him of the freedom he craved but didn't have. He brushed strands from his stubbled jaw, seeing not just a construction worker helper but a ghost of the athlete he once was. His vitality was now dulled by grime and exhaustion. Who had he become? The question nagged at him constantly. It was a deep ache that throbbed through the soles of his feet. He wasn't complacent; he was trapped.

A past he couldn't outrun forced him into a menial corner. He was defined by previously whispered lies about what seemed like a different person. His insecurity, a constant companion, chewed at his self-worth.

With a grunt, he kicked at the dirt, a protest against the sheer weight of his failure. This was never his plan. He'd envisioned a life of luxury fueled by his internal drive and natural talent. He had planned a social media empire. A sports career once begged for him. Maybe even the Olympics could have been reached.

Life circumstances made him a cog in someone else's machine. His strength had become a tool for others to use. The quiet desperation that simmered inside him wasn't about unfulfilled ambition. It was about a moral compromise and forced abandonment of the person he once was.

He was most irritated about not having the luxury of basic choices in his own life. After failing to find employment, his probation officer required him to interview for this humiliating job, which he hated, or face a probation violation. He thought it was a bad idea at the time, and his opinion hadn't changed. The issue wasn't the officer or the job. If he was being honest with himself, despite the fact that no one else had been for some time, this was his fate.

Destiny was merely a jagged pill swallowed with the lukewarm water of resignation. He had come to know that his status prevented him from doing a lot of the things that others take for granted, such as choosing a job that is a good fit. Sex offenders get the leftovers. Work like this is what is left on the plate after everyone else finishes.

He wasn't thrilled, but he'd come to accept it. Or else... what? He'd end up back in a cell, the cold concrete that society apparently preferred for him. The hollow thud of something hitting the ground picked Davis out of his contemplation. He didn't flinch. He didn't even glance back as the hard hat thudded onto the dirt beneath his feet. It was just another dull boom swallowed by the drum of the construction site.

"Hard Hat Area, dumbass," a voice shot at him, sharp as a chisel. Davis watched the reflection through the glass without turning around. He learned quickly not to look at people or face consequences. The distorted figure striding away from him was elongated and curved by the grimy surface. The daily disrespect tugged at him, but he wasn't about to start a conflict. He needed to keep this job.

His mouth moved to form a wordless curse. "Friggin' peasant," he breathed, the whisper lost in the wind whistling through the skeletal steel of the half-built structure. It struck him that he was not sure if his criticism was aimed at the retreating man or his own image.

His back screamed in protest as he stooped to pick up the orange hardhat. Backaches were more familiar than he had liked these days. The cheap plastic felt cool against his calloused fingers. He felt the pressure at his temples as he tried it on, the brim digging in. It was too small. The gesture of giving ill-fitting ger to him was a degrading joke.

He would never ask for a properly fitting one again. The memory of the last time: the explosive laughter from the crew, hot urine trickling across his forehead and down his neck as he put it on, was still a fresh trauma. He could still feel it soaking his shirt and could not forget the taste of it in the back of his throat. The bullying mirth of his "work buddies" was permanently fixed in his memory. It wasn't worth it.

They were just fucking with you, he thought. His daily dose of humiliation was an acrid flavor that he was gaining tolerance for. He adjusted the band the best he could. The activity served as a reminder of his place in the world.

A chunk of concrete, the size of a cat, whistled past his ear, narrowly missing him. He flinched; the dust from the impact stung his eyes. He couldn't worry about it. Ten hours stretched ahead, a brutal landscape of jagged bricks and rebar, a symphony of shouting and the screech of metal. He was a helper, he reminded himself. He had important work to do. He swept – swept DIRT from the DIRT– with a broom, the coarse bristles raked across grit that reeked of sweat and kerosine. His body ached from repeatedly bearing the weight of two-by-fours hauled up rickety ladders, the rough wood biting into his shoulders and palms.

Above, the men barked orders, their voices dripped with unearned authority. One of them tossed a coil of wire down, nearly hitting him in the chest.

"Hey! Watch it!" Davis yelled. His voice went unheard above the din. The only reply was a coarse laugh from the crew. He saw them looking down at him, silhouetted against the dust-choked sky, their faces hardened by years in the sun. They were members of a brotherhood. They spoke a silent language of shared purpose he couldn't understand. He was inferior, and they would never let him forget it.

A foreman with a face like weathered leather leaned down over the edge of the roof. "One wrong move, kid," he rasped, "you piss me off, and you'll be wishing from the joint that you were still here." Everyone knew. Everyone knew the probationary sword hanging over his head, a weight that pressed down on him. He had complained about the abuse in the past.

His probation officer, a man whose face seemed sculpted of granite and cynicism, merely shrugged, the gesture somehow more dismissive than any words. "I did what I could. You should be grateful. It isn't easy finding work for people like you. You ought to consider yourself lucky. Suck it up, or I can maybe get you a work detail in jail." The resolution to his concern was a clear indication of the support and care he deserved.

Davis understood clearly who "people like him" were. He had witnessed the judgment, felt the hatred, and experienced the blanket statement of societal scorn. He recognized his worth. He found no value in a world that regarded him as less than human. He was familiar with the chilling emptiness that consumed him. He also knew that he definitely wasn't one of them, and could never be.

He held this knowledge with valor, despite the scarlet letter etched into his soul by the system, another branding. He was aware of his own strength, his morality, and his capacity for love. This knowledge served as a mere umbrella against the storm raging within him.

The rusted lever of the time clock groaned, an antiquated, mechanical thunk echoing in the almost abandoned controller's trailer. Davis lagged behind everyone else to clock out before ending his day. It was definitely not an act of respect. It was one of avoidance. He slotted his timecard in the metal rack, the same card that happened to vanish prior to every payday, before heading for home. The safety lights hummed overhead, illuminating his path from the makeshift office to the parking lot.

His twenty-year-old sedan, a bruised plum under the early evening light, sat waiting. A deep dent marred its fender, and spiderweb cracks fractured the windshield like a map. He paused with his hand hovering over the dented door. Relief washed over him. It took a moment for him to realize why. There were no overturned trash cans this week. Maybe his friends didn't like him anymore. His heartbeat slowed to a hesitant rhythm.

He slid into the driver's seat and relaxed. The worn leather felt like paradise. A long, shuddering sigh escaped him. "Wishful thinking," he muttered, the words barely audible over the whine of distant machinery. He fumbled through his pockets, finally pulling out a zip tie holding two keys. One was for the car. The other would get him into his tiny, sparsely furnished apartment.

The keys felt heavy in his hand, as formidable as the unspoken anxieties that lived on him like a parasite. The engine sputtered, each gasping cough stretching the five-minute drive into an eternity. The familiar streets of the low-rent district made him feel uncomfortable. He gripped the wheel tighter, knuckles white against it.

Last autumn's move still felt fresh. He had turned twenty, and the fantasy of permanent residency in his childhood home was over. He couldn't keep subjecting his parents to the shame of living with a pervert. He had to move, like it or not. He couldn't stay there.

The car's tired engine gasped and died as he pulled into his reserved space. "Baltic and Mediterranean," he recalled describing his place to Travis when he made the deposit. While walking to his door, a knot of men with faces smudged with soot sat at a picnic table. They smiled and waved at him with a camaraderie he couldn't quite match. He doubted he would aspire to try. He reluctantly returned the gesture with a jerky nod. He hated everything about them... this. It was his worst nightmare.

The peeling paint of the apartment building welcomed him. He wrestled with his keys in the lock, which was perpetually sticky. The chipped paint on the door brushed against his shoulder. It left small shards of dried pigment on his shirt as it swung inward, revealing a space barely larger than a walk-in closet.

A dim ceiling light blinked on. It illuminated a small kitchen area. A single, overflowing trash can fought for space with a teetering stack of unopened mail, at least three weeks' worth, judging by the height of the pile. He didn't bother sorting it; a practiced flick of the wrist sent today's addition onto the top of the stack. Task accomplished. The microwave hummed a mournful drone as he heated a frozen pot pie, fresh from its cardboard tomb. Steam, smelling faintly of burnt vegetables, filled the cramped room. He didn't bother with a plate.

The bathroom mirror, cracked in a spiderweb style across its surface, reflected a stranger. He saw a face framed by unkempt hair, the color of spent oil, hanging past his shoulders. Dirt from the construction site clung stubbornly to the five-day-old stubble growing over his cheeks, highlighting the dark circles stamped around his eyes. Coarse black hair sprouted from under the collar of his shirt like weeds. He'd stopped trying to battle them... everywhere. He stopped fighting everything.

"Italian friggin' national forest," he mumbled with disgust, ruminating for a moment on the tangled nest that had formed between his legs. His stare drifted to a brown bottle perched on the shelf of the medicine cabinet. He didn't need to check the label. Medicine was now a stinging comfort, "time for my crazy pills." A practiced hand twisted the cap before dispensing two tablets into his palm. He swallowed them dry. He had become a pro.

The TV flickered to life, casting a silent, hypnotic glow. His pot pie sat, forgotten, beside him. The sounds of his environment were swallowed up by the volume of the television. This brought him peace. He sank deeper into the worn couch, the springs groaning a weary protest. Sleep, a temporary escape, was on the horizon. Unconsciousness was the only agenda that mattered.

Chapter 35: An Interrupted Meal

The plywood laminate table gleamed under the restaurant's overhead can lights. It reflected an unsteady nervousness in Davis as he reached for his water glass. The clatter of silverware against plates, usually a comforting Sunday sound, now felt amplified. Each clang was a foul discord grating on his already frayed nerves. Across from him, Travis and Macy ravenously dug into their salads.

Davis actively avoided eye contact. His focus darted, back and forth, between the cheap battery-powered candles hanging on the walls and the cartoonish floral pattern of the tablecloth. A wave of sudden nausea spilled over him. He felt suspicion and judgment from the other diners. This paranoia was nothing new, but it never faded or lessened in intensity.

He caught a glance of a teenager laughing. It wasn't about him, but it didn't matter. Davis recoiled and pulled his shoulders inward. He wanted to shrink. His height was no longer a source of pride but a target for unwanted attention.

"Relax, man," Travis's voice cut through the tension with a calming tone. "They're just people eating dinner." He gestured around the room with a nonchalant wave, "Nobody's looking at you like that."

Davis swallowed; the tightness in his throat made it hard for him to speak. "You don't understand," he mumbled. His words were forced... lost. "It's... it's different for me."

His mother, noticing his distress, reached across the table and squeezed his hand. "Again, with this? It's okay, sweetheart," she whispered, holding a tired weariness. The statement felt patronizing and awkward, like a poorly fitting shoe. He knew she meant well, but reassuring statements couldn't melt the icy core of his mind.

A deep-rooted fear lived in his soul, leaving him with a perception that wouldn't yield to logic. The warmth of his family, the vibrant energy of Travis, all of it was tainted with an undercurrent of self-hatred. The Sunday dinner night, a relatively new attempt at tradition, had morphed into a dreadful chore for him. Being anywhere in public was a struggle against his own inner demons. Ellen's eyes locked onto Davis with what appeared to be pity. The silence following closely behind her announcement sucked the air out of the dining room. She hadn't just swallowed a clown; she'd wrestled a rabid one and lost.

"So... we have decided," she sang, her arms waving a theatrical sweep over the table, as she revealed her "proposal" like a tray of poisoned chocolates. "To go back to the beach. It's about time, wouldn't you say?" She instantly shifted her attention to Travis. "We would love for you and Macy to come along. You've been such good friends to Davis."

The positive energy from her was almost comical. Travis watched with the cool detachment of a witness to an execution. Davis stared a laser through her. The insecurity he tried to mask with indifference had been pushed to its limit. He felt the sensation of hopelessness, which had become as commonplace as his pride once was. The beach. That beach. The memories that clung to it… Ghostly reminders of a horrid past gripped him tightly.

Davis sat up. "I have to work," he said, the words clipped, emotionless, like a dam holding back a flood. His voice, when he spoke, was a growl. A controlled fear was concealed beneath his unconvincing smile. He attempted not to draw attention to himself. He casually continued, "Why didn't you say anything to me first? I never want to go back there. Never!"

He then turned to Max and offered words firm enough to stand upright on the table independently. "This is the worst idea you guys have ever had. Count me out. Screw that noise." Max's hand landed with a solid thwack on Davis's knee. The impact vibrated through Davis's solid structure.

Max's wink was quick and mischievous. It crinkled the corners of his dark Italian eyes in a near-perfect impersonation of Davis's signature expression.

"We figured you'd say that," Max said. He held a cheerful tone. He leaned in, close enough for Davis to smell the remains of his morning shave. "We get it, Day. But… at some time, we need to move on. The place… it isn't the problem." He gestured with restraint. "There are more good memories there than bad, right? It's been a big part of our lives for a long time. Let's make it a symbol of us sticking together and not... that. It is important to your mother." His voice trailed off; the last word was an obvious attempt at coercion through guilt.

He noticed his son. The tightening flex of Davis's hands gave away an internal discomfort. A tinge of regret crossed Max's face, an atypical crack in his jovial presentation. Rather than continuing, he shifted control of the conversation back to his wife with a dramatic side-eye. It was a nonverbal cry for help.

Ellen, not missing a beat, met the challenge with pleasure. She knew, with a mother's intuition, that Davis needed to find his own way, but the fear of her own defeat slowly stabbed at her.

"And...," she began, with her 'I've got this' look locking onto his face. Her eyes widened slightly... a practiced maneuver. "We talked it over, and we'll cover any money you lose from taking time off." Max's hyperbolic cough, a theatrical display of disapproval, churned in his intestines. Ellen's hand, cool and smooth, settled over his. "We did, honey. Don't you remember? Of course, you do." Her lie was soothing silk. "It's a couple of months away, Day. Just take the time off. Rest." The sharp pat delivered on Max's hand was a final determination. The unspoken message lingered: Let me fix this. Her positive push returned to Davis. Her apprehension collided with her calm demeanor.

Macy intercepted, "I'm leaving for school next week. It's early registration. Travis is a free agent, though. He definitely could use a trip." A slow smile spread across her face as her boyfriend looked at her in shock.

Travis, never enjoying a net being tossed over him, caught the pass and attempted a fake. "C'mon, man." He coerced his friend, "You can make up for all the times you promised to take me as kids and brought Gr..." The oops face fell on him like a boulder. "Never mind. We should totally go."

Davis's face tightened with annoyance and shrank to the size of a postage stamp. A scream began to build from his core before he caught it and let out a genuine and audible sigh. He effortlessly relaxed his fists and allowed his hands to fall flaccid like autumn leaves. He gently pushed his plate away before placing his palms flat on the table in its place. Restraint was his challenge, and he was mastering it.

His eyes projected the ambition of a condemned man before he choked out his defense to his audience, "I'm... I'm paranoid all the time. There's girls and families, and little kids on the beach. They are all over the place. It's just." He paused with the regret of a thousand wars, "It's just not a place for people like me."

Ellen discounted his concerns. "What does that have to do with anything, Davis?" She looked at the others and passively chuckled, not intending to be condescending. The action ran through him like a hot iron, "My word!" She criticized as she tapped the table impatiently.

Davis's explanation transformed into a plea, which then became a sarcasm sharp enough to cut the world in half. His response came with managed force, "Nothing at all. That's the point. If I hear a baby crying, or laughing, or I even see one... it literally scares me. I always feel like everyone is looking at everything I do. I don't go to the gym or play soccer because I don't want anyone to see the scar. I don't like people to know what I am. You guys just don't get it! I haven't gone to the doctor since they made me go to jail after it happened." His voice escalated to a near roar, his drumming hands accented each point for clarity. "I feel guilty… GUILTY if I see a girl and think she is pretty. You're right… MOM… It has NOTHING to do with ANYTHING at all… FUUUUUCK!"

"DAVIS!" Ellen scolded. The population of the restaurant ceased to notice anything but the loud party in the corner.

Davis sat rigidly; his sculpted jaw clamped shut like a bear trap. A shadow fell across the table. Everyone was looking at him.

A server approached them with wide eyes, nervously canvassing the room with every step. She placed a tiny, crumpled napkin beside Davis's hand. It lay alone, a solitary white island in a sea of wood and floral tablecloth. She scratched out a statement, clearly feeling her interruption, "So sorry to bother you, sir. She… insisted." Then, she melted back into the room. Davis hesitantly unfolded the note after staring at it fearfully. His breath stopped. As he read it, he saw a death sentence in his hands.

'Look to your right.'

Panic flared in his eyes, a sudden storm in the depths of his troubled face. His head snapped right, jerky and frantic. Max, his thick, curly black hair catching the dim light, reacted instantly. His hand shot out, snatching the note before Davis could fully process it.

The tension on his face mirrored his son's. He scanned the room, his sharp surveillance missing nothing: the boisterous laughter, the hurried staff, the intimate whispers between couples. He stopped on a young woman across the room. She was subtly waving, her lips moving in silent words.

"It's her," Davis breathed without looking. His entire presence withstood a rocket of fear sailing through it. "If I'm near her, it's... a violation. I have to get out of here. I'll go to prison." He sprang to his feet, disrupting the table.

Travis placed a hand on his shoulder. "Easy, Davis," he said with intention. His grip was both powerful and gentle. Max joined in. He placed his large hand on Davis's other arm. The woman continued to wave from across the dining room. The fear in Davis's eyes was not retreating.

"It's not her, buddy," Travis assured him with a fraternal pat. "It's Cher... It's not her... She's not with her."

Max stood at full attention, staring at her with a vengeance. Dominance etched itself in his posture. "This stops now," a command that resonated between them. "Davis! Stay." He didn't wait for an answer. He moved toward the source of the written threat with the purposeful grace of a panther.

Davis watched, frozen. His reflection was distorted in the shine of the cheap gloss of the table, revealing a boy-man wearing a mask of mortification. I'm a dog, now? he thought. He saw Cher shaking her head at his father. A nervous flutter of denial seemed to define her words. Her fingers danced across her phone screen.

She was frantically looking for something and quickly found it. She slid the phone across the tabletop to Max; the plastic seemed to hypnotize him.

The images on the phone appeared to hit Max hard. The tight lines crossing his forehead loosened. His animated, protective, anger was replaced with something vacant. His eyes narrowed with contemplation. His masculine features softened more and more as he absorbed the material.

Reaching for a pen, he quickly scribbled onto a napkin. Then, with a quiet, almost reverent movement, he handed his message to Cher. Tears flashed in his eyes as he returned to his family. His strength appeared to have drained out of him, into the worn paths staining the carpet. As he walked, he motioned for Ellen to get the server's attention.

"We're paying. And we're taking this to go," he nervously spat out between breaths.

He placed his hand briefly on his son's head and mussed his long hair. It was an understood promise of protection. "Meet us at the house, Davis." The magnitude of his emotional pivot was unsettling.

Davis stood, paralyzed, once again, with genuine fear in his heart.

Chapter 36: Reunion

The living room was dim, setting the stage for blatant unease. Shadows shifted, distorting all movement, and increasing the tension gripping the space. Max sat, sinking into his worn leather armchair. The old material groaned beneath him. His eyes were fixed on a place beyond the far wall, finding a focal point for the anxieties tightening within him. A furrow etched his brow, showing concern he kept leashed behind his studied expression.

Beside him, Ellen perched on the edge of the sofa, habitually wringing her hands in her lap. Travis leaned forward in his seat. His elbows rested on his knees and his stare darted nervously between Davis's pacing and the emptiness of the unlit hallway.

Davis moved with the unhinged restlessness of a caged animal. Each footfall on the wooden floor was a countdown that seemed to hum in everyone's ears. His internal landscape was a tempest with an acerbic yearning for escape. Every movement he made was a presentation of inner distraction, an echo of his fractured thoughts.

Davis was obsessively drawn to the rectangular void at the end of the hallway. It offered a glimpse, a shadowed sliver of his empty room, a space haunted by his grandmother's mirror. It was an open invitation to retreat into the faded comfort of a past where these present horrors had not yet taken root; a time he would surrender anything to reclaim, a sanctuary now out of reach.

Outside, the sudden intrusion of the modern world shattered the precarious quiet. Headlights speared through the gloom, two white lances that breached the lace of the window curtains.

Patterns, formed by light through fabric, transformed the opposing walls into austere hieroglyphs. The soft shush of tires on the driveway followed. The sound was an alarm of her arrival. A sense of impending confrontation emerged.

Davis's voice, when it tore through the tension, was an unfinished tear in the environmental fabric. It showed the vulnerability he fought daily to conceal.

"What does she want?" he demanded of the awkwardness that had settled like a shroud over his childhood home. The question was formed of suspicion, defining the stare he fixed on Max. "Why did you give her our address?"

Outside, darkness slowly swallowed the white glow that lit the window. The sound of a halting engine arrested the throb in Davis's head. It was a brief respite before his anxiety surged again. A feeling of dread followed, softened only by the rush of his blood, a violent river moving through him.

Then, a shadow detached itself from beyond the window. It was a skeletal figure stretching through and across the hallway floor. It snaked its way toward the front door. Rapping knuckles against wood sounded like repeated gunshots. Each soft knock was a fresh scrape against Davis's rapidly fading control.

His eyes, shimmering with unshed tears, widened as his breath was stolen. He recoiled as if struck, sinking onto the plush cushions beside Travis. He sought the anchor of his presence to combat the churning sensation of his own apprehension. His chest felt constricted. His limbs became unresponsive as if bound by force. He couldn't even summon the will to turn his head to look at the door.

Ellen sprang into motion. Maternal reassurance poured from her. "Calm down, honey," she said softly as she hurried past him. Her odd rush revealed an underlying anxiety that her soothing words couldn't entirely conceal. "It's important, but..." Her voice trailed off, the end hanging in the unsettled quiet. A flicker of something unreadable shadowed her face.

Davis's head snapped toward his father with a jerk. Accusation was thick in his voice. "Wait, she knows, too?" His regard, honed to an edge by years of online skirmishes and defensive posturing, turned toward Travis. It demanded an answer he already feared. "You too?... Does everyone know but me? Am I just drowning here?"

The front door creaked open, its aged hinges letting out a sigh as Ellen extended her hand to greet their guest. Framed in the honey gold spill of porch light, Cher appeared in a luminous halo that seemed to canonize her. Her black hair resembled a raven's wing caught in the warm glow. This contrast accentuated the sharp angles of a face that was both enigmatic and poised, yet also bearing a rigid hardness.

Max welcomed her with warmth, but his dark eyes hinted at a hidden apprehension.

Ellen trailed behind Cher like an obedient puppy. A forced smile, very different from the warmth Max provided, was plastered on her face. "Please, make yourself comfortable, dear," an invitation Ellen offered with grace.

Cher moved through the space of the living room with a hesitant stride. The intensity of their stares was uncomfortable. She acknowledged Travis with a brief nod. Then her eyes slid over a brooding Davis. A sense of resolve traversed her features before she settled into a massive armchair. An enormous ottoman at her feet seemed out of proportion. It was an ironic metaphor for the awkwardness she felt. Cher's vacant stare locked onto Ellen. Dark eyeliner was purposefully smudged beneath apathetic eyes.

"I'm sorry. My name is Cher. Good to meet you, I guess."

Davis rose to his feet, impatiently. Accusation was coiled in his posture. His best defense attorney persona, sliced through the strained atmosphere. "What do you want, Cher?"

Cher absorbed his hostile tone without altering her expression. She rose from the depths of the armchair with mechanical precision. "I can go," she stated in a slow, laconic voice. Each word was measured, lacking emotion. "I just came with proof. Proof you never raped anyone. That's all. Don't be a dickhead."

Before his son imploded, Max intervened. A wave of warmth toward Cher flowed over her. His lumbering presence was a force in the charged space. He reached for Davis. The weight of the hand he pressed on his son's shoulder was a demand for restraint. Davis obediently returned to his seat, guided by his father's touch. His eyes narrowed onto Cher with suspicion, but he didn't move.

"Just wait, Davis... Cher, please, sit." Max extended his arm hospitably, imploring Cher's compliance. His action also served as an apology. He wasn't asking her to forgive his son's hostility. He was begging her to give him a chance, to offer the truth that might provide clarity for the mess around them.

Cher returned to the embrace of the armchair. She sank into its yielding fabric. Max signaled for her to speak with a kind smile. She felt the full force of the family's collective attention, a spotlight holding her in its grip. Each set of eyes was a question.

"Well..." Cher began. Her black nails were digging deeper crescents into the pale skin of her palm. A catch in her throat emerged. It was a slight sound that forced her to clear it several times before she continued. "This... this is way more awkward than I thought it would be."

The recollection, the memory of that night, hit her, robbing her of the ability to draw a proper draught. "It was... a year ago, maybe. We were at the ranch..." Her eyes shifted toward Ellen. A flush crept up her neck, staining her skin red and burning her cheeks. "Drinking. Smoking. That kind of thing..."

Her voice dropped to a whisper, her vision unfocused, as if speaking to shadows clinging to ghosts of that night. "Truth or dare," she continued, her voice a barely audible thread in the abyss of the moment. "Completely lame, I know, but... that's what we do sometimes. We were all... drunk. Well, they were. I couldn't stomach American beer. God, I hate American beer. Anyway..." She glanced at the worn rug and dusty bookshelf, anything to avoid Davis. His distaste for her was plain to see, and it filled the air, making her feel small.

"Gretchen was there," she blurted out in a rush. Words tumbled out in a stammer, a desperate attempt to find solid ground in the shifting sands of memory. "She... she was wasted. And Britney... Britney asked... she asked Gretchen if you raped her."

With her words, the air around them became colder. The impossible drop in temperature raised goosebumps. Suffocating silence amplified her icy stuttering. Her recollections, too fresh, too recent, too entangled with anxieties to be relegated to the past, pressed down on them all.

Davis, wounded by a clear reminder of the wreckage of his life, lashed out with virulent anger. His voice was laced sarcasm. "So what, Cher? I bet she told everyone that I never raped her, and now I am miraculously proven innocent... I'm sure all of this is just a nightmare, a trick my mind is playing on me. It's never going to happen. WHO... CARES?" He pushed out each word with a firm monotone; a wall of indifference standing on the foundation of his ruin.

Fueled by Davis's hostility, Cher drew deeper into the armchair, trying to vanish. The safety pins on her worn jacket gleamed dully in the dim light, tiny points in the oppressive darkness she felt closing around her.

"Umm... I'm not sure. I gathered... I don't know. Maybe you're right." Her voice eroded into a mumble. She dug through the pockets of her jacket. When her hand emerged, she was gripping her cell phone. Its dark screen reflected her face until she pressed it to life. She scrolled through the contacts with jerky movements; her brow danced with signs of anxious concentration. She paused to peer at Davis intermittently as she fumbled through her camera roll.

Cher's presence pleaded for understanding before she placed the device on the ottoman, where it could be easily seen by everyone. The heaviness of the moment crippled her.

She watched the guilt in her face slowly dissolve in the backlit glare. The small screen no longer reflected the fear and doubt carved into her expression. She was saved, at least from that. With a slow movement, her finger tentatively hovered before pressing her purpose into action.

The sound of adolescent voices held the room captive while the goth girl dissolved into the plush fabric of the chair. She stared at the ceiling as conflict churned in her stomach.

Chapter 37: The Game

The contents of the recording held everyone captive. Davis hovered inches over it, bathing his face in icy blue. His body heated with anxiety as he immersed himself.

In ridiculously high-cut denim shorts, Britney cartwheel across the frame. She wore a pair of boxer shorts on her head, covering her entire face. Her eye peered out of the gaping fly. Raucous laughter erupted from all sides, a sound that was now sickening. Doug stood behind her laughing and bashfully covering himself with both hands. Zack yelled at him, "Hands over your head, boy. Show it!" He refused to comply, but the bright red glow of his skin revealed the dare. Davis felt sorry for the kid.

Zack's voice was a trigger. It pulled Davis to relive it all again. He was called back to the barn. He could, again, feel the rough straw cutting into him, taste the iron-laden flavor of his own blood, and smell the decimation of his burning flesh. These sensations orbited his mind like witches, resurrecting the night that forever changed his life. 'Focus, Day, Focus, " he thought, pulling himself out of the pit.

The sight of Gretchen leaned against her boyfriend hurt, even now. It crawled through him with increasing pressure, seeping into the soles of his feet until even the floor beneath him felt stained. The ache was a feeling he couldn't understand or ignore.

The kids were huddled together in the same circle he remembered. Davis realized how they simply erased what remained of him. It ripped at him and picked at the soul he had left in the dirt they were playing on. He never existed.

Gretchen contorted her face into a mask. She kissed Justin with the same mouth that had delivered the lie that stole Davis's life. They were the same lips that had whispered promises that dissolved into dust that fell between his fingers and settled at his feet.

"I pick Truth," she slurred. She was obviously drunk. The others groaned. The outburst from the group was a chorus of boredom with her predictable game play. "I always do truth," she repeated. Inebriation colored her speech black. She flashed a coy smile that wasn't returned.

Davis felt cold seeping into his bone marrow. The grip of the betrayal he felt was a reminder of the innocence he once had. A hand rose to his chest for evidence he survived. On its surface, the phone's glass reflected the man staring into it: stripped bare, left with nothing but... nothing.

"Okay," Britney said with pointed boredom. "The truth, Gretchen... may you die if you tell a lie."

Gretchen eagerly replied through a giggle, "I will tell the truth... may I die if I tell a lie." Her kiss met Justin again with a peck before she pulled away and nodded at her inquisitor.

Justin, unaware of the rest of the group's irritation, beamed at her. Britney noticed and rolled her eyes, unimpressed with the boy's cluelessness. A slow, vulturine purse shrunk her mouth to a line, twisting her expression into something catty and sinister.

Her words, when they came, were barbed. "Did Ethan Cope and Davis Day ACTUALLY rape you?" Britney's laughter unearthed a hazing from her friends. The verbal assault that fell on her was a barrage of jeers. It was a hurricane of teenaged protection swirling to Gretchen's defense. Britney wasn't moved. She continued to stare, awaiting an answer.

Zack, lit by the firelight, fiercely intervened. "They did, Brit! What a bitch question. Ask her a different one."

Britney stood, indifferently. "I asked Gretchen, not you, Zack. Are you going to beat me up?" She glared at him until he looked away. She steeled herself again and turned to Gretchen for response.

Gretchen pivoted her head, looking at all of the eyes fixed on her and mumbled, "No problem... REALLY, Brit... I mean, REALLY?" Her voice became more articulate. "They went to jail, didn't they? There's your answer, bitch. By the way, that was two questions. I... call... foul." She laughed and plastered another sloppy kiss onto her boyfriend.

Behind the camera, Cher's voice, flat and sharp as files, rose over the others. "You didn't answer the question. You told us they went to jail. We all know that, but that wasn't the question at all. Was it, Gretch?"

Matt, a shadow of support in the corner, added his thoughts, meekly. "Yeah... she technically didn't. What's the problem? What does it hurt to say it if we already know the answer?"

Zack's eyes fired visual rounds at Cher. "She did answer the question, Cher. You're a fucking bitch... but fine, answer the question, Gretch! Get this shit over with." His fingers drummed on the same platform of hay that he delivered justice for his cousin on.

Justin encouraged her, "It's bullshit, babe, but show them how it's done." He patted Gretchen's back, empowering her. Gretchen, swaying precariously, steadied herself by placing her hand squarely on the top of Justin's head. Her body swayed slightly as she struggled to her feet. She seemed to be, oddly, battling the effects of liquor again. Around the fire, the circle of teenagers sat in the orange glow, silently assessing her. It felt like a trial.

"FINE!" she shrieked, with a theatrical whine," Yes, Queen Britney," she pressed, the emphasis dipped in scornful disapproval, "they did. But it wasn't... rape-rape," she sneered, the words categorical. "Because if it was that kind of rape," she hissed, her voice dropping an octave, "I'd be wearing their tiny mouse balls for earrings!" She paused for dramatic effect and formed a sly smile. "Just... regular rape. Happy now? Question answered." She threw her hands into the air and awaited approval from the jury.

Zack leaned back against his arms and laughed condescendingly. "You're a drunk bitch, cuz," he said with his own brand of condemnation. "What the hell is rape-rape anyway?"

Matt, confused and bewildered, chimed in. "Yeah! Fuck that! What's normal rape? Is rape just… normal now? Educate us, Gretch, we're all dying to know."

A viral chant began to ripple through the circle, the word "rape" repeated again and again, a hypnotic, unsettling rhythm echoing off the steel walls. Gretchen's giggles were thin, high-pitched, almost hysterical. Eerie shapes from the fire raced across her face, accentuating the blush blooming on her high cheekbones. She was thriving in the attention like a celebrity. Her hands hovered around her ears in mock protest, pretending to quell the rising tide of sound. Each repetition seemed to push her closer to relevance in the hierarchy.

"Even though that's… another question," she stammered, maintaining her balance with visible effort. "And since you're not going to shut up about it… I'll tell you, but your next turn's skipped, Brit. Rape-rape," she laid the words out like bricks, shooting each consonant through her teeth like cannon balls. "It's when someone… you know… FUCKS someone violently. Regular rape is different. You know… that's all." Her voice trailed off.

Cher's response, a horrified suspension, aimed at her like a laser sight. "No. That's not all. I… I don't know what you mean."

Gretchen's patience ended. She retorted with machine gun contempt. "Like when you agree to sex, and then find out it was a trick, and you wouldn't have done it if you'd known the truth ahead of time. THAT'S regular rape. That's what those fuckers did to me... both of them, but Davis especially. That cheating... fucker... got away with it for months."

The camera shook from Cher's stunned reaction. Its instability captured the storm of emotions battling through her. A moment passed. No one moved. The volume of Cher's repudiation challenged anyone to interrupt her. "That isn't rape. Davis's life is fucked. What the hell is wrong with you? Regret isn't rape! Do you understand that? DO YOU? This... this shitty thinking is why victims are doubted. Are you such a basic fucking BITCH that you can't grasp that?!"

Gretchen returned a furious howl. Her mask of toleration for Cher cracked, revealing the honest hate she felt for her. Angry tears dropped from her eyes, carrying layers of mascara with them. "I don't think you get it, Cher," she shrieked, bleeding with sincere offense. Her rage was an avalanche of hurled stones. "Don't you dare tell me what is and isn't rape! How dare you judge me? Do I need to be bruised and battered for it to count for you?" Her voice hit a high, keening pitch. "I was... cool at the time, but I never would have agreed if I'd known the truth. They lied to me. That's... that's coercion! THAT'S FUCKING RAPE! ARE YOU DONE?" She collapsed onto Justin's lap, inconsolably.

Unfathomable guilt was biting at the teenagers huddled in the barn. Matt broke the tension. "Zack...this is... fucked up. What did we do?"

Zack drew his mouth into a sharp, thin line. His eyes darted wildly. He was speechless for probably the first time in his life. There was an odd, clumsy aura around him while he formed a decision. "Shut up! Game over. Nobody says anything about this… ever. You hear me? This dies here." He circled the room, locking onto each face, individually, with a dismissive stare that guaranteed retribution.

His eyes caught a flash, something at the edge of the group. With dilated eyes, the small lens poking out of Cher's pocket snatched his attention. "Wait. Are you… recording this?" Zack came in to focus and then blurred with his approach. It zeroed in on him for a moment before plunging into darkness.

Chapter 38: A Flickering Light

Shock filling the room, was a ten-foot wall of isolation. Davis stumbled to his feet, sobbing silently with his face buried in his hands. Long brown hair obstructed the detail of his striking features.

Beside him, Ellen clutched a tissue with an empty expression. Her previous optimism had wilted around her. Max sat rigidly, staring forward. He mirrored his son's despair. Travis merely sat motionless, staring at the dark screen.

Cher's presence suddenly felt like a disruption to their intimacy. The subtle rustle of her backpack and the clink of loose change, disturbed by the drop of her telephone, were the only signs of life in the room. These slight intrusions cut through the quiet like a scalpel.

She rummaged through her bag. The annoying rustle went unnoticed by everyone but her. Within seconds, a hand emerged, holding a small silver flash drive, embossed with tiny figures of bats. Cher stared at it for a moment with thoughtful contemplation.

She took a deep breath and placed it on the ottoman, still warm from where her telephone had been. Her fingertip reverently grazed the plastic. She finally spoke in a whisper. "It's on here... here. It's for you, Davis."

Looking at him, she stiffly held her position. She felt empty as well, hoping for a closure that wasn't coming. "I'm going now. I... just thought... you should have this. Maybe... clear your name. Or something like that."

Only after Davis glanced an acknowledgement in her direction, she stood. Her slowness emphasized the gravity that seemed to want to hold her in place. "I'm sorry... I've been... carrying it around for a long time, hoping to... run into someone. I know it's... fucked up. Maybe... this can help... undo some of the... damage." The honesty bled from her like an open wound.

She shifted her weight from foot to foot, searching for some sign of what she should do next. Nothing. She nodded and began to creep away from the group like an unwanted shadow.

Davis managed a sterile, "Thank you." The heartbreak visible in the way he shook, struck her like a blade. With a sharp breath, she did the best she could to compose herself before inching toward the exit she needed.

The brass knob was frigid against her palm. Her failure to ask questions at the time felt inherently wrong in hindsight. It was steadily creating a feeling of complicit guilt for all the pain that might have been spared.

The creak of the hinges brought all of the deception she carried home to die. There was no turning back now. Her sweaty palm stole the coolness from the worn metal in her grasp. She turned to look at Davis. It was an admission, an incautious search for something... understanding? Forgiveness? She watched him for a moment, lingering on the lines formed deep in his face by despondency.

"I'm sorry, Day," she breathed. The statement seemed meaningless, almost criminal, to say. "I know... we barely knew each other. We only met once. I... I didn't believe you without even knowing you. She seemed so... broken, or whatever. It really doesn't matter now, does it?"

Regret painted her mind red. She knew there was no point to her elaborations now. Their relevancy had passed long ago. Her explanations couldn't undo the damage. He knew. They both knew. Davis, tall and angular, met Cher's regard. His eyes, the color of warm honey, held unwarranted compassion.

"It matters to me," he said. That was all.

Cher stared at him softly, "Please understand this wasn't a setup." She blinked, her breath not knowing where to land. A strand of hair fell across her cheek. She was a striking beauty, despite hiding it under black and grey cosmetics.

She swallowed and drew her gaze toward her scuffed, clunky black boots. She couldn't bring herself to look at him while speaking. "Who knows what you think about me now? I was just... recording the game... My life... or what passes for it. I don't even know why I picked that night... being sober for once, I guess. And then... that happened."

Davis's mouth curved into a barely-there smile, offering gratitude. "No apologies needed," he said quietly. "You didn't do anything."

She remained fixated on her boots, ashamed. The silence was stretched taut with endless things. "I know I didn't do anything," she mouthed, "I know I didn't. No one did. That's the reason I'm sorry, Day."

Cher's statement hit Ellen like a slap, but she stood with grace. Her hand reached to her son with a gentleness that spoke volumes. Her fingers brushed the back of his neck and a peaceful smile consoled her. She offered a gesture toward Cher, a single open palm from across the room. Cher accepted the gift with the intention it carried, feeling it was much more than she deserved.

The goth chick pushed her shoulders back, avoiding eye contact, and returned to the comfort of her apathetic normality. "Okay, this... this got weird. I'm... I'm gonna just... go." The statement was finite. With nothing more to be said, she exited into the darkness, gently pulling the door closed behind her without a click. The night seemed much brighter than the place she was leaving.

Chapter 39: A Bright Path Forward

A crinkled plastic grocery bag, serving as a trophy, felt like redemption in Davis's hand. He laughed, genuinely, as he stared at his shorn locks spilling over the edge. He had cut it himself, but didn't care. They were remnants of a past he was finally able to leave behind.

The bathroom mirror still reflected a stranger, yes, but not the stranger he'd been. This face, clean-shaven, skin marked with the ghost of past trauma, pulsed with something hopeful, something like resurrection. Hope? No, something fiercer. Victory.

He raked his fingers through the curls he hadn't seen for what seemed like a lifetime. Their texture was alien yet strangely familiar. His practiced smile also returned, feeling like a weapon, a defense. He'd rehearse it a million more times if he had to. The apologies, when they came… and they would come… would be a symphony of regret, a chorus to his vindication.

"Tomorrow," he sang like a hymn holding deep promise. The difficult weeks since Cher's visit served as a purging.

Sweat that stung his eyes during daily runs with Travis helped him feel alive again. The pounding of his feet on the trail blazed a path away from the spirits of his past. Even the soul-crushing monotony of his crappy job now felt like a prelude, a final indignity he must suffer before his life was given back to him.

The visions that swam through his mind weren't fantasies; they were plans for his freedom. He relished the explosion of truth coming out to confront the accusers who had condemned him with lies.

Three years of loyalty and support from what was left of his meager, yet devoted, social media following will be rewarded. The validation the truth offered would be as sweet to him as the tears of his betrayers. He would savor it. The world laid open before him and he intended to be ready for it.

More importantly, IT had to be ready for HIM. His body screamed in protest from the daily workouts. Each repetition and every set was an act of contrition for the hell and hatred he subjected himself to since his arrest. This wasn't a basic reputation overhaul. It was going to be work that he was more than willing to do. He was forging a new shell, hard and gleaming, to banish the injustice levied upon him.

Tomorrow morning, in the attorney's office, will be a battlefield, he thought. His misplaced shame? It would signal the system's defeat. He would wear it like a crown. Each spire would be a reminder of the many times he had to overcome the judgment of others.

He rehearsed his gratitude speech to his probation officer, the words sounding like heaven pouring from his mouth, a necessary penance. The money... oh, the money sang an angel's song in his ears, an ode to justice and retribution. The city's coffers were soon to be his. He could almost feel the crisp weight of the bills in his hand, each one a well-earned slap in the face to those who'd dared to underestimate him.

His body, a loose marionette, jerked into a joyful dance in the bathroom. He didn't care about the chipped sink, the grimy shower curtain, or the overall damp neglect of the room. Excitement vibrated within him. He had all but forgotten what it felt like. He glanced down, noticing the slight jiggle of his belly.

'Work out more', he thought. The words snapped with the force of a rubber band. He slammed an energetic, motivational fist into his palm. "I'm gonna keep running with Travis every day! No wimping out." He leaned against the cool, damp tiles of the wall and breathed deeply. The horrid scent of mildew was strangely comforting. Everything was.

He closed his eyes; the faintest hint of a smile lived on his face. He felt... different. This peace, this... rightness, was a feeling entirely new but ever so natural. He'd almost reached for his phone. Dating apps were calling him. His hand froze. He wouldn't answer that one. Not today.

He thought about the three years of persistent fear he had endured. The experiences over this time were a pain in his heart that flared. He would soon stand free from all of them. He finally captured the elusive, fragile relief from the icy grip of his past with a silly video. He finally got to win Truth or Dare, after all.

A vision sparked: Cher. The way she returned to his life, when she didn't have to, unsettled him in a way he couldn't fully process. For a change, it was a good unsettling. A wave of pure, unadulterated appreciation rushed over him, strong enough to pull him under. He felt it physically, a lightness in his soul, a warm sensation spreading from his heart outwards to eternity. He wanted to thank her, to give her a diamond necklace to show his gratitude. It would be beautiful against her skin. The fantasy ignited something powerful within him.

It would be a surprise. The thought brought a bubbling childish excitement to him. This was an emotion he'd almost forgotten he was capable of. A mental list, only half-finished, built a harmony for him: Parents… mortgage, Travis… his own car, Gretchen… straitjacket. He laughed out loud, strong enough to cramp his stomach because he didn't want to think about her. He'd stared into the abyss for too long; he wouldn't let anything bad into his heart again.

Against his wishes, an involuntary grimace invaded his face, triggered by the image of Gretchen tumbling down a flight of stairs. A trickling xylophone scale accompanied her descent, ending with a comical bass drum beat when she hit the bottom. He quickly pushed that thought away as well. Everyone deserved happiness, even Gretchen and Zack. However, it was acceptable that he felt a twisted kind of glee at the thought of anything else.

Getting back to business, he turned away from the mirror to further assess his body. As he pivoted, his reflection revealed only a glimpse of the brand seared into his flesh. It was not fully visible in the small mirror but revealed enough to prove it was there. The jagged scar, the intended mark of a rapist, now held a different meaning for him.

His brand was far more powerful than a scar. He had plenty of scars, a mere peasant in the realm of injuries. A brand had to be the top friggin tier! He was definitely keeping it for good now. The shiny R on his hip was now a phoenix rising, engraved deeply into his skin. Resilience. Retribution. Resurrection.

Shame? He spat that word out; the texture was too nasty to chew. He wouldn't let it touch him... not ever again. Feeling satisfied with his appraisal, he finished preparing for the day.

Davis sat eagerly in his living room and waited. The tick-tick-tick of a mom-van's engine announced his best friend's arrival. "Ready to go?" Travis called from the parking lot.

"Let's do this," Davis shouted, jogging to meet him. The engine thrummed to life. The waterfall awaited. A distant boom, a signal of freedom, was just over the horizon.

Chapter 40: A Contradiction of Ideologies

Polished wall panels reflected hopeful smiles on the faces of Max and Ellen, waiting patiently. Davis couldn't contain his excitement. His feet tapped a drumroll under his chair. His mother sat next to him with a comforting hand rubbing his shoulder. Across the room, Gerald's secretary occasionally glanced up from her work to offer a positive nod.

After a while, the hinges groaned to announce the opening of Gerald's office door. Before the sound could fade, Davis exploded from his chair. A flash of movement, a blur of limbs... and he was gone, swallowed by the world beyond the dark wood. Gerald's booming laugh increased the hope of his parents, following behind their son with much more composure.

"Hello, Max... Ellen... Long time no see. I received the package." Gerald gestured with a broad, welcoming sweep of his hand. "Come in, come in." Ellen nodded and settled back into the leather armchair she had used in the past. Its familiarity was relaxing to her this time. Max followed, copying her quiet refinement. Davis peered from his chair in the center and spoke before his attorney could sit down, his eyes wide with breathless expectation. "Did you watch it?"

"I did," Gerald said. His reply arrived through an almost too-bright smile. "Quite an extraordinary bit of documentary film there, eh?"

Max squared his shoulders and sat tall with authority. "Yeah," he breathed with relief washing over his face. "We've been waiting for this. We were... excited and worried when we saw it."

Davis, rocking rhythmically in his chair, let out a shaky laugh. "We can use it to undo everything."

The brightness leached from Gerald's face. His head tilted to study his desk calendar momentarily. A deep sigh with the weight of the world followed. "Oh, boy," he said quickly. He looked at Max with a blank curiosity. "How... how do you mean?" His tented fingers tapped against each other with an uncomfortable fidget.

Ellen leaned forward, "Well... it proves our boy didn't rape her. The little witch said it herself," she snapped without compromise.

Max slapped his strong hands together. The sound echoed from the walls around him. "We have the real story now," he declared with self-importance.

Davis had already become impatient. He exploded with manic questions. "Will she go to jail? Can I sue her? I need to sue the city!" He looked to Gerald for answers with a face that had become a mask of desperate hope.

Gerald's hands flattened against the shiny wood of his desk, and he leaned into them, obviously in contemplation of his direction. He searched Davis's face with a slow appraisal. A deep breath of weariness opened the conversation. He responded in a matter-of-fact tone that suggested forthcoming disappointment. "I was afraid of this," he rasped. He locked eyes with Davis and uttered a eulogy for the kid's dream. "Son," he said, his voice slow and remorseful, "it doesn't work that way. There's nothing to undo." The confusion from the Day family felt like a vise pressing down on the spacious office, which had suddenly become very small.

The space they occupied was a vacuum. No one spoke. The only identifiable sound was the rhythmic tick-tock of the clock behind them. Ellen remembered that sound. She realized that the sound of clocks were always premonitions of tragedy in her life. She sat frozen in her seat.

Max's jaw dropped. His incredulity was a painted earthquake that rattled the room. "Nothing to undo?" The question rose from him like a missile. "We sent proof… irrefutable proof that our son didn't commit the crime. A crime he's already paid for ten times over." Gerald remained a statue.

Davis's eyes flicked nervously between his parents and his attorney. He seemed to understand only bits and pieces of the exchange. He was not prepared for anything but what he had planned. No variation could make sense to him.

Ellen slammed her fist onto her thigh, the sharp thud shocked the men in the room. "Let me get this straight," she snarled. Uncontrolled passion radiated from her like heat. Her finger, stiff with rage, stabbed toward her son, who swiveled in his chair. The expression on her boy's face only showed a snippet of the damage he had suffered over the past three years. She was not going to allow any more destruction.

"Nothing to undo? What about this? What about three years stolen from our lives? I'm not stupid. I know we cannot rewrite the past!" She was unstoppable and had no intention of walking out of the office again in defeat. Not today, "but this felony... based on vicious, deliberate lies... surely, that can be undone." She stopped and waited with her arms crossed.

Davis attempted to regain control with suave confidence. "What do I need to do?" he asked without the suggestion of knowing what was happening around him. "Paperwork? How much? Just tell me how much it costs." He immediately looked to his father for reassurance.

Gerald paused to read the hurt in each of their faces. His compassion wasn't a stated fact, but it was clearly evidenced in the slight softening of his jaw and the sluggishness of his hand while reaching for his pen. He spoke; his voice measured with each word, carefully chosen. "I know... this is... overwhelming," he said, pausing slightly on the last word. "But this," he continued, his face firming, "this is a separate thing entirely."

Max released a porcine snort. Disgust rolled from him in angry bursts. He opened his mouth to speak, but Gerald raised a hand, to silence him with an authority that only years spent navigating such emotional minefields could provide. The gesture was successful. Max simply leaned back and glared over folded arms.

"This," Gerald resumed, "points toward... something else entirely. A...civil matter, perhaps. It is outside my area of expertise. I wouldn't even begin to..." He trailed off, noticing Max's purpling face and increasing irritation.

"So, you won't help us," he blurted. "You got us into this... this shit show with your 'excellent' plea deal. It's a life sentence! It destroyed him. Look at him!" He boldly pointed at his son, who was rapidly shifting his eyes, looking to settle them on anything that might help him.

Gerald's attention followed Max's, settling on Davis. When their eyes met, he was changed. He was swallowed by the expensive furniture and the shadow of the hopeful young man who was sitting there moments ago.

Unshed tears, catching the light, defined Davis's presence. Twin lakes of molten silver sat in the corners of eyes holding a devastation too deep for words. Gerald didn't waver in his expression but instead returned to Max with a glacial calm.

"I gave you an option," he said in a smooth drone that somehow felt sharper than any shout. "I was completely transparent. He didn't go to prison. Your son chose wisely." The statement was made of carefully placed stones. Davis's hands, now knotted into nervous fists, bounced against his knees.

"But I didn't rape her," he pleaded through strained words, "You said you watched it. You can see I didn't." His eyes, wide and unfocused, darted around the office again, aimlessly.

Gerald leaned back. His voice was a smooth baritone. It was soothing, yet assaultive. "That's exactly right, Davis," he said. "You did not rape her. The court never said you did. Do you understand?" Davis blinked; he stared at some unseen point beyond Gerald's shoulder.

His lips moved, but no sound emerged. Gerald continued, almost condescendingly. "The plea deal was for Gross Sexual Imposition involving a minor. The video, this recording, proved what was already established. It's not going to change anything."

Davis's whisper fought for clarity. His Adam's apple jumped in his throat as he tried to find breath. He asserted with despair running, full blast, through him.

"But... you told me..." he gasped, the words pressing deep into flesh like splinters. "To take the deal... remember? I said... trial... I didn't do it! You said... prison..." His tears finally won and washed down his face. An audible cry tore through him. It was an animal-like sound that erased the somber hush.

Davis looked to his mother to save him. That is what she always had done. He needed her to do it now. Instead, she sat motionless, her face resembling death. It was apparent she was not going to.

All he could do was bow his head. There, in the carpet, he seemed to search for something: a shard of hope someone may have dropped, a fragment of his former self. His question was an agonized scream. "What choice did I have?"

The attorney looked at Davis. His hand, surprisingly gentle, reached across the polished wood. Davis didn't reach for it; he didn't look at him.

"I know this is hard," Gerald whispered. "But I didn't tell you to take that deal. I presented the facts as they were, then the options. You chose." He tapped his pen against the desk, habitually. "It took you until almost the day of the hearing, if I recall correctly, to make a decision." He paused before adding, "It was a good deal, Davis. A good deal."

The words stung, but Davis didn't show it. He chose to focus on the rasp of his own breath. He didn't see the good deal; he saw the shattered pieces of a life taken away, given back, and then stolen again. The crushing weight was his despair.

"But it was for something I didn't do," Davis whispered, resigned. His tears had dried, leaving behind pale salt paths spanning his cheeks and ending at the base of his chin.

Frustration tightened Gerald's shoulders. He stood up, a sudden shift, his demeanor altered drastically. He became a different man, almost robotic. His hands pressed firmly on the desk as he leaned forward, his voice now hard yet compassionate.

"No, Davis. It's for exactly what *did* happen. You had sex with a minor. At least once. She was intoxicated. High on drugs, alcohol, or both." He paced in a short line. The pile of the plush carpeting shifted color beneath his shoes. He assessed Max and Ellen before continuing his explanation. "She said she didn't consent. Consent requires a sound mind. Does your video, even if it were admissible... which it isn't... show a sound mind? Think about it." He paused dramatically.

"You pleaded to one count of GSI, not nine counts of rape. To the letter of the law, I did my job, and we did well. Nothing you showed me in this video disputes those facts. In fact, it supports them. She was so wasted that she could barely stand. Even if the video were relevant, do you honestly think any court would allow it to be shown?" He shook his head with finality. "Hell no." Gerald sank back into his chair, his closing argument was slowly settling on the family like dust.

He waited for a hint of something: acceptance?, resolution?, in Davis's eyes.

"Let's go. Max, Davis. Let's go!" Ellen's voice sliced through any remaining sentiment.

Davis fumbled with the tail of his shirt. "Wait? Am I really... not going to be innocent? I don't understand." His voice was chaotic, a buoy floating on the rising tide of another failure.

Gerald, offered a piece of paper to Max with a scrawled message clutched in his fingers. "I want to give you a referral to a very good..." The crash of Max's disgust stopped his words. He didn't even acknowledge it. He moved toward the exit with fluid momentum, pulling the heavy door open with a force that sucked the air out of the room.

"One more word," he snarled from the doorway, "I dare you. You can take your referral and shove it up your ass—" Gerald remained rooted until he was jolted by the sound of his door slamming closed behind his clients.

Davis leaned against the lobby wall as he gathered his thoughts. A profound wave rushed over him. His shoulders slumped, and the weight of the past three years visibly melted away. Confusion warred with a dawning clarity. A strange and unexpected comfort blossomed through his sadness.

Ellen's voice rang with optimism. "We'll find another attorney," she declared with maternal resilience. "One with some common sense. We found this one; we will find another one."

Her son offered a smile, the genuine kind that crinkled the corners of his eyes. He stopped her and pulled her into a hug, hoping to provide comfort. Her body pressed against him, and she broke down. He could feel her tears soaking the fabric of his shirt.

"Let's give it a rest," he said, touched with a surprising lightness. "Honestly, I'm… okay." He grinned at his mom as he released her. "I don't understand it, but it is the system. Crazy, right?" His statement was accompanied by a chuckle. "I can't believe how okay I am. But we can't keep doing this to ourselves. I can't keep doing it, anyway."

Davis's voice was quiet, almost a murmur. "Everyone's been telling me that for years," he admitted, a hint of self-deprecating humor coloring his tone. "I'm hard-headed, though… yeah. Am I disappointed? Sure. But… I'm at peace with it. I didn't see it before, I guess, but he's right. These were all my decisions, and I gotta own them." He moved toward the exit, leaving the historic weight of the legal battle behind him.

No tears streamed down his face, only a quiet determination. With a reassuring touch, he guided his parents toward the waiting car. They left the sterile office and its memories far behind. The future, uncertain yet promising, stretched ahead. It was time to move forward.

Max's hand strongly settled on his wife's back. The fierce anger that had drilled itself onto his face moments before, softened. He looked at his family with pride.

Chapter 41: Butterfly

Gravel crunched underfoot before softening to a deep, resonant thud as Travis and Davis jogged away from the asphalt parking lot and onto the packed earth of the trail for the warm-up. The woods opened before them like a living cathedral. Towering pines and ancient oaks reached upward through the filtered light, their trunks gnarled with age, layered with moss, and dark in the creases where rain had soaked in deeply. Some leaned like old men mid-whisper, while others grew straight and still, as solemn as statues.

Shafts of sunlight pushed through the canopy, striping the forest floor in soft gold, catching particles midair like fireflies frozen in place. Ferns fanned out from the roots, lush and layered, while ivy curled over fallen logs and crept along tree bark with quiet determination. Birds called from somewhere overhead, but their songs were hushed by distance, as though even they knew not to disturb the stillness. The breeze carried the deep scent of pine needles and wet stone; the kind of air that filled the lungs and made you slow down without thinking.

The place felt etched into memory, a sacred spot untouched by the world's rush. The trees didn't move, but they seemed to watch, not menacingly, just present, like guardians protecting something valuable. The sun, warm on Travis's face, contended with the cool, steady breeze that tousled his short, light brown hair. This natural contrast of warmth and coolness mirrored the balance between the two of them: Travis's bright energy and Davis's wild, unpredictable swagger.

Travis glanced at Davis, his long legs eating up the trail with ease. Davis, tall and lean, moved with a fluid grace, but there was a tension in his shoulders that Travis noticed. Davis didn't meet his eyes. He kept his focus on the path ahead, his breathing steady but just a touch labored. The rhythm of their footfalls, thud, thud, thud, blended into the organic symphony around them.

The waterfall remained distant. Its flow was a gentle hum, in harmony with the accompanying nature. The air carried the scent of pine and damp earth, and a fine mist caressed their faces, cool and refreshing. Far below, the river's low murmur grew more pronounced with each step, yet it remained a soft, distant sound beneath the trees.

"Another perfect day, huh?" Travis called out over the quiet background, his voice barely audible, but there was warmth in it. His green eyes crinkled with that signature warmth he always carried, always there to lift those around him, especially Davis. The challenge in his tone was playful, but there was an undertone of camaraderie, a feeling of togetherness, as they shared this time together.

Davis nodded with a broad grin, but it was more a reflex than genuine enthusiasm. His focus never left the trail in front of him, and Travis could see the faint tension in his friend's jaw, with his hands clenched at his sides to steady himself.

"Yeah," he panted, the word was wedged in the effort of his breathing. "Another one." The trail curved, revealing its full magic. Sunlight pierced through the trees, scattering into a thousand fragments as it hit the dew-covered leaves, casting light in every direction.

Travis felt that familiar sense of comfort, a grounding sensation in this shared space. There was something about this trail, this place. It was a part of their routine, something that had woven its way into the fabric of their lives. He couldn't put it into words, but it was in the way they moved together, in the ease with which they communicated without speaking. The sunlight, the earth beneath their feet, the challenge ahead, all of it wrapped them up in a familiar embrace.

"What's with the panting, Davis?" Travis called again, teasing but with an undercurrent of care. His voice carried that rich warmth, with a playful chuckle slipping out, filling the humid air between them. "I'm not going easy on you today!" Davis, his face flushed under the dusting of sweat, struggled for breath. His tall frame paused for a moment, his breath coming in jagged, uneven pulls. A single bead of perspiration traced a path down his cheek, highlighting the sharp angles of his face, as if time had worked harder on him than it ought to have.

His laughter was strained, breathless. "Going easy on me?" he rasped out, his voice cracking slightly. There was defiance in his eyes, but beneath it, the weariness of someone who wasn't used to letting his guard down. "You've been kicking my ass on the daily, Trav." He forced a smile.

Travis's grin only widened. Without breaking his stride, he increased his pace, his movements fluid and effortless. He passed Davis with ease, then pivoted on a heel, running backward, his bright green eyes fixed on his friend. It was a challenge, but more than that, it was Travis's way of motivating Davis, of keeping him in the fight.

"Come on, man!" Travis called out, a challenge laced in his tone, but there was something else there, something that said, "You've got this. Don't back down."

There was a moment of silence, other than the rhythmic percussion of Travis's steps and the soft sound of Davis's struggling lungs stretching between them. Travis glanced back at him again, not slowing down, but maintaining a manageable distance, as though he knew precisely how hard to push without losing him.

Davis broke the silence. "Wait," he gasped, holding up a hand. His voice was strained but clear, a quiet admission of his need to slow down. "I call Mercy... Just a sec." He bent forward, his fingers digging into his thighs, his body in full stretch as he tried to catch his breath. The movement was slow and intentional, almost methodical, as if he were trying to regain control of the moment.

"I forgot to stretch," he muttered. He was aiming for a weak attempt at humor, but there was sincerity in the words.

Travis slowed, but not by much. He approached Davis, his footsteps became lighter as he moved. He offered his hand to his buddy, not to help, but to act as a subtle nudge. A pat on the shoulder, almost dismissive in its lightness, but there was a warmth there, a reminder. "Whaaat?" Travis's voice carried a teasing quality, but there was a deep affection beneath it. "That's like half, no, less than half of what you've already done. We just got here, bro. You ain't wimping out on me."

Davis looked up, meeting Travis's eyes for the first time during the entire run. There was a flicker of something, maybe gratitude, maybe uncertainty, but something real. "I know, dude," Davis croaked.

His breath was hard, but his eyes softened. "You're right. I'm just... I need a second. It's been a rough week. Stress, I guess. I'm fine." The words were more than an explanation; they were a confession. He wanted to keep moving, to keep up with Travis, but the weight of the last few days had been more than he expected.

Travis didn't speak. He didn't need to. He simply stayed there, standing over Davis, letting the silence sit between them. There were no empty words, no promises that would make it easier. All that was required was his unconditional presence.

"You're a good friend, man," Davis finally whispered, his voice quieter now, as if the words were harder to say than anything else. His eyes searched Travis's face, looking for something.

Validation, maybe. Or just a reminder that, despite it all, he wasn't alone. "The best."

Travis's grin softened. "Damn right, I am," he said with playful ease. He placed a hand on Davis's shoulder, squeezing it in reassurance. "You know it."

Davis looked at him, a blush creeping over his cheeks. "I love you, man," he added, almost as an afterthought, the words loaded with meaning.

Travis blinked, then burst out laughing, his bright, open grin spreading wide. He blew a lighthearted kiss at Davis. "Seriously? I love you, too, man. No homo. But you're still running this thing," he teased, his voice playful and full of warmth.

Davis's face flushed even deeper, but he brushed it off with a quick, sarcastic wave. "Yeah, yeah," he groaned, still tight, but it was lighter. The tension was beginning to ease out of him. "I just... I need a second. Let me stretch, and then I'll show you what I'm made of."

He straightened slowly, then began patting his pockets. The confidence faded from his face. His eyebrows pulled together.

"Crap," he mumbled, barely above a whisper.

Travis turned, eyebrows raised. "Now What?"

Davis's hands moved to the back of his neck, fingers pressing into the tight muscle there. He didn't look up. "I left my friggin' phone in the van. That little pocket in the door. I meant to grab it."

Travis narrowed his eyes, half amused. "You? Leave your phone? That's a first. I'm surprised you don't shower with it. I figured you would have had it surgically attached to you by now."

"I know," Davis muttered, his voice strained. "But I did. And now I'm gonna obsess about it the whole friggin' time. I needed to film today."

Travis exhaled slowly, his expression softening with recognition. "Use mine. I'll send it to you later."

Davis wrinkled his nose in mock offense. "You know I need my phone, Travis," he whined. "My camera's better. Plus, if I don't have it, I'll just think about NOT having it the whole friggin' time. You know it's the truth." A playful pout, almost cartoonish, twisted his lips. "We're not far. Could you, please, go get it for me?"

Travis sighed, shook his head, then tossed the keys with a lazy flick of his wrist. "Heads up."

Davis caught them clean. He grinned, already smug. "If you go get it, I can sit here and stretch and then TOTALLY kick your ass when you get back."

Travis gave him a long look, then exhaled through his nose as he took the keys from his friend's outstretched hand. "You're right," he said. His words were edged with irritation. "You are a real pain in the ass sometimes, buddy."

Davis snorted. "I know. Love ya, man."

Travis, already halfway down the path, called back, "Oh God! That again? Geesh." His voice trailed behind him, dry and amused. His stroll quickened, powerful legs devouring the uneven ground beneath each stride. Davis watched him go. The friend, the athlete, the man, the brother, all of it faded into the lush, verdant backdrop until his figure was barely visible among the trees. Then, even the shadows swallowed him whole, leaving behind the faint, rhythmic echo of retreating footsteps dissolving into the woods.

The forest now held Davis in its hush. In its cool, damp embrace, he felt the sting of something tangled. Solitude, yes. But also, an unshakable, almost aching affection for Travis. He looked down at his hands, slowly bending each finger as if trying to read his own bones. A quiet pause overtook him. He thought of his friend. Of his parents. Of the fragile architecture of his life. His chest rose with a long, full breath, satisfied but tinged with resignation.

Something finally went right, he thought, the words forming like a whisper in his head. Then, as if an invisible switch had flipped inside him, he sprang to his feet and launched himself from the trail toward the beckoning call of the gorge's edge. He was all energy, uncontainable and electric, like a power plant come to life. He had felt that way all day. He felt guilt for lying to his friend, but it passed quickly as he moved. The underbrush cracked beneath him, wild foliage exploding in protest as sharp, whiplike branches snapped against his face without mercy.

The cool wind reminded him he was alive and running for his life. The river's whispers grew louder, shifting into soft mumbles as he neared the edge. He paused with solemn reverence, gazing out at a view he had seen a thousand times. This time, though, he saw it through a different lens, sharpened by urgency and truth.

The gorge stretched before him, beautiful and expansive. Its depth no longer threatened him. Instead, the vast shadows wrapped around him with a strange, comforting grace. What had once loomed as a menacing threat now opened like a sanctuary, offering salvation from what felt like a lifetime of misunderstanding, poor choices, and bad luck.

"I am not bad," Davis whispered, a quiet reassurance meant only for himself. He thought about his mother, who had spent his entire life giving him everything she could. He loved her. What he dreamed of right now, though, was freedom. For the first time in his life, he had to pursue that dream alone.

The funny thing about dreams is, he recalled, we don't take them with us. They take us with them.

He pulled his arms around himself with strength, squeezing harder, giving himself the embrace he needed in that moment that his circumstances made difficult and society refused to provide.

The distant sound of a familiar voice ended his hold. A single tear traced his cheek, falling to his chin. It wasn't a tear of sadness or regret. It was one of defiance, a quiet acceptance that he was proud of. The voice called again, closer now. "Davis!" Urgent, desperate. He turned toward it, just once, before breaking into a run.

His steps quickened, the ground hard beneath him, until he reached the rail. Without hesitating, he jumped toward it, planting his foot firmly on the top of the barrier. Using it as a springboard, he propelled himself forward into the open air. The metal bolts creaked under his weight. His body arced cleanly, legs extended, chest lifted.

For a fleeting moment, he hung above the gorge, suspended in silence, the wind cutting across his face and tugging at his clothes like invisible fingers. The horizon bowed around him, vast and unbroken. It was framed by jagged trees and rock walls that fell away beneath him like a curtain parting. His shadow passed below the rim and was gone.

He raised two fingers in the direction of the voice, a gesture of understanding, a fragile peace, an apology. The air rushed around him, thick and violent, pressing hard against his face and forcing his eyes to squint. It pulled at his clothes and clawed at his skin. His hair whipped backward in sharp, frantic lashes. The rush came with weight and speed. It filled his chest and curled around his legs, shaping the moment with a flurry of unstoppable motion.

The rim of the gorge disappeared over his head, and the shadows surged upward to meet him. They gathered around his arms and legs, moving fast and soundlessly. They slipped across his chest, filled the hollows behind his knees, and wrapped around the curve of his back. The temperature dropped as they closed in, not suddenly, but steadily, and unmistakably. The light above him narrowed and vanished. The fall had a shape now, a form, and the shadows moved with it. They didn't flinch or slow. They closed over him fully, folding him into their depths with quiet certainty. There was no resistance. There was no return.

The world tilted and spun. It had to be you, buddy. I'm sorry. The thought passed through him quietly, not as a farewell but as a truth. Before it settled, his contemplation was interrupted by his destiny.

***

"Here we go again," Travis muttered under his breath as he opened the van door with a resigned pull. "Stupid phone," he whispered as its rattle echoed from its plastic pocket. He snatched it up, eager to finish this unnecessary trip back to the van and get back to the trail.

A yellow note stalled his breath as it slipped from his trembling grip and floated onto the empty passenger seat. Something didn't feel quite right all of a sudden. Anguish rose as the scrawled note's words settled in his focus like the dust of a fallen star, a cold, alien residue that dimmed the familiar world.

"Travis, give this to my mom." The simple, devastating instruction tore a scream from him. He spun and bolted back towards the trail, without pause. His legs burned as they carried him back to where he could have stayed but did not. "Davis!" he bellowed, a tearing sound that felt capable of fracturing the very sky. He saw the trail unroll ahead of him.

Dread and duty powered his frantic stride. His muscles burned like a numb inferno. "What are you doing?" His voice cracked, strained by the force behind it. "I found your phone!" He wasn't calling out for answers. He was reaching for a connection.

The words burst from him with panic behind every syllable. His legs pounded the trail, faster, harder, until every step felt like it might break him. His breath came ragged. The air stung his throat. His eyes scanned the path ahead, wide and wild, barely registering anything beyond movement. The trail narrowed and stretched as he ran. Trees whipped past in streaks. Roots and rocks blurred at his feet. His whole body surged forward, chasing something that mattered more than the air.

"Davis!" he shouted again, louder, voice cracking under the weight of it. His mind screamed for a glimpse, a sound, a shadow. The world rushed by in motion and noise, but none of it slowed him. He drove himself deeper into the path, arms pumping, lungs screaming, heart full of one name and nowhere left to send it.

"What's up, man?" His desperate pleas remained swallowed by the indifferent woods. He reached the place on the path where he had left Davis. And there, in that ordinary spot, the weight of his brother's absence slammed into him. He crumpled to his knees. "God! Please!" he screamed, the words ripping from his throat.

His voice cracked and caught, but the sound kept pouring out. "Please!" again, louder this time, desperate and unraveling. The noise didn't sound like a voice anymore. It came from somewhere deeper, somewhere he didn't recognize. His arms locked around his body, trying to stop the feeling from spilling out. He bent forward until his face pressed into the dirt, and still, the sound kept coming. Screams twisted into broken cries.

His breathing turned fast and shallow; each inhale was sharper than the last, each one harder to take in. He kept pushing it out, his voice hoarse and uneven, with a body shaking under the pressure of it all. He clawed at the trail. His jaw clenched so tight it sent pain through his face. His chest heaved. Every new breath was a wound.

The sound refused to die, a persistent echo of his shattered world. The place where Davis had stood held him captive, refusing to release his ghost. The very spot where Davis's shadow still remained seemed to physically constrict his lungs, vacuuming the air from them. His world dissolved into blackness.

"You're not here," he choked out, a broken whisper as he fully collapsed. The truth didn't arrive gently. It crashed through his chest, slammed into his ribs, and kept going. There was no preparation possible for this devastation, no shield strong enough to deflect its impact. Every cell in his body was filled with unbearable, absolute knowledge. There was no corner within him strong enough to contain its immensity. "You are my fucking brother!" he wailed with no expectation of a response. He knew the boy better than anyone else did.

He was enveloped by the glaring, agonizing realization that he was already gone.

***

A soft breeze, born of the river's passage through the verdant chasm, stirred the leaves. It wandered slowly across the canopy, tracing the arms of trees that had stood for generations. Their trunks bore the deep scars of time, and their roots pressed against the earth with patient insistence. Sunlight filtered through the branches in fragmented ribbons, catching on suspended dust and the translucent threads of drifting spiders. Insects hummed low and aimless through the stillness.

Far below, water pushed over stone in endless conversation, its rhythm patient and consistent. It whispered to the rocks and reeds with the comfort of a long memory. The forest was steeped in silence but not emptiness. It was full. It carried roots, breath, and memory. The pristine wilderness, a tapestry of earthy browns and vibrant greens, evoked a poignant sense of eternity and ephemerality. Ferns curled upward toward the light. Moss clung to bark like a language written in time. The cliff's edge remained still and solemn. It bore witness. It had seen storms and sunrises and now, something far quieter.

Distant from the rivers edge, a boy slept, nestled amongst a fragrant bed of clover and wildflowers. The blossoms had opened wide to greet the morning, unaware of what lay among them. Delicate petals brushed his temple. Davis's elbow bent with a relaxed ease. His other arm stretched gently beside him with fingers softly curled as though he had only just let go.

The bright orange of his soccer shirt cut through the greens and browns around him. It was loud and alive, a color that did not belong to this silence. His hair stirred with the breeze. His chest did not. There was no rise, no fall. No rhythm. No breath.

The body that had once outrun defenders that had laughed, and ached, and burned with fight, now lay still. The world pressed around him. It was vibrant and in motion, but nothing moved through him anymore. He had already joined the landscape.

He was not asleep. He was not at peace. He was gone. Untouched. Unbroken. Whole.

There was no violence, no carnage, no disturbance, with the exception of the gentle flutter of a monarch butterfly seeking a resting space. It descended proudly onto his shoulder... and became... still.

Finis

www.ingramcontent.com/pod-product-compliance
Lightning Source LLC
Chambersburg PA
CBHW062112040426
42337CB00043B/3710